Continuous SCHOOL IMPROVEMENT

MARK A. SMYLIE

A JOINT PUBLICATION

CORWIN
A SAGE Company

LEADERSHIP for LEARNING

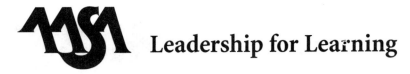

Leadership for Learning

Series Editors

Willis D. Hawley and E. Joseph Schneider

Joseph F. Murphy
Leadership for Literacy: Research-Based Practice, PreK–3

P. Karen Murphy, Patricia A. Alexander
Understanding How Students Learn: A Guide for Instructional Leaders

E. Joseph Schneider, Lara L. Hollenczer
The Principal's Guide to Managing Communication

Kenneth A. Strike
Ethical Leadership in Schools: Creating Community in an Environment of Accountability

Karen Hawley Miles, Stephen Frank
The Strategic School: Making the Most of People, Time, and Money

Ellen Goldring, Mark Berends
Leading With Data: Pathways to Improve Your School

Sharon D. Kruse, Karen Seashore Louis
Building Strong School Cultures: A Guide to Leading Change

Mark A. Smylie
Continuous School Improvement

Please call our toll-free number (800-818-7243)
or visit our Web site (www.corwinpress.com)
to order individual titles or the entire series.

To James H. Smylie

For information:

Corwin
A SAGE Company
2455 Teller Road
Thousand Oaks, California 91320
www.corwinpress.com

SAGE Ltd.
1 Oliver's Yard
55 City Road
London EC1Y 1SP
United Kingdom

SAGE Pvt. Ltd.
B 1/I 1 Mohan Cooperative Industrial Area
Mathura Road, New Delhi 110 044
India

SAGE Asia-Pacific Pte. Ltd.
33 Pekin Street #02-01
Far East Square
Singapore 048763

Printed in the United States of America

Library of Congress Cataloging-in-Publication Data

Smylie, Mark A.
Continuous school improvement/Mark A. Smylie.
      p. cm.—(Leadership for learning series)
"A Joint Publication With the American Association of School Administrators."
Includes bibliographical references and index.
ISBN 978-1-4129-3689-7 (pbk.)
    1. School improvement programs—United States. I. American Association of School Administrators. II. Title. III. Series.

LB2822.82.S66 2010
371.2′070973—dc22   2009033590

This book is printed on acid-free paper.

09   10   11   12   13   10 9 8 7 6 5 4 3 2 1

Acquisitions Editor:	Arnis Burvikovs
Associate Editor:	Desirée Bartlett
Editorial Assistant:	Joanna Coelho
Production Editor:	Veronica Stapleton
Copy Editor:	Jeannette McCoy
Typesetter:	C&M Digitals (P) Ltd.
Proofreader:	Charlotte J. Waisner
Indexer:	Terri Corry
Cover Designer:	Scott Van Atta

Contents

Foreword

Every now and then a phrase will pop up that warrants acceptance just because it captures in a few words the need to improve one of our basic institutions. One such phrase is "health care reform." Another is "continuous school improvement." Mention "health care reform" or "continuous school improvement" to most people and heads will start nodding in agreement. Sure. We need to reform health care. It's busted. By all means, schools need continuous improvement. Let's get the job done.

But reforming the medical system is complicated and when the options are presented the head nodding stops and people begin to think twice about the urgency of reform. Continuous school improvement is a whole less controversial. Nevertheless, confusion about its exact meaning and skimpy evidence about its success have begun to tarnish the label.

Mark Smylie, in this important book, points out that educators have embraced continuous improvement without a good sense of what it is and what it might and might not accomplish. He argues that if continuous improvement is to be pursued in schools at the pace and with the force with which it is being promoted, now is a good time to take an in-depth, analytical look at it.

Smylie understands the attraction of continuous improvement. He believes meaningful change takes time and substantial support. School "reform" is, in the words of Richard Elmore and Milbrey McLaughlin, "steady work." Smylie does not support the adoption of innovations or short-run efforts at turnaround, knowing full well that while claims for their alleged success may be measured by standardized tests, the adopting schools lack the capacity for sustaining the improvement over time.

What Smylie encourages—and writes about clearly in his book—is the need to build the capacity in schools for meaningful continuous improvement. The book implicitly rejects the idea that programmatic solutions to school improvement can be universally effective. Education has been, and always will be, an uncertain technology. Goals are varied and constantly changing. Strategies that work in some settings don't work in others. Students come to school with diverse needs, motivations, and experiences that require educators to continuously adapt while upping the outcomes expected by a nation that believes that its future depends on the skills and character of its people.

To say that education is an uncertain technology is not to say that educational practice cannot and should not be driven by evidence and the search for better answers. There is a difference between solutions and problem solving just as there is a difference between innovation and innovativeness. If there is a concise description of continuous school improvement, it may be that it is the process of evidence-based collaborative problem solving that results in day-to-day innovation where its effectiveness is persistently questioned.

As Smylie notes, few schools manifest continuous improvement and the institutional capacity to support such development is weak or nonexistent at the district, state, and federal levels. This book is designed to help educational leaders develop and sustain school structures, cultures, and processes that will enable them to enhance the learning opportunities and outcomes of all their students and to do so over time.

Smylie's book might be called an exercise in practical theory—that is, theory that fosters situationally appropriate and effective practices. The author draws on research on successful education, business, and government organizations to develop a set of principles to guide action in different contexts. While this is not a "how-to" handbook, it contains many examples of effective practice.

This book argues that schools can become continuously improving a number of specific ways. What matters is that these different paths to continuous improvement are consistent with a set of principles and preferred states. Smylie examines these principles and preferred states in some detail. He believes that the effectiveness of their enactment through specific practices depends on how school personnel define continuous improvement, "theorize" about it, and "translate" these principles and preferred states to particular contexts in real time and place.

Smylie's book is one of a series that is part of the Leadership for Learning initiative of the American Association of School Administrators (AASA). Its primary purpose is to provide school leaders with support in strategic allocation of limited resources to maximize student performance and foster continuous school improvement.

Willis D. Hawley and E. Joseph Schneider

Preface

It is difficult to read about education reform and school change these days and not run head-long into the idea of continuous improvement. It is ubiquitous. Continuous improvement is at once a buzzword, mantra, and a potentially effective way for schools to succeed in an uncertain and demanding future.

The call for schools and school districts to engage in continuous improvement comes from many quarters. It is seen in the pages of practitioner and scholarly publications and heard from the podiums of professional and academic conferences. It is promoted by professional education associations, consultants, and academics alike, including the Executive Committee of the American Association of School Administrators (AASA), the North Central Association (NCA), the Southern Association of Colleges and Schools (SACS), the American Federation of Teachers (AFT), the National Education Association (NEA), the National Association of Elementary School Principals (NAESP), and the National Association of Secondary School Principals (NASSP).

The education literature is replete with models and strategies for schools and school districts to engage in continuous improvement and with stories of those that claim to have "done it." A search of *Books-In-Print* reveals that between 1988 and mid-2008, 216 books were published on the general subject of continuous improvement. Almost one-third of those books concern continuous improvement in education. In late 2008, the ERIC Clearinghouse listed more than 580 papers and articles on continuous improvement in elementary, secondary, and postsecondary education.

So why another treatment of continuous improvement? The short answer is that while there is growing attention to the subject and while there are increasing calls for schools to engage in it, there has not been a systematic effort to examine the subject in a comprehensive way. Much of what has been written about continuous improvement in education tells what a school or school district has done, makes an argument about what a school or school district should do, or presents "how-to" steps for doing it. Continuous improvement is often discussed and promoted as if the concept and the theory or logic behind it were self-evident and unproblematic. Little attention has been paid to empirical evidence of its effectiveness. Few connections have been made in the education literature to the more fully developed conceptual, theoretical, and empirical literatures outside of education. The idea of continuous improvement is not new. It has at least a century-long lineage, but its history has gone largely unexamined. We are barreling toward continuous improvement without a good sense of what it is and what it might and might not accomplish. If continuous improvement is to be pursued in schools at the pace and with the force with which it is being promoted, it is a good time to take an in-depth, analytical look at it.

PURPOSES OF THE BOOK

The purposes of this book are twofold. The first is to analyze the concept and theory of continuous improvement and to synthesize what is known about its practice and its effectiveness in schools. This means addressing several questions: What does the concept of continuous improvement mean? Where does the concept come from? What are the reasons for engaging in continuous improvement? What are the anticipated outcomes of continuous improvement in schools? What is the evidence about the effectiveness of continuous improvement? How is continuous improvement practiced in schools? What processes are used? What organizational supports are needed for these processes to be successful? What does continuous improvement look like "in action"? And finally, what are the practical implications of answers to these questions for schools as they pursue continuous improvement?

The second purpose of this book is to inform the practice of continuous improvement. This is not a conventional "how-to" book. It is not a "step-by-step" action guide for implementing continuous improvement. There are a number of these guides now available, and they can be quite useful (e.g., AdvancED, n.d.b; National Education Association, 2008; Lezotte & McKee, 2002, 2006; Zumda, Kuklis, & Kline, 2004; see also Fidler, 2002; Leithwood, Aitken, & Jantzi, 2001).

This book takes a different approach to informing the practice of continuous improvement. Rather than focusing on specific strategies and activities, this book considers the "best practice" of continuous improvement in terms of a set of overarching principles and "preferred states of being," here school organizational being. It argues that there are a number of specific ways that schools can effectively become continuously improving. As argued at several points in the book, what matters is that these different paths to continuous improvement are consistent with this set of principles and preferred states. This book examines these principles and preferred states in some detail and argues that the effectiveness of their enactment through specific practices depends a great deal on how school personnel define continuous improvement, how they "theorize" about it, and how they "translate" these principles and preferred states to particular contexts in real time and place.

This reasoning follows that of Chris Argyris and Donald Schön (1974) who stress the importance of the relationship between theory and practice. They argue that our behavior—our practice—is driven in large part by our knowledge, our assumptions, our mental frameworks, our "theories" about phenomena and relationships among them (see also Nisbett & Ross, 1980). While many factors play a role in the enactment and outcomes of our theories (Argyris & Schön, 1974), what we are able to accomplish in practice is contingent on how good our theories might be. The more well informed we are and the better our theorizing, the better our practice. In psychologist Kurt Lewin's (1935) famous words, "There is nothing so practical as a good theory."

HOW THE BOOK WAS DEVELOPED

This book is the result of a study of continuous improvement that began several years ago. This study started with a search of the education literature and branched out to literatures from business and management, the organizational sciences, and public administration. The search went wherever the library's reference systems led. There were dead-ends aplenty, but the result was a compilation of a substantial amount of literature, much of which has not made its way into writing in education.

While these literatures were surveyed broadly to understand the "state of the art" of past and present thinking about continuous improvement, the book itself focuses primarily on subsets of several literatures. It draws primarily on conceptual and theoretical analyses, reports of original empirical research, and analytic syntheses of original research. The characteristics, strengths, and weaknesses of these literatures are discussed in several chapters.

This book draws on a great deal of material from outside of education because so much of the theory and empirical evidence about continuous improvement comes from studies of non-education organizations. And this raises a perennial issue about the applicability to schools of theory and empirical evidence developed through the study of non-educational organizations, particularly businesses and industries. One perspective posits that schools are unique organizations. Their missions and functions, their "core technologies" of teaching and learning, their work with children and youth, among other things, are so completely different that knowledge about other types of organizations is not relevant and applicable.

This book adopts a different point of view, one advanced by Seymour Sarason (1996), Kenneth Wilson and Bennett Daviss (1994), and others. This perspective, in Sarason's words, "gives up the myth that in regard to the design and redesign process schools are unique social systems" (p. 359). It holds that schools are only a different type of organization. Again, in Sarason's words:

> It seems so obvious that we overlook or fail to see the myriad similarities among organizations. Indeed, we [educators] are likely to resist a point of view that holds that organizations are different; they are not unique. And the *practical* consequences of seeing them as different but not unique are enormous. . . . (pp. 317–318)

In his historical analysis of the relationship between education and business, Larry Cuban (2004) encourages his readers not to automatically write off business-inspired efforts to improve schools even though "their purposes, authority, and outcomes differ in fundamental ways" (p. 12). Instead he urges "even-handed analysis" and "balanced judgments" (p. 14). And in introducing their analysis of "turning around" failing schools, Joseph Murphy and Coby Meyers (2007) argued the following:

> PreK–12 education can learn a good deal . . . by carefully studying work afoot in other industries and organizations. . . . Yet these insights are conspicuous by their absence from the education turnaround literature. Indeed, there is an insularity and parochialism in the turnaround literature in education that is as arrogant as it is ill advised. Our message is that there are lessons from turning around other institutions . . . that can help us more effectively undertake recovery work in failing schools. (pp. 4–5)

A message of this book is similar—there are lessons from continuous improvement in other organizations that can help us more effectively understand and undertake continuous improvement in schools.

That said, there is no intention here to privilege or deify non-education organizations. Nor is there any suggestion that any particular organizational type "has it over" schools and establishes the model for schools to follow. Instead, this analysis looks across literatures about different organizations for similarities and differences in theories and research findings. These organizations include schools, businesses, industries, nonprofit organizations, and public agencies. The idea is that where convergence exists, we can have greater confidence in the relevance and applicability of ideas and findings to schools. As will be clearly evident throughout this book, there is a substantial amount of convergence.

One other matter concerning the development of the book is important to note. The study focused predominantly on continuous improvement at the school level. It did not explore in any systematic way continuous improvement at the school district level. The reason is twofold. First, there is virtually no literature related to continuous improvement of the central office or at the districtwide level. Second, while ideas about continuous improvement at the school level could have been applied hypothetically to the central office and to the district level, it would have required many more pages than are here. The reader is invited to consider how the ideas and findings discussed throughout the book might apply to the central office and to the district level. It is likely that many will.

ORGANIZATION OF THE BOOK

This book is organized in seven chapters. Chapters 1, 2, and 3 focus primarily on the theory of continuous improvement and evidence of its effectiveness. Chapters 4, 5, and 6 focus primarily on the practice of continuous improvement. Chapter 7 takes stock and engages a number of issues related to schools becoming continuously improving organizations.

Chapter 1 is an assessment of the changing conditions of schools, the ability of schools as they are currently organized and operated to succeed in these conditions and in the future, and the attendant call for schools to engage in continuous improvement. Chapter 2 explores the meaning of continuous improvement—in the education and non-education literatures—and it presents a number of key, common definitional properties of the concept, the theory or logic of continuous improvement, and the benefits that are expected to come from it. This chapter also traces the historical roots of continuous improvement, noting several related concepts and theories of organizational change. Chapter 3 contains a review of findings from research about the effectiveness of continuous improvement in schools and in different types of non-education organizations.

Chapter 4 explores the processes of continuous improvement. It presents a basic process model and then examines the historical and contemporary application of this model in schools. It reviews several contemporary process models of continuous improvement in schools and concludes by distilling and analyzing their common properties. Chapter 5 further explores the practice in terms of organizational design elements needed to support continuous improvement processes and the implementation of particular initiatives that might be generated by them. Chapter 6 presents four vignettes of continuous improvement "in action." These vignettes feature two elementary schools, one middle school, and one high school. They illustrate the development of continuous improvement processes over time and various organizational design elements that are integral to their success. They reflect key aspects of continuous improvement processes discussed in Chapter 4 and organizational design elements discussed in Chapter 5. They also reflect some of the changes and uncertainties in school context discussed in Chapter 1. Additional examples of continuous improvement "in action" are found in the discussion of research in Chapter 3.

Chapter 7 provides a summary of the book and, using ideas and evidence developed in the first six chapters, engages two questions. The first question is, *Should schools pursue continuous improvement?* And the second is, *If they pursue it, how might they do so successfully?* The answer to the first question constitutes a basic argument of the book. In brief, the argument is that there is a very good reason and good enough evidence to pursue continuous improvement as a process of school improvement and as a way to organize schools. It is a potentially powerful option for preparing schools to be effective in a demanding and uncertain future. However, the pursuit should not proceed without study and reflection. A good deal is known about continuous improvement in educational and non-educational organizations, but there is much more to be learned. While this book does not lay out an agenda for research on continuous improvement in schools, it is not difficult to see where inquiry is warranted. Making inquiry a central focus is perfectly consistent with the theory of continuous improvement, for it is through continuous inquiry, among other things, that continuous improvement is achieved.

At the end of each chapter is a short series of questions for study, reflection, and action. These questions are designed primarily for practicing educators and for readers preparing to become school leaders, although all readers should find them helpful in one way or another. Posing these particular questions aims to achieve several specific objectives. One objective is to stimulate thinking about and promote deeper understanding of particular ideas and arguments presented throughout the book. A second objective is to prompt readers to "test" these ideas and arguments against their own experiences, to see how well they hold up in relation to particular school settings. A third objective is to introduce readers to several aspects of the actual work of continuous improvement. In one way or another, each series of questions evokes some important aspect of this work, be it assessing future challenges and opportunities; identifying and clarifying the mission, vision, and core values of a school; assessing and choosing different process models of continuous improvement; assessing organizational capacity for continuous improvement; identifying and assessing the quality of evidence and using evidence to make assessments and support decisions; deciding how to assess implementation and outcomes of continuous improvement; and so forth. These questions communicate important "how-to" information, and they provide some initial experiences in putting the ideas of this book to work.

Acknowledgments

The study of continuous improvement in schools that resulted in this book began as a project of a graduate class on educational change in the College of Education at the University of Illinois at Chicago. For the better part of a semester, five students and I explored various literatures on the subject inside and outside of education, and we began to develop the ideas around which this book became organized. For the ground they broke, I thank Tony Corte, Minerva Cruz Familar, Dan DiCesare, Patricia Garza, and Julie Greenfield. I thank Kelly Hallberg and Cristal Mendlin, two other graduate students, who helped carry on the work. Their particular contributions are acknowledged by coauthorships of Chapter 2 and Chapter 6. Thanks to David Mayrowetz and Shelby Cosner for reading early drafts of chapters and providing very useful comments and suggestions.

Special thanks go to Bill Hawley for the opportunity to write this book, for his guidance and patience, and for his keen and cogent insights about arguments and audiences. I thank Joe Schneider for his constructive suggestions and the editors and staff at Corwin Press, especially Arnis Burvikovs and Desireé Bartlett for their insights, and Veronica Stapleton and Jeannette McCoy for guiding this work through production. Thanks to the Spencer Foundation for the sanctuary of a residential fellowship that was invaluable to moving the writing forward. And finally, I am deeply grateful to Sallie, Lauren, Anna, and Rachel for their love, encouragement, and support. I don't get very far in this life without them.

Corwin gratefully acknowledges the contributions of the following individuals:

Margarete Couture, Elementary Principal
South Seneca Central School District
Interlaken, NY

Douglas Gordon Hesbol, Superintendent
Laraway Community Consolidated School District 70-C
Joliet, IL

About the Author

Mark A. Smylie is Professor of Education at the University of Illinois at Chicago (UIC). He received his PhD from Vanderbilt University and BA and MEd degrees from Duke University. Professor Smylie's research concerns school organization and processes of school organizational change, administrative and teacher leadership and development, and urban school improvement. His work has appeared in the *American Education Research Journal, Educational Researcher, Educational Administration Quarterly, Educational Evaluation and Policy Analysis, Educational Policy, Journal of School Leadership,* and *Review of Research in Education.* He has contributed chapters to numerous books on teachers and teaching, leadership and administration, and educational change.

Professor Smylie has been Chair of the Educational Policy Studies Department in the College of Education at UIC and Secretary-Treasurer of the National Society for the Study of Education. He also served as a Director of the Consortium on Chicago School Research at the University of Chicago. He has been awarded a National Academy of Education Postdoctoral Fellowship, the William J. Davis Award from the University Council for Educational Administration, and the American Educational Research Association's Research Review Award. He has been a Residential Fellow at the Spencer Foundation. Before his work in higher education, he was a high school history teacher. He has maintained a close relationships with schools and school districts through joint projects and professional development activity. He has consulted with numerous regional and national professional and policy organizations concerned with education.

The Context and Call for Continuous Improvement

1

The future ain't what it used to be.

—Yogi Berra, 2001

A relationship, I think, is like a shark. You know? It has to constantly move forward or it dies. And I think what we have on our hands is a dead shark.

—Woody Allen as Alvie Singer in *Annie Hall,* 1977

There are at least two ways to interpret Yogi Berra's famous aphorism about the future. One is the way that the iconic New York Yankees catcher himself explained it, "Honestly, I don't think much about the future—not like I used to—but just enjoy life. It's too short to worry about" (p. 162). Another way to interpret the aphorism is that the future we expect is not likely to be the future we will experience. In relatively stable times, our expectations for the future—derived from presumptions past and present—stand a decent chance of coming to fruition. But in turbulent, rapidly changing times, those chances can be long shots. Thus, the aphorism can be understood to warn us that the future we experience ain't likely to be the one we expect it to be.

The latter interpretation lies at the heart of a current argument about schools. There are three basic parts to this argument. First, these are rapidly changing and unpredictable times. Populations, economies, and employment; communications and technologies; geographic boundaries; the nature of communities and social relationships; civic, social, and religious institutions—all are changing in unprecedented and often contested ways. To many, these changes are threatening and destabilizing. [1]

Old beliefs and assumptions that once guided, governed, and gave meaning no longer work so well. Ambiguity is ascendant. The future will be defined by rapid change, systemic uncertainty, even chaos. Where it will all lead, no one really knows. Former U.S. Secretary of Defense Donald Rumsfeld's (2002) now infamous statement about the early stages of the war in Iraq makes the point well:

> [T]here are known knowns; there are things we know we know. We also know there are known unknowns; that is to say, we know there are some things we do not know. But there are also unknown unknowns, the ones we don't know we don't know. . . . [I]t is the latter category that tend (sic) to be the difficult ones (sic).

So too does the remark he made a year later to deflect criticism that the Bush administration lacked an effective reconstruction plan for "post-war" Iraq, "Stuff happens!" (Rumsfeld, 2003).

The second part of the argument is that schools are not prepared for such a future. Most of today's schools are yesterday's schools, built for purposes and contexts disappearing or gone. They are oriented toward the past, not the future. They are built to promote stability and to be stable themselves, not to change on their own or to be changed very easily by others. They are not oriented or organized for the types and magnitudes of change that are occurring now and that will likely occur in the future. In short, they are ill suited to a future that ain't what it used to be.

This leads to the third part of the argument. Schools must change in fundamental ways in order to perform effectively in this future. They must become more flexible and adaptive, better able to deal with increasing complexity and ambiguity, more proactive than reactive, and reoriented toward different objectives. As change accelerates around them and as demands on them intensify, schools must begin to move and keep moving. They must improve and keep improving. Otherwise, the argument concludes, they will become like Woody Allen's shark—if not dead, then moribund and largely ineffectual.

And thus the call for schools to take on organizational properties and adopt the processes of continuous improvement. Continuous improvement is a concept that has a long history and a variety of meanings. The definitions, the logic, and the history of continuous improvement are explored in Chapter 2. This first chapter sets the stage. It examines the context and the call for continuous improvement by exploring several contexts or "terrains" of schooling that are changing dramatically and will likely continue to do so. In particular, I look at growing demands for schools to promote new types of learning, to improve performance continually, and to be more accountable.[2] From this discussion, I turn to the challenges these changes pose to schools and to an analysis of schools' current capacity to respond. And then, I introduce the call for continuous improvement.

SHIFTING TERRAINS OF SCHOOLING

The contexts in which schools operate are changing dramatically. William L. Boyd (2003) observed that we are in the midst of broad social, political, economic, and demographic transformations that portend crisis for public schools as we know them now. He saw schools as having entered a period of "trial" that will challenge them at their core. He argued that a "paradigm shift" has been developing in the United States since the 1980s:

This shift is marked by a change in focus from inputs *to* the system to the outcomes and accountability *of* the system, by a shift in the attitudes of key constituency groups, and by a critical reexamination of what public education means and how it can or should be delivered. (p. 7)

It is unclear where such changes will lead. At minimum, they will create a future for schools that is more complex, more contested, and more demanding. As Boyd (2003) saw it, these changes may constitute an "unusual convergence" of institutional forces that not only makes "deep changes" in schools possible but perhaps inevitable. What transformed schools might look like and how transformed schools might function in this future is not particularly clear. This raises the very difficult question of how schools might organize themselves and operate now for a future that is certain to be uncertain and a future in which schools' form and function are part of the unknown.

There are several areas in which changes are occurring that are especially salient to schools. These include (a) jobs for which schools prepare students; (b) politics and control of education; (c) school funding; (d) the characteristics and conditions of children and youth; and (e) demands on schools for new learning, higher performance, and greater accountability. There are other areas that might be examined, but these represent particularly important dimensions of a future that schools will confront. I adopt the language of "shifting terrains" that Lugg, Bulkley, Firestone, & Garner (2002) used to analyze the increasingly complex, variable, and volatile contexts facing educational leaders at the beginning of the 21st century. Important to their analysis and to mine is the idea that these contexts are not independent or mutually exclusive. Instead, they constitute a dynamic, unpredictable, systemic environment in which schools must find ways to succeed.

The Transformation of Jobs

Jobs in the United States are undergoing fundamental transformation. There have been and will continue to be substantial changes in the nature of work and substantial shifts in employment among different sectors of the economy. These shifts are due to a number of broader changes that include but are not limited to the explosive development and expansion of computer, robotic, and information technologies; the rapid pace of globalization of markets and work; and deregulation of key industries (Lerman & Schmidt, 1999; Levy & Murnane, 2004).

Economists Frank Levy and Richard Murnane (2004) tell us that between 1969 and 1999, the proportion of adult workers in managerial or administrative positions and in professional occupations (e.g., teachers, lawyers, engineers) rose from 8% to 14% and from 10% to 13%, respectively. The proportion of adult workers holding service-related jobs (e.g., janitors, cafeteria workers, security guards) rose from 12% to 14%, and the proportion in sales-related jobs rose from 8% to 12%. At the same time, the proportion of adult workers in blue collar, manufacturing, and administrative support positions fell from 56% to 39%.

Some of these changes in percentages seem small, but they represent tens of millions of jobs. In more a more recent analysis, for example, Murnane (2009) found that between 2000 and 2006 the number of jobs in production and manufacturing fell by almost 2.1 million, and the number of jobs in office and administrative support fell by 1.6 million. At the same time, jobs in service occupations, in the professions, and in management, business, and financial operations rose by 3.2 million, 2.5 million, and almost 1.3 million, respectively. Such changes will only continue.

The U.S. Bureau of Labor Statistics (2007) projects that the number of goods-producing jobs (e.g., manufacturing, mining, construction) will fall 3% between 2006 and 2016. This follows a 4% decline in these jobs that occurred between 1996 and 2006. At the same time, the number of service-producing jobs (e.g., trade, professional and business services, educational and health care services, etc.) will increase by 13%, adding to 17% growth in these jobs the previous decade.

These trends are reflected in the U.S. Bureau of Labor Statistics' (2007) projections of the industries that will experience the largest employment increases and declines between 2006 and 2016. The 10 industries with the largest projected employment increases are mostly professional, managerial, and heath service industries, and elementary through postsecondary education. The 10 industries with the largest projected job losses are in all areas of manufacturing (from apparel to computer equipment, to motor vehicle parts), crop production, and industries supporting print and wire communications. Overall, the number of manufacturing jobs is projected to fall 11% during this period.

Politics and Control

Lugg and her colleagues (2002) map a political terrain of schooling that is "increasingly marked by contests at the local, state, or national levels [over] resources, as well as over the scope and direction of public education" (p. 21). They observe that as a "contested public good," education involves a large and variable cast of stakeholders and constituencies competing to determine "who gets what, when, and how" (p. 21; see also Wirt & Kirst, 2005). This cast includes but is not limited to students, parents, educators and their unions, civic leadership, policy makers, and the general voting public. It also includes vast networks of suppliers and vendors, publishers, consultants, and other members of what Brian Rowan (2002) calls the "school improvement industry." Lugg and her colleagues contend that this terrain has become and will continue to become increasingly contested with regard to funding, governance and control, and even the general purposes of schooling. Contests will be waged not only on the basis of economic interests, exacerbated by growth in the privatization of public services and market-based reforms, but also ideology.

Boyd (2003) observed that in the past few years, efforts to cast the future direction for public education have come largely from outside the education system. More and more, recommendations for reform reflect "the thinking of corporate leaders, policy analysts, foundations, and critics of public education" (p. 1). Boyd argued that American public education is caught up in a "double crisis" of performance and legitimacy and this crisis is providing the foundation for a fundamental shift in control of schools. The performance crisis is based on critiques of low student performance and poor preparation of students for the needs of a global "knowledge-based 'information society'" (p. 3). The issue of performance is discussed in more detail later in this chapter. The legitimacy crisis comes from difficulties the educational system has had to accommodate the "demands of an increasingly diverse society divided by 'culture wars'" (p. 3).

Boyd (2003) also argued that as the country becomes more diverse, multicultural, and multilingual, "and at the same time more unequal," the "character, values, and legitimacy of our society and of its public school system are increasingly called into question" (p. 12). He observed that globalization is forcing states to recognize growing pluralism and, as a result, tensions are mounting as public education's universalistic system tries to accommodate increasing diversity without betraying its "common school" history and philosophy. Boyd saw the politics of education intensifying as social change becomes more obvious and unavoidable. "Put another way," he concluded, "there is less social consensus, more 'pluribus' than 'unum,' and the 'one best system' approach to public education has collapsed along with the 'myth of the unitary community'" (p. 12).

Accompanying these changes in social and political dynamics have been shifts in the governance and control of public education. Lorraine McDonnell (2008) observes a clear evolution of governance relationships characterized by growing centralization of control at federal and state levels and greater devolution of responsibility for compliance to the local level. This shift is perhaps best illustrated in the growth of state standards-based accountability reforms of the 1990s, culminating in 2001 with the *No Child Left Behind* reauthorization of Title I of the federal Elementary and Secondary Education Act. These reforms raise the bar for local school performance and outcomes and introduce sanctions for non-compliance. At the same time they leave it to local districts to find the means and resources to comply. McDonnell observes that with increasing centralization has come greater fragmentation. There are larger numbers of actors with a greater range of economic agendas and political stakes that represent a growth of potential sources of external political influence. Such expansion adds to the fragmentation of control but also increases the prospects of growth in total external influence over public schools.

Shifts in and expansion of control are manifest in other ways too. Boyd (2003) observed that the historical separation of educational and municipal governance in big cities is beginning to disappear as more and more districts are moving toward mayoral control. Superintendents are being replaced with greater frequency not by other educators but by people outside of education, including city government officials, military leaders, and corporate executives. Charter schools and choice and voucher plans are growing in number while home schooling is flourishing. Boyd also forecast the development of more online learning and "cyber-schools." Each of these developments contributes to the "externalization" and fragmentation of influence and control over schools to a wider array of sources.

School Funding

Total revenue for public elementary and secondary education in the U.S. schools has been increasing steadily since the mid-1980s (Education Finance Statistics Center, 2005b). Between 1985 and 1995, total revenue, which includes all revenue received from federal, state, and local sources, increased almost 40% from $249 billion to $348 billion. Between 1995 and 2005, total revenue rose another 40% to nearly $488 billion.

The vast majority of total school revenue comes from local and state sources. A relatively small percentage comes from the federal government. Overall, the federal share has gradually increased since 1990 (Zhou, 2008). The increase since 2001 may be due in part to additional revenues associated with *No Child Left Behind*. In fiscal year 2006, 90.9% of all revenue came from the state and local levels, and 9.1% came from the federal level. Trends and variations in federal, state, and local "shares" of public school funding are perhaps best seen at the regional level (Education Finance Statistics Center, 2005a). Across different regions of the country, the federal share has varied by as much as four percentage points. Trends in state and local shares vary even more across regions. These differences are indicative of a number of broader demographic and economic changes occurring across the nation. They suggest a growing need in some regions for states to assume a larger share of school districts' general operating expenses as districts experience difficulty raising revenues from property taxes and other local sources (Lugg et al., 2002). But as discussed later, states are experiencing their own economic troubles and may find it increasingly difficult to "make up the difference."

Perhaps a more meaningful way to assess changes in school funding is trends in per pupil revenue. According to the Education Finance Statistics Center (2005b), average revenue per pupil has risen since 1985 but at a smaller rate than total revenue. Between 1985 and 1995, revenue per pupil rose 24% from $6,348 to $7,894. Between 1995 and 2005 it rose another 27% to $9,995. Yet wide disparities in per pupil revenue can be seen at the state and district levels (Hill & Johnson, 2005; Zhou & Gaviola, 2007). In 2005, for example, median school district revenues at the state level ranged from $6,823 to $17,865 per pupil and district-level per pupil revenues ranged from $7,021 to $19,680 (Zhou & Gaviola, 2007). These disparities are likely to continue well into the future if not addressed.

District-level funding can vary tremendously, even within the same states, depending on local districts' political will and "ability to pay." Because district-level revenues are tied closely to property values and other sources of local taxation, low-income communities are often at a tremendous disadvantage. Jason Hill and Frank Johnson (2005) found that in 2003, differences between highest- and lowest-funded districts exceeded 200% in five states. They found differences between 100 and 200% in another 19 states.

Several studies have documented wide gaps in funding among school districts serving large and small concentrations of low-income students. In one recent national analysis, Carmen Arroyo (2008) found that districts serving the highest concentrations of low-income students received, on average, $938 less per pupil in state and local revenues than districts serving the lowest concentrations of low-income students, a gap unchanged since 1999 (adjusted for inflation). When "commonly used" adjustments of costs of educating low-income students were applied, Arroyo found that the gap increased to $1,532 per pupil. With this adjustment applied, the nationwide funding gap between districts serving the highest and lowest concentrations of minority students was $1,275 per pupil. This study also found substantial variation among states in per-pupil funding gaps between high- and low-poverty districts.[3]

A recent study from the Center on Budget and Policy Priorities (McNichol & Lav, 2008) suggests that despite trends in revenue growth, there is likely to be trouble ahead to fund education adequately and to address funding inequities such as those described before. This study identified 29 states facing revenue shortfalls for fiscal year 2009 and three more states expecting to experience shortfalls in fiscal year 2010. These shortfalls are attributed primarily to loss of tax revenue and growth in spending obligations. Local property tax revenues, once a relatively stable source of revenue for school funding, are now expected to decline with long-term structural problems in housing markets. Local governments and school districts will be looking for more and more to states to help relieve the squeeze on general operating and education budgets.

This will place additional pressure on states that are wrestling with their own shortfalls. According to the Center on Budget and Policy Priorities (McNichol & Lav, 2008), as many as 34 states have begun to cut "real per-pupil aid" to elementary and secondary school districts. This has resulted in districts having to raise local fees, shorten school days, lay off personnel, and reduce student transportation. States have also begun to use funds that would have gone in the past to education to cover other costs such as health care for state employees and entitlement programs such as state Medicare. In some states, health costs now surpass education costs for the first time. Furthermore, notes the Center's report, "Many states never recovered from the fiscal crisis in the early part of the decade. This fact heightens the potential impact on public services of the deficits states are now projecting" (p. 4). In the future, earlier reductions in state education funding are not likely to be made up. Indeed, reductions are likely to continue. The report ends with a rather dismal conclusion that states have few options to avoid further reductions. Their "rainy day funds" and other reserves are depleted, and public service spending has been cut substantially, leaving tax increases as the most viable financial option but the least viable political option available to them.

It is important to note that these studies of school funding were conducted before the recession began at the end of 2008.

Characteristics and Conditions of Children and Youth

Substantial changes are also occurring in the characteristics and conditions of children and youth. The population schools serve is growing larger and is becoming more diverse racially, ethnically, culturally, and economically. Large proportions of children come to school without early educational experiences and without particular academic readiness skills. Moreover, the systems of support available to many children and youth are changing.

The U.S. Bureau of the Census (2004) predicts that between 2000 and 2050, the population from birth through age four will increase by 46%, and the population between the ages of 5 and 19 years of age will increase by 32%. There will be 28.6 million more children and youth below the age of 20 in 2050 than in 2000. Increases can already be seen in school enrollments (Hussar & Bailey, 2007). Between 1991 and 2004, the number of students enrolled in pre-kindergarten through 12th grade rose 15% from 47.7 million to 54.9 million students. Enrollment is expected to increase another 9% between 2004 and 2016 to 59.8 million students.

School enrollments will continue to become more racially and ethnically diverse (Orfield & Lee, 2007). Between 1968 and 2005, the number of white public school students fell nearly 20% while the number of African American students rose 33%, and the number of Latino students rose 380%. In 2005, public school enrollment across the United States was 57% white, 17% African American, 20% Latino, 5% Asian American, and 1% American Indian. Growth in racial and ethnic diversity has occurred at different rates in different regions of the country with the west and the south experiencing the greatest increases.

Growth in diversity has occurred throughout the country. Between 1993 and 2002, minority proportions of public school enrollments in central cities rose from 56% to 65%. In the urban fringe, it rose from 31% to 37%. In towns it rose from 22% to 30% and in rural areas it rose from 17% to 21% (Kewal Ramani, Gilbertson, Fox, & Provasnik, 2007). In 2007, one in 10 of the nation's 3,141 counties had a population that was more than 50% minority, an increase in "majority-minority" counties from the year before (U.S. Bureau of the Census, 2007a).

The U.S. Department of Labor (1999) projects that by 2050, immigration will account for almost two-thirds of the nation's population growth. Net migration from abroad—immigration less emigration—added 5.5 million persons to the population between 1990 and 1997 and another

4.1 million between 1998 and 2002 (U.S. Citizenship and Immigration Services, 1998). In 2005, 4.3% of children under the age of 18 were foreign born (Kewal Ramani et al., 2007). That year, almost 11% of Latino children were foreign born as were 23% of Asian American children.

With increasing immigration and ethnic diversity comes greater language diversity. In 2004, almost 20% of children 5 to 17 years of age spoke a language other than English at home (U.S. Bureau of the Census, 2007b). About two-thirds of all Latino and Asian American children spoke a language other than English at home. Among children who speak Spanish at home, 28% speak English with difficulty (National Center for Education Statistics, 2007). Among children who speak Indo-European and Asian and/or Pacific Islander languages at home, 21% and 28% respectively speak English with difficulty.

The proportion of children living in poverty has increased in recent years with growing differences among racial and ethnic groups. Between 2001 and 2005, the proportion of children under the age of 18 living in poverty rose from 15.8% to 17.1% (U.S. Bureau of the Census, 2007b). The proportion of white children living in poverty rose from 12.8% to 13.9% while the proportion of African American children living in poverty rose from 20.0% to 34.2%. Across this period, approximately 27% of Latino children lived in poverty. In 2005, 41% of all American 4th graders were eligible for the federal government's free or reduced-price lunch program (Kewal Ramani et al., 2007). About 24% of white 4th graders but 70% of African American and 73% of Latino 4th graders were eligible that year.

Family structures continue to change. According to the U.S. Bureau of the Census (2007b, 2009), smaller proportions of children under the age of 18 are living with both parents. Between 1990 and 2006, the proportion of children living with both parents fell from 73% to 67%. Proportions of children living with only their mothers increased from 21% to 23% and with only their fathers from 3% to almost 5%, as did the proportion of children living with neither parent. There are substantial differences in family structure among children of different races and ethnicities. In 2006, 74% of white children, 66% of Latino children, but only 35% of African American children lived with both parents. Eighteen percent of white children lived with their mothers compared to nearly 51% of African American children. Children in female-headed households are more likely to live in poverty than children in two-parent households (Kewal Ramini et al., 2007). White children are eight times more likely to live in poverty if they live in female-headed households than in two-parent households. African American children and Hispanic children are, respectively, four times and about three times more likely to live in poverty if they live in female-headed than in two-parent households.

Growing proportions of young children are involved in early educational experiences (U.S. Bureau of the Census, 2007b). Between 1970 and 2005, the proportion of young children enrolled in preprimary programs (e.g., nursery school, kindergarten) rose considerably. Still, substantial proportions of young children across the country do not have these experiences. In 2005, about 35% of white children, 38% of African American children, and 44% of Latino children were not enrolled in such programs. According to the U.S. Bureau of the Census (2007b), substantial proportions of children between three and five years of age have not developed certain "school readiness skills." About 25% of children in this age group cannot recognize letters, and about 40% cannot count to 20 or higher or write their names. Almost 30% have not begun to read or cannot pretend to read storybooks. Sixty percent of children lack three or more of these skills. White children are generally "better prepared" for school in terms of these indicators than African American or Latino children. Moreover the readiness skills of children living in poverty are less well developed than the skills of children not living in poverty.

Between 1995 and 2005, the number of children and youth diagnosed with physical and mental disabilities increased 20% from 5.1 to 6.1 million (U.S. Bureau of the Census, 2007b). The largest proportions, between 45% and 51%, have specific learning disabilities. About 20% have speech or language impairments. And in 2007, 8.1 million or 11% of children in the United States under the age of 17 had no health insurance, and 4.4 million or 6% had no regular source of health care (Federal Interagency Forum on Child and Family Statistics, 2009).

Demands on Schools

In addition to these changes in jobs, politics, control, funding, and characteristics and conditions of children and youth, demands on schools are increasing. There are demands to promote new types of learning. There are demands for improving levels of performance and outcomes. And there are demands for greater accountability. These demands are intensifying and they are not completely in sync. There are tensions and contradictions among them that create additional challenges for schools.

New Learning

In the future, schools will need to change course from promoting student learning that might have been appropriate in the past to promote learning that will be required in the future. In the introduction to its seminal report *How People Learn,* the National Research Council (2000) laid out the change this way:

> In the early part of the twentieth century, education focused on the acquisition of literacy skills: simple reading, writing, and calculating. It was not the general rule for educational systems to train people to think and read critically, to express themselves clearly and persuasively, to solve complex problems in sciences and mathematics. Now, . . . these aspects of high literacy are required of almost everyone in order to successfully negotiate the complexities of contemporary life. The skill demands for work have increased dramatically, as has the need for organizations and workers to change in response to competitive workplace pressures. Thoughtful participation in the democratic process has also become increasingly complicated as the locus of attention has shifted from local to national and global concerns. . . . Above all, information and knowledge are growing at a far more rapid rate than ever before in the history of humankind. . . . More than ever, the sheer magnitude of human knowledge renders its coverage by education an impossibility; rather, the goal of education is better conceived as helping students develop the intellectual tools and learning strategies needed to acquire the knowledge that allows people to think productively . . . [to become] self-sustaining, lifelong learners. (pp. 4–5)

This imperative for new learning is echoed by many others. According to Robert Lerman and Stefanie Schmidt (1999), most economic analysts believe that employers will seek different skills than in the past. They observe that changes in the occupational and industrial structures of the economy that took place between 1960 and the mid-1980s led to a growth in demand for cognitive and interpersonal skills and a decline in demand for motor skills. They report the findings of a recent survey of firms in major U.S. metropolitan areas that among lower-level workers holding jobs that do not require a college education, 70% must work directly with customers, 61% must read and write paragraphs, 65% must perform arithmetic operations, and 51% must use computers.

Levy and Murnane (2004) argue that the general nature of work has been shifting for some time from routine to nonroutine. They report that between 1969 and 1999, the number of jobs requiring routine manual tasks—those organized around *a priori* rules—declined 3%. The number of jobs requiring routine cognitive tasks declined nearly 8%. On the other hand, jobs requiring nonroutine tasks increased substantially. The number of jobs requiring expert thinking—solving problems for which there are no rule-based solutions—rose 14% while the number of jobs calling for complex communication—for example, interactions with other people to acquire information, explain it, and persuade them of its implications for action—rose 9%.

Levy and Murnane (2004) also maintain that the growth of computer and information technologies has had its most negative impact on blue collar and clerical workers in rule-based jobs. This "bias" against "less-skilled" workers will continue, they predict, and will expand to other jobs with large rules-based components, such as tax preparation and computer programming. They suspect that "the major consequence of computerization will not be mass unemployment but a continued decline in the demand for moderately skilled and less skilled labor" (p. 152). Job growth will be greatest in higher-skill occupations in which computers complement expert thinking and complex communication.

Consistent with the National Research Council's (2000) statement, Thomas Friedman (2006) argues in his best-selling book *The World Is Flat* that young people will need to develop new sets of skills and attitudes to prosper in the future. The first and foremost is the ability to learn how to learn, "to constantly absorb and teach oneself new ways of doing old things or new ways of doing new things" (p. 302). While one's intelligence quotient (IQ) will still matter, Friedman believes that the importance of continuous learning will make curiosity and a passion for learning imperative. Having good "people skills" will be even more important in the future. Friedman contends that "there are going to be a whole slew of new middle jobs that involve personalized, high-touch interactions with other human beings—because it is precisely those personalized high-touch interactions that can never be outsourced or automated and are almost always necessary at some point in the value chain" (p. 306). Finally, the future will demand substantially greater development of "right-brain" capacity such as "forging relationships rather that executing transactions, taking novel challenges instead of solving routine problems, and synthesizing the big picture rather than analyzing a single component" (p. 307). Jobs that can be reduced to a set of "rules, routines, and instructions" are migrating overseas to less expensive labor markets and are being supplanted by new technologies. Friedman concludes that if workers in other countries can do such "left-brain work" as well and for less money, "we in the United States must do right-brain work better" (p. 308).

Others have argued for the need to expand learning beyond that required for employment. Levy and Murnane (2004) contend that in addition to developing new skills that will be required for the labor market of the future, it will be imperative to prepare young people for the "challenging political time" that will accompany economic and occupational changes and the redistribution of wages that will follow. The skills needed to excel at expert thinking and complex communication in work are skills that will also be important for engaging myriad social and political issues that lie ahead. They conclude, "The skills critical to expert thinking and complex communication are just as important to meeting [social and political] goals as they are to earning a living in a work world filled with computers" (p. 156).

Psychologist Howard Gardner (2006) is even more explicit. "The world of the future," he argues, "will demand capacities that until now have been mere options" (p. 2). Gardner speaks of the need to cultivate five minds for the future. The first is the *disciplined mind*. It will be important for persons to master at least one distinctive mode of thinking, of cognition associated with a particular scholarly field or discipline, craft, or profession. The second, the *synthesizing mind*, allows one to take information from disparate sources, understand and evaluate it objectively, and put that information together in ways that make sense to the person and to others. The capacity to synthesize will become even more crucial as information is produced and accumulates at "dizzying" rates. The third, the *creating mind*, builds on discipline and synthesis to "break new ground." This mind of the future "puts forth new ideas, poses unfamiliar questions, conjures up fresh ways of thinking, arrives at unexpected answers . . ." (p. 3). The fourth, the *respectful mind*, recognizes that now and in the future, one can no longer remain socially isolated. It "notes and welcomes differences between human individuals and between human groups, tries to understand these 'others,' and seeks to work effectively with them . . ." (p. 3). The fifth, the *ethical mind*, considers the needs and desires of self and society. This mind conceptualizes "how workers can serve purposes beyond self-interest and how citizens can work unselfishly to improve the lot of all" (p. 3).

Each of these five minds has been important historically and each, Gardner argues, will be more important in the future:

> Whatever their importance in times past, these five minds are likely to be crucial in a world marked by the hegemony of science and technology, global transmission of huge amounts of information, handling of routine tasks by computers and robots, and ever increasing contacts of all sorts between diverse populations. Those who succeed in cultivating the pentad of minds are most likely to thrive. (p. 163)

With these minds, a person will be equipped to engage not only the expected but also the unexpected. Without them a person will be "at the mercy of forces that he or she can't understand, let alone control" (p. 2).

Higher Performance and Outcomes

Demands are also increasing for schools to perform more effectively and to achieve better outcomes for greater numbers of students. In short, schools are being asked to do more and do better without commensurate increases in resources (often with fewer resources). While assessing the overall quality and performance of schools is not a simple matter and while that assessment is politically contentious (e.g., Berliner & Biddle, 1996), these demands nevertheless exist and are coming from a larger number and a wider range of sources. Demands for higher performance are related to but can also be seen as different from demands for new learning. That is, independent of specific learning sought, schools are seen generally as under-performing organizations that fail to serve all their students well.

Recent demands for improved performance and outcomes often begin with critiques of the preparedness of students for jobs, of trends in student academic achievement (particularly as measured by standardized test scores), and of the academic performance of American students in international comparisons.[4] The basic argument is that current levels of school performance and outcomes are unsatisfactory and current levels will be even more unsatisfactory in the future. An increasingly complex, contentious, and changing world requires ever-increasing levels of performance from schools if the nation is to remain economically competitive and preserve if not improve its global standing.[5]

Demands for higher performance and outcomes also arise from critiques that schools are working much better for some students than for others. Recent data from the National Assessment of Educational Progress (NAEP) show that while there has been some long-term progress (Perie, Moran, & Lutkus, 2005), substantial gaps exist in the academic achievement of white, African American, and Hispanic students (Planty et al., 2008; see also Hedges & Nowell, 1999). Achievement of students in high-poverty public schools lags substantially behind the achievement of students in low-poverty schools. Students in central-city public schools tend to achieve at significantly lower rates than students in schools in rural areas and the urban fringe (National Center for Education Statistics, 2006). While dropout rates have been declining nationally since 1972, the dropout rate for African American students is almost twice that of white students (Planty et al., 2008). The dropout rate for Hispanic students is almost twice that of African American students. Demands for addressing the under performance of low-income and minority students reflect equity and social justice concerns. Boyd (2003) observed that as the general population becomes more diverse and as minority populations constitute larger proportions of the workforce, the equity agenda and the economic agenda may converge into a more unified set of demands for schools to serve all students well.

There are other factors that portend a future of increasing demands on schools to perform better. The introduction of market-based reforms, particularly choice policy, the growing school improvement industry, and increasing privatization of school services embody demands for ever-increasing performance (see Boyd, 2003; McDonnell, 2008; Rowan, 2002). These demands are implicit (or explicit) in the threats that competition poses of losing clients—students—and the funding attached to them, losing control, and losing opportunities for "doing business." And several political phenomena all but guarantee the continuation, even the intensification of demands on schools, no matter how well they are performing. These phenomena manifest themselves in many ways, including the familiar sound bite of election-year politics: "If I'm elected, I will demand more from the public schools."

Some time ago, Anthony Downs (1972) observed that issues—such as education—keep coming back to the political agenda because they never get solved. Progress is made, perhaps, but satisfactory resolution is not achieved. Pointing to what he called the "issue-attention cycle," he argued that multiple issues compete for public and political attention and that our attention to any particular issue tends to be relatively short. Attention never stays focused on large, complex, difficult-to-solve issues very long. Issues that command attention at any given moment are likely to recede as other issues are perceived as more interesting or pressing. Attention returns to earlier issues as they seem more interesting and pressing again and as current issues lose salience.

Some years later, David Tyack (1991) pointed to lags between political and policy cycles and practice cycles (see also Tyack & Cuban, 1995). The former tend to be much shorter than the latter, meaning that improvement in practice (e.g., school performance and outcomes) almost always lags behind the political demand for it. Thus, the demand will never go away. There will be more recurrent "policy talk" about change than actual change in practice. But as Tyack reminds us, education policy talk is not simply about school improvement. It constitutes an "arena" within which enduring arguments about deep social values and social futures take place. As these arguments are unlikely to be resolved (see Cuban, 1990), so too will demands continue for schools to do better.

Yet another reason that demands on schools will likely continue is the political need to "keep problems alive." According to Sandra Stein (2004), problems are often perpetuated in order to attract support—both political and financial—to preserve individual and group influence, particular political positions, and specific policies and programs (see also Kingdon, 1995). Thus, even as progress is made, the political system provides incentives to continuously "move the goalposts." If a problem gets solved, the need for support goes away. And if support goes away, then positions, policies, programs, and influence are put at risk. All of this is to say that the political process itself is wired in such a way that demands for ever-better performance, and outcomes will continue to be an important part of the future of schools.

Greater Accountability

Demands for better performance and outcomes, as well as for effective and efficient use of scarce resources, are related to calls for schools to be ever more accountable. Boyd (2003) observed, "A race is on among political leaders to see who can promote the toughest testing and accountability programs for schools" (p. 3). Indeed, almost every state has implemented some education accountability agenda. And then there is *No Child Left Behind*. The focus is shifting from accountability for the use of inputs (e.g., funding) to the "production" of student outcomes (Lugg et al., 2002). The push for increased accountability is fueled by multiple agendas including dismantling of the current system of public education (Boyd, 2003). For whatever the range of agendas, one reason for the turn to accountability is what McDonnell (2008) sees as the failure of policy makers to find reforms that "penetrate the classroom" and lead to deep, long-lasting improvement in school performance and student outcomes. Being thwarted in other attempts to bring about change, policy makers have resorted to increased specification of outcomes and sanctions should they not be achieved. How those outcomes will be achieved is left largely to schools and school districts. It is a logic of, "We can't figure out how to improve you, so you do it yourselves. And if you don't, there will be consequences."

The push for greater accountability has followed two general tracks: mandates and sanctions, and market mechanisms (Hannaway & Woodroffe, 2003; Lugg et al., 2002). The former establish objectives and consequences. The latter seek to make schools more accountable to a broader range of non-educator stakeholders, including parents, through increased competition. Specific accountability programs and policies have proliferated, among them standards and high-stakes testing programs; school report cards and other public reports of school performance; ending student social promotion; plans for state takeovers and reconstitution of failing schools, sometimes under private, for-profit management; privatization of services; vouchers;

charters. School choice provisions, and support for home schooling. Even the changes discussed earlier that shift political control of schools from professional educators to parents, non-educators, and the private sector.

Such demands for school accountability are clearly illustrated by *No Child Left Behind*. This legislation places substantial emphasis on standards, standardized testing, disaggregation of data to monitor and promote the progress of different student groups, and sanctions for lack of improvement. It also combines standards-based accountability with market-based accountability by requiring that school districts provide students in failing schools additional support and if schools fail to improve the ability and means for students to choose to attend more academic-effective schools.

Ironically, the mechanisms for change evoked by *No Child Left Behind* and other accountability policies may not necessarily be conducive to schools' efforts to meet other demands placed upon them, particularly the demands for new learning. Several recent studies of how schools respond to external accountability imposed by high-stakes policies suggest just this (e.g., Darling-Hammond & Rustique-Forrester, 2005; Farkas & Duffett, 2008; Mintrop & Trujillo, 2007; see also McNeil, 2000). These studies illustrate how these policies can narrow the curriculum, shift instruction toward subject matter tested, and sacrifice subject matter that is not tested, that may be controversial, or that is difficult to teach (Schwartz, 2005). They can direct teachers to work more closely with some students than with others and to engage students in more review and test preparation and less instruction in new subject matter. For some students, particularly those in high-minority, low-achieving urban schools, instruction may be pushed in the direction of the most shallow and basic skills required for the greatest numbers of students to "pass" the test (Maudus & Clarke, 2001; Rhoten, Carnoy, Chabran, & Elmore, 2003). Even where tests purport to measure higher-order skills and analytic capacities (e.g., the ACT), there is evidence that so much time may be devoted to test preparation that instruction to develop the skills and capacities to be tested is sacrificed (e.g., Allensworth, Correa, & Ponisciak, 2008; Nagaoka & Roderick, 2004).

Current research on school choice provides little evidence that competitive, market-based mechanisms promote school improvement and innovation (e.g., Fiske & Ladd, 2000; Hess, 2003).[6] Some preliminary findings suggest that students in schools faced with competition may perform better on standardized tests than students in schools that do not face competition. Some schools may become more alert to the needs of their students, adopt new outreach practices, or adopt new programs that might appeal to students and families they might lose. However, there are few studies and little evidence that show that competition spurs innovation or more substantial improvements in school organization and educational processes. There is some evidence that competition can promote some undesirable side effects, especially an erosion of professional relationships that may be important to promote school improvement and innovation. According to Fiske and Ladd (2000), principals and teachers in some competitive contexts have become "less willing to share pedagogical and other ideas with their counterparts at schools with which their school is competing for students" (p. 9). As will be discussed in Chapter 2, such behavior is consistent with the general tendencies of organizations under external stress to become more protective and insular.

Demands for ever-better performance and outcomes and for greater accountability reveal a curious ambivalence about schools that is also likely to be part of the future. At the same time that schools are blamed for poor performance and outcomes and failing to prepare students adequately for the future, they are also asked to take on more and are entrusted as a primary solution to our educational, economic, and social problems. There is a certain amount of irony that in this age of increasing expectations and accountability, schools find themselves left largely on their own to find the means—both the strategies and the resources—to improve and to achieve outcomes for which they are held accountable (Hargreaves, 2003; Hopkins, 2001). The logic can be viewed either as extremely optimistic about the ability of schools to improve on their own and to perform at higher levels or as deeply cynical.

MEETING THE CHALLENGES

These shifting terrains point to a future for schools of increasing complexity, change, and uncertainty, a future where it is not clear what schools should look like or do to be responsive and successful. As Gardner (2006) observes, schools are organized around educational goals and practices that may have been useful "for the world of the past, rather than for possible worlds of the future" (p. 17). He continues, "No one knows precisely how to fashion an education that will yield individuals who are disciplined, synthesizing, creative, respective, and ethical" (p. 19; see also Fink, 2000; Friedman, 2006). The question is whether schools are suited to succeed in this future. There are a several reasons to believe that most are not.

Most schools may find it difficult to succeed in a future of change and uncertainty because they are organized for stability. As Pallas, Natriello, & McDill (1995) note, they are organized as if their tasks were "predictable and routine" (p. 43). They are not organized, as Goh, Cousins, & Elliott (2006) suggest, for a future of continual adaptation to meet the needs and demands of their many stakeholders. Schools are organized as if they exist in stable environments. As a rule, they lack the capacity, the "competence," and some might say the inclination to be flexible, to adapt quickly, and to innovate (Hopkins, 2001; Timar & Kirp, 1987). Conventional mechanisms that might be employed to promote flexibility and change—such as teacher professional development, supervisory and evaluation practices, staff incentive and accountability systems, information gathering and analytic capacity, even leadership—are typically weak. The "grammar of schooling" or the "genetic codes" of school organization seem programmed for persistence, for reactive rather than proactive behavior, for defending rather than prospecting (Laughlin, 1991; March, 1991; O'Day, 2002; Tyack & Cuban, 1995).

Andy Hargreaves (2003) contends that even schools that are trying to move toward the future may be trapped by organizational structures and processes of the past. He describes the most future-oriented schools that he recently studied this way:

> [Even] schools that were preparing young people for the rapid change and complexity of a postmodern, postindustrial world were actually locked in modern—even pre-modern—principles of the factory and the monastery. Schools were still ruled by clocks and bells, periods and classes; children were grouped by age and taught memorizable knowledge via a standardized curriculum that was conventionally tested. Much of this conventional "modernism" of our school systems persists through the actions of professionals and bureaucrats who look inward to the custom of certain of their own expertise and routines rather than outward to the concerns of students, families and communities. (p. 21)

These tendencies are reinforced in a number of ways. Traditionally, principals have been rewarded by their central offices not so much for their own performance or the performance of their schools, but for the lack of disruption, the lack of problems, and the lack of change (Smylie & Crowson, 1993). As Robert Crowson and Van Cleve Morris (1991) observed in their study of central offices, the traditional stance of the superintendent has been, "I leave my principals alone to run their schools. But I tell them 'No surprises.'" (p. 207). This may be changing in the present period of increasing accountability for student outcomes to something like this, "I leave my principals alone to run their schools. But I tell them 'No surprises. And get your test scores up!'" Larry Cuban (1990) described a "grand bargain" struck between principals and teachers. Principals agree not to press teachers too hard to do things differently if teachers agree to provide support needed to maintain their schools' stability and credibility in the eyes of those who monitor and control them—parents, tax-paying citizens, and state and federal education agencies. There are also, as David Tyack (1974) has described them, the historical inclinations of school systems to develop and perpetuate the "one best system" as a means of centralized control over local school operation.

Yet another reason that schools may find it difficult to succeed in the future is the broad range of external forces that reinforce convention and suppress differentiation and innovation. One of these forces consists of the institutional demands on schools to reflect what is valued and expected of them by broader society. Such "deep structural" expectations dictate what schools should look like, how they should to operate, and what they are to achieve (Tye, 2000). It is the notion of the school system "encapsulated" by its external environment (Sarason, 1973, 1996). This phenomenon is related to institutional isomorphism—the idea that broad environmental norms and expectations press organizations to emulate each other to reflect those norms and expectations (Meyer & Rowan, 1978; DiMaggio & Powell, 1983; Scott, 2007). By reflecting them, organizations gain credibility, legitimacy, and the support of the environments on which they depend often for survival (Weiler, 1993; see also Shipps, Kahne, & Smylie, 1999). The net effect is more similarity than difference among organizations that perform "like" functions and more stability than change.

Cuban (1990) brings these ideas together in an argument that a primary reason why schools tend to "reform again, again, and again" but not progress very much is that they confront strong external pressures to comply with a limited number of historical expectations or scripts. These scripts relate to performing basic, traditional functions of maintaining order and producing students who appear to have learned what is valued and expected by the larger society. Change tends to occur within the "boundaries" of these scripts. Cuban contends that these scripts constrain more expansive change and innovation. School systems pay close attention to their policies and practices and how they "signal to the public that the schools are really schools and are doing what they are supposed to do" (p. 11). Departures are carefully "scrutinized" for potential risks.

Such institutional arguments assume that larger environments are generally stable, predictable, and very slow to change. They suggest that whole "institutional fields" must shift in order for organizations to change in more than incidental ways. But even as organizations are able to achieve "symbiotic" relationships with their environments through mostly small and incremental adjustments (e.g., Burke, 2008), these relationships can fall severely out of alignment either because organizations do not manage these relationships well or because institutional environments can indeed change in significant ways (Weick, 1993). As noted at the beginning of this chapter, Boyd (2003) believed that such significant changes in institutional fields may be happening now. The irony is that the ways in which organizations tend to respond to extensive external pressure for change may not be particularly productive or conducive to improvement over time.

Long ago, James Thompson (1967) observed that when confronted with uncertainty and threats from their environments, organizations seek to reestablish certainty and ameliorate those threats in ways that are consistent with their core beliefs and functions, that is, their "technical cores." When uncertainty and threats intensify, organizations protect their cores, even when it means compromising their performance and productivity. When organizations experience extreme external stress from uncertainty or from other sources, their responses tend to be even more protective and potentially dysfunctional (March, 1994; Simon, 1986; Weick, 1993; see also O'Day, 2002). Organizations under extreme stress tend to adopt short-term, often symbolic strategies to ameliorate the stress. They tend to rely on current knowledge and assumptions that restrict information processing and learning. And they revert to familiar behaviors rather than engage in more risky behaviors of experimentation and innovation. Organizations under extreme stress tend to centralize and consolidate authority to increase their sense of internal stability and control. They abandon collective activity and revert to individual action. They "circle the wagons" and buffer themselves against external influences, which may cut off sources of support and limit access to solutions to problems.

Such responses can be seen in the findings of research discussed earlier on instructional responses to high-stakes testing policies and sanctions. They can also be seen in findings of other studies on school organizational responses to these policies. For example, these policies have been found to induce new sources of stress into teachers' relationships with students and parents and create disincentives for teachers to assume the risks of trying to change and presumably improve their classroom practice (e.g., Schwartz, 2005; Valli & Buese, 2007). They have been found to "crowd out" or "swamp" other types of reforms aimed at developing organizational and professional capacities that may be conducive to school improvement and performance in the long run (Lipman, 2002; O'Day, 2002; Smylie & Wenzel, 2003). A recent study of Chicago public elementary schools found that following the ascendance of centralized high-stakes testing, school probation, and "ending social promotion" policies was a systemic erosion of elements of social and organizational infrastructures of schools (Sporte, Smylie, Allensworth, & Miller, 2003). These elements included principal instructional leadership; teacher influence and inclusiveness of teachers and parents in decision making; teacher collaboration and their collective focus on and responsibility for student learning; teacher inclination toward innovation; teachers' commitment to their schools; and outreach to parents, parent involvement in school, and teacher-parent trust. Ironically, these organizational elements have been found in other research to be related positively to school effectiveness and instructional improvement (Sebring, Allensworth, Bryk, Easton, & Luppescu, 2006).

THE CALL FOR CONTINUOUS IMPROVEMENT

Because of their orientations and tendencies toward persistence and stability, most schools will find it difficult to meet the challenges of the future. It will be difficult for them to adapt effectively to changing conditions and to meet demands for new learning. It will be difficult for them to achieve greater performance and outcomes. This takes us to the call for schools to organize for "increasingly elusive certainty" (Pallas et al., 1995, p. 43), to adopt the organizational properties and the processes of continuous improvement, to become continuously improving organizations. The call is summarized well in Nobel Prize winning scientist Kenneth Wilson and Bennett Daviss's (1994) argument about the need for redesigning education:

> To effect fundamental meaningful reforms, *all* educators must first be able to admit and agree that our traditional guiding vision of education is no longer relevant in a postindustrial, knowledge-based society. . . . Second, educators must accept, then build on, the model that the needs of a new society demand. Finally, when our schools do acknowledge education's new paradigm, they will need an ordered process of change that will enable them to exchange the patterns rooted in an antiquated structure of ideas for those needed to enact a new vision . . . a process of continuous, guided innovation. (pp. 20–21)

As was noted at the beginning of this chapter, the idea of continuous improvement is not new. I will present a brief history of the concept in Chapter 2. For now, it is useful to recall from the pages of Michael Fullan's (2005) recent book on leadership and long-term school success a challenge Donald Schön issued more than 20 years ago:

> We must become able not only to transform our institutions in response to changing situations and requirements; we must invest and develop institutions which act as "learning systems," that is to say, systems capable of bringing about their own continuing transformation. (pp. 15–16)

Fullan (2005) further develops Schön's idea in terms of his own concept of "sustainability." He defines sustainability as "the capacity of a system to engage in the complexities of continuous improvement consistent with deep values of human purpose" (p. ix). He argues that sustainability requires ongoing movement and improvement in the face of complex challenges that "keep arising" (p. 22; see also Koberg, 1986). Fullan contends that the strategies that may have brought success to a school in the past might not bring success in the future or help a school achieve greater performance or outcomes. And he argues that it is not just the outcome of continuous improvement that matters. It is also the development of the organizational system itself that can "display dynamic sustainability" (p. ix; see also Fullan, 1993). Andy Hargreaves and Dean Fink (2006) extend this idea further arguing that sustainability, or shall we say continuous improvement, should go beyond developing new organizational systems that "last" in rapidly changing and uncertain times. Those systems should have the capacity to develop "deep learning for all that spreads and lasts, in ways that . . . create positive benefit for others around us, now and in the future" (p. 17).

QUESTIONS FOR STUDY, REFLECTION, AND ACTION

1. What changes have you seen in the following terrains of your school and school district in the past five years? Ten years? What evidence can you point to that shows these changes?

   - Jobs and the nature of work for which students are to be prepared
   - Politics and control of education

- School funding
- The characteristics and conditions of children and youth
- Demands for new learning, higher performance, and accountability

2. What changes do you anticipate occurring in these terrains in the next five years? Ten years? On what evidence or rationale do you base your projections?

3. What challenges and opportunities do such projections pose for your school and school district to educating all students effectively in the years ahead?

4. How prepared is your school and school district to meet these challenges and opportunities? Explain your assessment, pointing to particular strengths and weaknesses of your school and district.

5. How does the issue of inertia manifest itself in your school and school district? What are the likely sources of it? What evidence is there of inertia and its sources? What might be done to confront and overcome it?

The Meaning of Continuous Improvement

2

With Kelly Hallberg

> *Ecclesia reformata, semper reformanda.*
>
> —Presbyterian Church USA

> *Change is what we do everyday. Change is the way we are.*
>
> —Teacher at Blue Mountain Secondary School, Ontario, Canada

"Ecclesia reformata, semper reformanda" is often referred to as the "motto" of the Presbyterian Church USA. Roughly translated from the Latin, it means, "The church reformed and always to be reformed." Traced from the Protestant Reformation in Europe and first appearing in 17th century theological writings, the statement challenges the church to be always open to change, indeed to pursue change. Theologian Anna Case-Winters (2004) interprets the challenge this way: "[W]hile we honor the forms of faith and life that have been bequeathed to us, we honor them best in a spirit of openness to the Word and the Spirit that formed and continue to reform the church."

According to Case-Winters, there are at least three reasons why continuous reformation is important to the church. These reasons form a logic that is much like the logic of continuous improvement that is the subject of this chapter. The first is an understanding about the church itself. In Case-Winters' words, "The church is a frail and fallible pilgrim people, a people on the way, not yet what we shall be. The church, because of who we are, remains open to always being reformed." The reason for continuous reformation rests not only on who the people are and what the church is; it also rests on belief about God. God is a living God whose existence and will is continually revealed but can never be fully known or understood. The church must remain open to continuous reform as God continually reveals God's self and will to the church. The world is also always changing, requiring the church to continually reform to reflect its ever-changing understanding of God's will for the church in the world. Another element of this statement is relevant to our discussion. It is the stipulation that reform is never only for reform's sake (Case-Winters, 2004). While the church is assumed to have some will in the matter, the intent of the early reformers was for continuous reformation to be grounded in evolving understanding the Scripture as the Word of God. Reform was to be in service of the church's core mission and belief. It was to be intentional and directional (strategic even), and it was to be informed by faith and continuous search for the meaning of God's Word.

The second statement that heads this chapter introduces a number of dimensions of the concept of continuous improvement. The quotation, "Change is what we do everyday. Change is the way we are," is used by Andy Hargreaves (2003, p. 156) to demonstrate what he calls an "essential truth" about a school that developed the structures, processes, and ethos conducive to continuous improvement. The quote explains why this school was able to learn and improve continuously, withstand internal difficulties, and "absorb and rework externally imposed changes in ways that protect[ed] and preserve[d] [its]mission" (p. 155). It was because change is what the school is and what it does everyday. This gets to the heart of the meaning of continuous improvement. It is at the same time three things: It is a way to think. It is a way to act. And it is an identity, an organizational way of life.

DEFINING CONTINUOUS IMPROVEMENT

Continuous improvement has been defined in many ways. In this section, I examine a sampler of contemporary definitions found in the education literature and in the broader organizational and management literature. After this sampler, I identify common properties of these definitions to suggest some shared meaning. First, I take a brief look at the history of the concept.

A Brief History of the Concept

This chapter began with a little tongue-in-cheek suggesting that today's concept of continuous improvement can be traced to the Protestant Reformation. While there may be something to this, most scholars consider the idea of continuous improvement to be a direct descendent of the principles of scientific management developed in the late 19th and early 20th centuries (Bhuiyan & Baghel, 2005; Taylor 1911). These principles were first applied in industrial and manufacturing organizations and then to other types of organizations, including schools and school districts (Callahan, 1962). They focused on managerial use of "scientific methods" to improve the quality of products and to solve production problems related to quality control and production efficiency.

These early principles developed throughout the 1920s as seen prominently in Walter A. Shewhart's (1931) statistical methods of quality control. Shewhart's work laid the foundation for the "quality movement" in the United States (Zangwill & Kantor, 1998). According to Reed, Lemak, & Montgomery (1996), the catalyst for this movement was the U.S. Department of Defense's adoption of statistical quality control to regulate its procurement of munitions early in World War II. Later in the war, the federal government promoted principles of quality control through the "Training Within Industry" program that was designed to increase the country's industrial output (Bhuiyan & Baghel,

2005). This program was introduced in Japan at the end of the war by U.S. military forces and by management experts such as W. Edwards Deming (2000), Frank and Ernestine Gilbreth (1948), and Joseph Juran (1992). The Japanese eventually developed their own ideas and methods of quality control, which grew into a larger management philosophy and process for ongoing organizational improvement.

The Japanese approach to quality management became known as *kaizen*. Popularized in the United States by Masaaki Imai (1986) and others, the rough translation of kaizen is *kai*, meaning *change*, and *zen*, meaning *good* or *good change*. More recently, kaizen has been equated with continuous improvement—"the never-ending attention to detail that reduces the effort and time that it takes to conduct operations" (Reed et al., 1996, p. 181). During the 1950s and 1960s, management experts such as Deming, Juran, Philip B. Crosby, Armand Fiegenbaum, Kaoru Ishikawa, Genichi Taguchi, and others took the quality movement beyond statistical control to "reliability engineering and quality assurance."

Emphasis on quality management waned in the 1970s but reemerged in the mid-to-late 1980s as Total Quality Management (TQM). Despite its ubiquity through the early 2000s, it has been difficult to pin down a clear and common meaning of TQM (Hackman & Wageman, 1995; Yong & Wilkinson, 1999). Still, across the numerous conceptualizations of quality management, continuous improvement is usually identified as one of its several "critical components" (Anderson, Rungtusanatham, & Schroeder, 1994; Lillrank, Shani, & Lindberg, 2001). James Dean, Jr. and David Bowen (1994) understand continuous improvement in TQM as "a commitment to constant examination of technical and administrative processes in search of better methods" (p. 394). They see in it the belief that by improving processes, "organizations can continue to meet the increasingly stringent expectations of their customers" (p. 394). Richard Hackman and Ruth Wageman (1995) also identify continuous improvement as one of several broad principles of TQM. They contend that behind the various models and practices of TQM is the idea that the long-term health of an organization depends on "treating quality improvement as a never-ending quest" (p. 312). As they view it, opportunities to develop better methods for carrying out work will always exist and organizational commitment to continuous improvement "ensures that people will never stop learning about the work they do" (p. 312).

Contemporary thinking about continuous improvement is also related to a number of other concepts of organizational change and improvement that developed during and after the 1970s. These include concepts of organizational self-design, organizational improvisation, high reliability organizations, and organizational learning. It is well beyond this chapter to explore these concepts in the depth that they deserve. For an introduction to these concepts, the reader is referred to the respective literatures.[7]

A Sampler of Contemporary Definitions

For as much as continuous improvement has been written about in the education literature, there are very few efforts to define the term directly or analyze it conceptually. Much contemporary writing on continuous improvement proceeds as if its meaning is self-evident. Among the few efforts to define continuous improvement in schools and school districts are the following examples (see also Fullan, 2005 and Hargreaves & Fink, 2006).

- James Detert, Karen Louis, and Roger Schroeder (2001) conceptualize continuous improvement as a cultural value of school organization. Consistent with that value, "Teachers and others in the school should devote time and energy to make things better. This is a never-ending process" (p. 191).

- AdvancED (n.d.a, b), the umbrella organization for North Central Association and the Southern Association of Colleges and Schools, names continuous improvement as one of its standards for school accreditation. It defines continuous improvement as a commitment of schools to "being better today than they were yesterday." It is a "quality improvement process that yields results for students." This process articulates a vision and purpose; maintains a "rich and current description" of students, their performance, school effectiveness and the school community; employs goals and interventions to improve student performance; and documents and uses the results to inform what happens next.

- The National Education Association (2008) and Willis Hawley and Gary Sykes (2007) define continuous improvement as a means by which "organizations work in steady, systematic fashion to improve their results" (NEA, 2008). Change in effective schools is a constant. Continuous improvement focuses attention on "discovering and implementing ways to achieve core goals related to student learning. [T]he persistent and collaborative analysis of the reasons for differences between goals for student learning and actual student performance is the engine that drives coherent collective action" (NEA, 2008).

- Lawrence Lezotte and Kathleen McKee (2002) define continuous improvement as "a never-ending cycle of self-examination and adjustment" (p. ix). School improvement is an endless succession of incremental change. The effective school and school district will continually ask, "How are we doing? What can we do better? How can we better serve our students?" (p. ix). Continuous improvement is both "an attitude and a set of concepts and tools" (p. 35). "The underlying attitude," they contend, "is that anything and everything can be improved" (p. 35). The process of continuous improvement is a cycle of action, evaluation, and reflection that should result in continuous adjustment of activities in response to changing environments, new research on practices, and the success or failure of present efforts. Continuous improvement is a "cycle of self-renewal" (p. 7).

If we look to the broader organizational and management literature, we find that continuous improvement is defined in at least three general ways. One way is as a set of values and beliefs or as an orientation of an organization. For example, Nadia Bhuiyan and Amit Baghel (2005) define continuous improvement as a "philosophy" and as a "culture" of an organization that manifest themselves in improvement initiatives to increase success, eliminate waste in systems and processes, and reduce failures. James Dean and David Bowen (1994) define continuous improvement as "a commitment to constant examination of technical and administration processes in search of better methods" (p. 395). John Anderson and his colleagues (1994) define continuous improvement as a "propensity of an organization to pursue incremental and innovative improvements of its processes, products, and services" (p. 623). According to this perspective, leaders, organizational members, and stakeholders believe in the importance of continuous improvement. They are committed to ongoing learning and growth. This is accompanied by a sense that the organization can always be better and stronger.

A second way that continuous improvement has been defined is as a strategic organizational process. Robert Burgelman (1991) calls continuous improvement a process of "strategic renewal . . . through which an organization can indefinitely maintain adaptive[ness]" (p. 255). Sarah Caffyn (1999) defines continuous improvement as the "ability of an organization to gain strategic advantage" (p. 1138). In similar fashion, Martha Feldman and Brian Pentland (2003) define continuous improvement as a "metaroutine" of an organization, in other words, a routine for "changing routines [and] to generate change" (p. 94). Sometimes definitions of this type will focus on specific managerial models and practices that purport to help organizations respond to new demands or to innovate.[8]

Continuous improvement has also been defined as an organizational property. Continuous improvement is not just what an organization does. Continuous improvement is what an organization is. It is how an organization is organized and how it continues to organize over time. John Bessant and David Francis (1999) have called continuous improvement a "dynamic capability" of organization. They define it as "a collection of attributes which are built up over time in highly firm-specific fashion and which provide the basis for achieving and maintaining competitive edge in an uncertain and rapidly changing environment" (p. 1106). Shona Brown and Kathleen Eisenhardt (1998) consider continuous improvement "a core competence" of organization, "endemic" to the ways that successful organizations compete in rapidly changing environments.

Others have fashioned more comprehensive definitions. Two particularly useful examples are those of Yoram Mitki and Paul Lillrank and their respective colleagues. First, Mitki, Shani, & Meiri's (1997) definition:

> Continuous improvement is a process that involves everyone, employees and managers alike. It is a process that involves the ongoing rearranging and redesigning of elements of the organization; it requires the continuous rethinking of the patterns that connect and relate different elements of the organization and connect them with the environment; it is a process that bundles together data collection, interpretation, research, experimentation and diffusion; and it involves the individual, the team, and the total organization. As such, continuous improvement seeks to develop new cognitive frameworks, interpretive schemes and actions on ongoing bases. (p. 429)

And Lillrank and his colleagues' (1998) definition is as follows:

> Continuous improvement is a purposeful and explicit set of principles, mechanisms, and activities within an organization, designed to achieve positive and continuous change in deliverables, operating procedures, and systems by the people who actually perform these procedures and work under these systems. Continuous improvement takes place in increments that, taken separately, will not constitute a fundamental change in the operating structures, processes, and mechanisms of the organization, but over time may have a fundamental impact on how an organization operates. . . . (p. 50)

A few years later, Lillrank and his colleagues (2001) extended this definition to refer to "ongoing, systematic, and cumulative improvement" in deliverables, operating procedures, and systems rather than simply "positive and continuous change (p. 44) ." They went further to indicate that continuous improvement was "a response to environment conditions that call for organizations to develop methods for adaptation" (p. 42). This response is subject to "conscious and goal-oriented managerial effort" that can be described as "a set of design requirements" for an organization to achieve continuous improvement in a systematic way (p. 42).

Taken together, these various definitions consider continuous improvement as something that organizations do and are, and something that organizations strive to achieve. Continuous improvement is both a "means" and an "end," a noun and a verb. The concept embodies the notion of continuously getting better, performing better, and achieving objectives more effectively. The concept also embodies ideas about organizational orientations and processes by which such outcomes are achieved.

Considering the Meaning of *Improvement*

While the meaning of the word *improvement* in continuous improvement may seem obvious, it is important to remember that it connotes something more than change and something more than organizational adjustment and adaptation to internal or external demands. Neither change nor adjustment and adaptation require improvement. Both can serve to reinforce the status quo, which may not be bad sometimes. Both can also represent regress or change in an unproductive direction. Improvement requires change in the direction toward some valued objective.

Considering the word *improvement* with the word *continuous*, the something valued is not some goal or end state that can be finally achieved. No final "mission accomplished." To be sure, there is progress to be made, successes to be attained, and objectives to be met. But improvement in the sense of continuous improvement is never fully achieved. The valued outcome is the organization getting better and better and better at what it is, at what it does, and what it achieves, ad infinitum. It is the stance that good is never good enough.

Common Characteristics

If we look across different definitions of continuous improvement, it is possible to identify eight common descriptive characteristics that connote some core of shared meaning:

1. Regular and ongoing

2. Oriented toward small incremental changes

3. Intentional and strategic

4. Proactive as well as reactive

5. Focused on the whole organization

6. Inclusive of all organizational members

7. Oriented toward the organization's mission and core values

8. Integral to an organization's mission, identity, design, and basic functions

These characteristics can be elaborated as follows. Continuous improvement is something that an organization attends to all the time. As will be discussed in Chapter 7, this does not necessarily mean that an organization is actually changing all the time. There may be periods when very little change takes place. However, it means that an organization is attending all the time to the prospects for improvement. It is regularly assessing its environment as well as its own capabilities, operations, and outcomes in search of problems and opportunities. Organizations engaged in continuous improvement are always "on the look out" and are always developing capacity to get better instead of merely adapting to sustain the status quo. They are continuously "prospecting" rather than "defending" (Fox-Wolfgramm, Boal, & Hunt, 1998).

Continuous improvement is accomplished through small, incremental advancements. Continuous improvement is not solely reflexive or solely reactive, although there may be times when it will be. It is deliberate and strategic. It assumes that the organization has agency and that its actions are not simply determined by external forces.

Continuous improvement is focused on all aspects of the organization. Everything is under scrutiny. Every aspect of the organization is "in play" and subject to improvement. Continuous improvement is not the sole province of executive leadership or a particular individual or organizational unit. Everyone is involved, perhaps not in everything all the time. But all organizational members are committed to continuous improvement and everyone "touches" and is touched by the work of continuous improvement somehow at some time. Finally, continuous improvement is central to what an organization is and what an organization does.

The principle of *equifinality* is also important in thinking about the meaning of continuous improvement. Referring to Ludwig Von Bertalanffy's (1950) work on general systems theory, W. Warner Burke (2008) describes equifinality as the idea whereby "an organization can attain the same goal from different starting points and by a variety of paths" (p. 53). Equifinality holds that different organizations, in different contexts, and starting from different places may need to use different strategies and take different routes. With regard to continuous improvement, equifinality means that different organizations may achieve continuous improvement in different ways. The literature indicates that there are common elements of processes and organizational design characteristics that are particularly conducive to continuous improvement. I will explore these processes and design characteristics beginning in Chapter 4. The literature also indicates that continuous improvement can be pursued successfully through a wide variety of specific strategies and practices. Those who study continuous improvement observe that different organizations are likely to use different combinations of practices and change those combinations as situations warrant (e.g., Bhuiyan & Baghel, 2005; General Accounting Office, 1994; Lillrank et al., 1998). I will return to this idea later.

THE LOGIC OF CONTINUOUS IMPROVEMENT

At the end of Chapter 1, we began to discuss the rationale for continuous improvement in schools. We resume that discussion here, looking in particular at the theory or logic of continuous improvement and its presumed benefits. In Chapter 3, we will examine the empirical evidence regarding such outcomes.

The Need for Continuous Improvement

In her book on modern, symbolic, and postmodern perspectives on organizations, Mary Jo Hatch (2006) recounts that classical management theorists and early modern organizational theorists nearly always focused on identifying "the organizational principles and structural elements that lead to optimal organizational performance in the belief that, once basic laws governing these relationships were discovered, the perfect organization could be designed" (p. 109). Hatch continues that such "stability-centered" views of organizations will no longer do. Instead, "change-centered" perspectives will need to play a larger role in organizational development and operation. According to Hatch, these perspectives are rooted in predictions of rapidly changing environments, technologies, and social, economic, and political institutions. She concludes that in order to keep up and to survive, organizations of the future will have to be built for change.

Beginning in the 1960s, contingency theorists urged organizations operating in uncertain and turbulent environments to adopt flexible, organic structures and processes so that they could adapt to ever-changing markets, customers, and competitors (e.g., Burns & Stalker, 1994). James Thompson (1967) argues that some organizations employ "intensive technologies," that is, ever-changing "custom" combinations of strategies and activities because of uncertainty in their environments, their inability to control inputs for production (e.g., raw materials), and the absence of organizational processes that could produce consistent results given that environmental uncertainty and lack of control. More recently, Carrie Leanna and Bruce Barry (2000) suggest that focusing on organizational stability "impedes adaptation for nearly all organizations as their environments become increasingly unpredictable" (p. 754). According to Wanda Orlikowski (1996), "In a fast-paced world, stability is out, change is in" (p. 63). She continues that conventional perspectives of organizations, "grounded as they are in the prior discourse of stability," are poorly suited to a world where change will be "a way of organizational life" (pp. 63, 64).[9]

The rationale for continuous improvement is linked to the premise that change is no longer a choice for most organizations. It is an imperative. Given rapidly changing environments, organizations will need to assess their surroundings and themselves continually and change accordingly. The issue is not whether to change; it is how to change and where to direct the change. Organizations will need to adapt, improve, and even innovate on an ongoing basis. Organizations will need to change in small, incremental ways and in fundamental ways. Organizations will need to understand that any current state is or may soon be insufficient. This will require more than organizational reflex; it will require strategic agency (Hatch, 2006). It will require reconceptualizing the idea of organization as continuously "emergent." This is similar to Haridimos Tsoukas and Robert Chia's (2002) idea of "organization becoming" and to Weick's (1979) preference of the verb "organizing" to the noun "organization" when describing how organizational participants constantly construct and reconstruct their organizations by doing their work, by formally and informally gathering and analyzing information, and by making decisions and taking actions based on their analysis. Organizations are evolving enactments.

As described at the end of Chapter 1, the call for continuous improvement comes from the argument that as currently organized, most schools will find it difficult to adapt effectively to a rapidly changing and uncertain environment. It will be difficult for them to meet demands for new learning and to achieve higher and higher levels of performance and outcomes in that environment. Recall Wilson and Daviss's (1994) argument that schools will need to adopt "an ordered process of change that will enable them to exchange the patterns rooted in an antiquated structure of ideas for those needed to enact a new vision" (p. 21). Recall Schön's observation of the need to develop schools "capable of bringing about their own continuing transformation" (in Fullan, 2005, p. 16). And recall, Fullan's (2005) and Hargreaves and Fink's (2006) calls for the development of new educational organizational systems that can "display dynamic sustainability" in rapidly changing and uncertain times and that can continuously improve to achieve higher levels of performance and greater outcomes to benefit all.

Fullan provided an early rationale for continuous improvement in his 1993 book *Change Forces*. There he argues, "change is ubiquitous and relentless, forcing itself on us at every turn" (p. vii). He called for a "paradigm breakthrough" in how we think about and act in relation to this reality. "It is a world," he observes, "where change is a journey of unknown destination, where problems are our friends . . ." (pp. vii–viii). Change or its demands are not always predictable. This is why, he argues, schools need to develop "more generative capacities that can anticipate and rise to the occasions of change in a continuous basis as they occur" (p. viii). Fullan continues, "You cannot have an educational environment in which change is continuously expected alongside a conservative system and expect anything but constant aggravation" (p. 3). The new problem of change, as he put it, is to make the educational system "expert at dealing with change as a normal part of its work, not just in relation to the latest policy, but as a way of life" (p. 4). Schools must be able to contend with and manage the forces of change on an ongoing basis if they are to achieve their broader moral purpose—"to make a difference in the lives of students regardless of their background, and to help produce citizens who can live and work productively in increasingly dynamically complex societies" (p. 4).

Richard Elmore and Deanna Burney (1998) extend the argument by first drawing distinctions between the rationale for continuous improvement in public schools and the rationale for continuous improvement in the private sector. They observe that the core idea of continuous improvement in the private sector is that firms that work in competitive, quickly changing environments must develop internal processes for monitoring performance relative to competitors, seeking out and implementing state-of-the-art service and industrial processes, and implementing these processes through improvement cycles. The faster competitive environments change, the faster and more efficient these internal improvement processes must be. In the private sector, "continuous improvement takes its meaning mainly from a focus on improving the quality of services and products . . . in response to external competitive pressures" (p. 5). In public education, they contend, continuous improvement has a related but somewhat different rationale. Continuous improvement in public schools takes its point of departure less from competitive pressures, although those pressures may increase as states provide a greater variety of and choice among schools, and more from external pressures of accountability:

> Schools and school systems will begin to discover the demands of continuous improvement as they move into a period where state policy increasingly focuses on accountability for measurable student performance. (p. 6)

Arguments of Benefit

The basic idea behind continuous improvement is that making continuous, strategic, incremental changes can help organizations adapt to internal changes and changes in their environments. This will help organizations constantly improve their performance and productivity. And making strategic incremental changes across the organization as a whole can add up to fundamental changes in organizational structures, processes, and cultures (Orlikowski, 1996; Weick & Quinn, 1999). Concentrating on and investing in regular incremental changes can keep an organization flexible and nimble. Focusing on regular incremental change can foster innovation by making improvement part of organizational life rather than relegating it to an infrequent ancillary activity. According to Ty Choi (1995):

> Continuous improvement [CI] changes are incremental, and those people who institute them focus on making small-step changes rather than an instantaneous, large-scale change. . . . CI changes, which occur gradually and constantly, are less dramatic than abrupt and volatile changes, but their effects are long term and long lasting. The key advantage of such changes is that they readily become part of work routines. (p. 615)

The logic of continuous improvement is analogous to the logic of what Kerber and Buono (2005) call *guided changing*. Guided changing is an "interactive process" that begins with initial identification of problems and opportunities, the design of initiatives to address those problems and opportunities, implementation of and improvisation on those initiatives, learning from the effort, leading to ongoing reinterpretation and redesign of initiatives. They argue that "the resulting spiral of learning, innovation, and development contributes to both continuous improvement of existing change efforts as well as the ability to generate novel changes and solutions" in the future (p. 28).

There are other ways that continuous improvement is thought to promote organizational improvement and effectiveness. These include reducing the need for and costs of major organizational change, reducing what is called "threat-rigidity," mediating isomorphic tendencies, enhancing the prospects for productive organizational learning, and avoiding vicious circles and creating virtuous ones. Threat rigidity and isomorphic tendencies are two factors introduced in Chapter 1 that make it difficult for schools to change in significant ways.

Reducing the Need for and Costs of Major Change

The organization and management literature indicates that continuously improving organizations are not immune to the need to make major changes. Even though they may make small, incremental changes continually, there will be times when large, revolutionary changes must be made. All organizations will confront "big jolts" from their environments and engage the prospects of major change at times in their life spans. For schools, major changes may emanate from a number of sources, including but not limited to external policies and mandates (e.g., recent high-stakes testing and accountability systems), rapid changes in student populations (e.g., increases in immigration and racial and ethnic diversity), and severe reductions in funding or significant changes in staffing and leadership.

Major changes can be very disruptive and costly. They can exact a tremendous toll on organizations and individuals within them. Indeed, they can threaten organizational survival (Burke, 2008; Hannan & Freeman, 1984). In their review of the literature on the major change strategy called organizational "turnaround," Joseph Murphy and Coby Meyers (2007) found that turnaround efforts are more likely to result in failure than in success. They cite one source that claims that on average only one in four companies that attempt such major change recover successfully (Slatter, 1984). They cite a study of the American Management Association that estimates the success rate even lower, at about one in ten (Shuchman & White, 1995).

M. Anjali Sastry (1997) identified a number of high-impact risks associated with major organizational change. He argued that such change can be highly disorienting and debilitating. It can strain, drain, and destroy organizational competence and capacity and in the process lead to organizational failure. It can create extreme stress on employees and organizational processes and use a substantial amount of resources that may be necessary for organizational performance and survival. Sastry also argued that major change can cause organizational failure if it does not meet demands of the environment. In other words, the change may not address the problem that spawned it in the first place. Change can be too slow or lack the scope and intensity needed to bring the organization back into alignment with the environment, thus leading to additional stress and the prospects of failure. The change can be overly responsive to external demands, further draining necessary resources and exacerbating the lack of "fit" between the organization and the environment.

Another consequence of major change is the disruption it can cause in relationships between organizations and other actors and entities, including customers, clients, stakeholders, suppliers, competitors, and sources of political or financial support. Michael Hannan and John Freeman (1984) argue that organizations depend on such relationships for their productivity and survival. These relationships take time and resources to cultivate and manage. Organizations are able to accomplish things through these relationships that they are not able to alone. Hannan and Freeman contend that major organizational change can introduce a "liability of newness" and reset the liability of newness "clock" back to zero (p. 160). Major organizational change can introduce uncertainty and risks into these relationships, meaning that organizations must often spend considerable time and resources reestablishing them. This drives up the costs and risks of major change and, according to Hannan and Freeman, increases the death rate of organizations the longer the duration of the change process (see also Haveman, 1992).

Continuous improvement may help reduce the need for major change. By making ongoing adjustments and improvements, organizations may be able to lower the likelihood that the "gap" between performance and goals or the "misfit" of the organization to the environment would become so great as to require major transformational change. In the event that major change becomes necessary, continuous improvement may help organizations engage that change more productively. It may help reduce its costs and liabilities by having established the organizational capacity and expectations for change. In theory, organizations that have developed resources and routines for change and the inclination and orientation for it do better and are more efficient at making changes whether those changes are large or small. Organizations that establish and maintain relationships with other entities in their environments based on expectations and routines for continuous improvement are less likely to have to spend resources and assume liabilities of reestablishing relationships each time they change (see Haveman, 1992). Those relationships would be built around the expectation of ongoing improvement and innovation, not the expectation of stability.

These prospects are evident in the literature on organizational turnaround. Murphy and Meyers (2008) tell us that organizational decline that precedes the need for turnaround is often associated with a deterioration in an organization's ability to adapt to its environment. They tell us that decline can begin when an organization fails to anticipate or recognize problems with its own processes and performance and then fails to make the necessary improvements. On the flip side, the earlier that problems are recognized, the higher the probability that an organization can respond effectively and avoid the need for risky, radical change. The inference is that processes of continuous improvement may help an organization recognize signs of trouble and address problems before those problems become so great that major change is needed.

Reducing Threat-Rigidity

Alaistair Bain (1998) observed that organizations often possess socially constructed defenses that can suppress and limit their ability to learn and to change. These defenses are used to buffer individuals and organizations from excessive stresses and threats. They can exist in an organization's structures and routines, in its procedures and information systems, in the roles of its members, and in its culture. By reducing the ability to learn and to change, these defenses can be maladaptive.

In their study of the airline industry between 1962 and 1985, Dawn Kelly and Terry Amburgey (1991) examined the role of routines as a source of organizational stability during this period of deregulation and rapid environmental change. Older companies were more likely than newer companies to rely on existing routines and were constrained by them in their responses to new demands from the environment. The changes older companies made tended to be limited to areas of earlier changes of the same type and magnitude. Jesper Sørensen and Toby Stuart (2000) made similar findings about organizational age in their study of the semiconductor industry. They found that as companies grow older, they accumulate experience and develop competences and routines that help them increase the efficiency of their operations and help them innovate at greater rates than newer companies. At the same time that they may become more innovative, older companies have more difficulty maintaining a fit between their organizational capabilities and outcomes and the changing demands of their environments. Sørensen and Stuart (2000) found that gains in efficiency and effectiveness of organizational routines that come with age are likely to be achieved, in part, by simplifying assumptions about the state of the environment and by narrowing organizational capabilities in a manner consistent with those assumptions. With this narrowing comes the possibility that organizations will lose the ability to "assimilate and exploit new information" in particular domains (p. 87). If reinforced over time, these assumptions and capabilities are difficult to update, as are the routines that flow from them. These tendencies become a source of inertia and create conditions whereby organizations can drift out of alignment with their environments and put themselves at risk.

According to Barry Staw, Lance Sandelands, and Jane Dutton (1981), organizations tend to exhibit "maladaptive" tendencies as they confront changes in their environments that they perceive as threats and other forms of adversity (see also March, 1994; Simon, 1986). When organizations sense threat, they tend to become more anxious, more "rigid," and more persistent in their thinking and in their behaviors. Organizations tend to rely on "well-learned" assumptions and responses that may not be appropriate to or effective under new conditions (see Thompson, 1967).

Staw and his colleagues (1981) observed that threats, particularly severe ones, may result in "restriction of information processing," such as narrowing fields of attention, simplifying ways to think about information, and reducing the flow and sources of incoming information (p. 502). When they sense threat, organizations tend to simplify and reduce the number of alternatives they consider. They rely on experience and prior knowledge and restrict alternatives to those that are consistent with this knowledge and experience. Organizations under stress do not necessarily reduce their search for information or alternatives, but they focus that search on information that confirms choices rather than generates alternatives. Staw and his colleagues also observed that when they sense threats, organizations tend to centralize authority, consolidate control, and reduce autonomy and discretion. Organizations also redirect members' actions toward reducing the threat and away from more productive activity. They emphasize efficiency over effectiveness and intensify internal accountability. Such behavior may be counterproductive to an organization's responses to demands from its environment, be those responses in the form of change, engagement, or buffering. As discussed in Chapter 1, these tendencies have been found in several recent studies of schools under severe stress from external accountability (e.g., Lipman, 2002; O'Day, 2002; Smylie & Wenzel, 2003).

Continuous improvement may help organizations confront and reverse these tendencies toward rigidity and thus help them improve under conditions of heightened external threat and stress. Continuous improvement may establish a different set of routines and social constructions to displace maladaptive defenses (Sørensen and Stuart, 2000). Continuous improvement may help organizations manage the tensions and "break points" between stress and inertia (Huff, Huff, & Thomas, 1992). That is, continuous improvement may help organizations manage threat and stress so that they are not overwhelmed and default to inertial tendencies. It may also help organizations fight inertial tendencies so that threats and stress may be confronted and engaged more productively.

Mediating Isomorphic Tendencies

Institutional theory contends that organizations have a propensity to emulate, even mimic, the structures, operations, and symbols of organizations around them, particularly seemingly effective and innovative organizations (DiMaggio & Powell, 1983; Meyer & Rowan, 1977; Scott, 2007). Organizations make "social comparisons" to evaluate their own practices and their relationship to other organizations in their environments (Greve, 1995). They tend toward isomorphic behavior for several related reasons. One reason is that by emulating others, organizations can bring themselves in line with the expectations of their environments and develop the legitimacy and credibility that are often important to their function and survival (Scott, 2007; Weiler, 1993). A second reason is that by creating such alignment, organizations can reduce the risks associated with being out of alignment.

The problem is that such tendencies are not necessarily a good thing. As Haveman's (1992) study of savings and loan associations illustrates, organizations often engage in this behavior without serious consideration of the alternatives. It is easy for organizations to "take-for-granted" the idea that the largest, most successful organizations in one's market or sector should be imitated. Yet, at the same time that it might be helpful, isomorphic behavior can reduce the capability of organizations to innovate, to adapt effectively to the demands of their own local environments, and to improve continuously.[10]

Continuously improving organizations might be prone to isomorphic tendencies by continually looking beyond their boundaries to assess their operations and performance and to identify potentially more productive practices. However, continuous improvement could mitigate these tendencies by focusing an organization's external search beyond the biggest and presumably best organizations in the environment to others whose practices may be more conducive to local problems and contexts. Moreover, continuous improvement would likely make emulation of other organizations' practices continually provisional as those practices are regularly "tested" in action and even better practices sought.

Enhancing Productive Organizational Learning

Another presumed benefit of continuous improvement is its prospect for enhancing productive organizational learning. Organizational learning can be very important for an organization, but it cannot be presumed to always be productive. It can be limited, distorted, and misdirected in a number of different ways. It can reinforce existing beliefs and practices when those beliefs and practices might be sources of organizational problems. And it can take an organization in directions that are not conducive to achieving its goals (Locke & Jain, 1995).

The literature tells us that organizational learning can be problematic in several ways. It can be limited by "systematic errors" of interpretation and inference. Barbara Levitt and James March (1988) identify two of these errors as competency traps and superstitious learning. They contend that trial-and-error learning, problem identification, and search for alternatives depend on the evaluation of an organization's outcomes as successes and failures. Such evaluation is likely to be affected by the tendency of decision makers to interpret their initial objectives and outcomes in such a way as to consider themselves or their decisions successful, although that may be far from the truth (see also Locke & Jain, 1995). This is what is meant by a competency trap. Levitt and March (1988) argue that superstitious learning occurs when an organization attributes outcomes to actions when little or no connection exists between them or when an organization attributes outcomes to the wrong actions. Both competency traps and superstitious learning distort an organization's interpretations of its experiences and what it believes it has learned from them (see also Hedberg, 1981).

March (1991) observes that organizational learning can involve both the "exploration of new possibilities" and the "exploitation of old certainties" (p. 71). He maintains that an important challenge for organizations is to manage an appropriate balance between the two. Exploration to the exclusion of exploitation is likely to "incur the costs of experimentation without gaining many of its benefits" and result in "too many undeveloped new ideas and too little distinctive competence" (p. 71). On the other hand, exploitation to the exclusion of exploration is likely to leave organizations trapped in "suboptimal stable equilibria" (p. 71). March argues that organizations, even adaptive ones, have a tendency to "substitute exploitation of known alternatives for the exploration of unknown ones, to increase the reliability of performance" rather than improve the means of performance (p. 85). And this, he concludes, degrades the prospects for productive organizational learning and is potentially "self-destructive."

Organizational learning can also be limited or misdirected by emotional defenses and political barriers. Individuals and groups conduct themselves in part on the basis of their emotional responses to organizational issues. This includes efforts to avoid emotion. Russ Vince (2002) contends, "emotions . . . create both the possibilities for making the most of strategic moments and the capacity for ignoring them" (p. 79). Emotions can be an impetus for learning and change and they can discourage and impede learning and change. Among the more problematic emotions are perceived challenges to personal value systems and frames of reference, anger, embarrassment, threat, fear, sense of loss, tension, and anxiety (see Bascia & Hargreaves, 2000; Evans, 2001). Myeong-Gu Seo (2003) also points to problems of defensive reasoning and controlling political behavior that can flow from emotions triggered by change.

According to Herbert Simon (1991), organizational roles and processes "tell organizational members how to reason about problems and decisions that face them" (p. 126). They direct members where to look for "appropriate and legitimate" information and premises for goals and evaluation. They also communicate what members might do in "processing these premises" (p. 127). The idea is that continuous improvement can provide these messages as well as the structures and processes to manage potential impediments to organizational learning that come from competency traps and superstitious learning. They can provide the frameworks for emotional responses to learning and enhance the possibilities of "cognitive confrontation" that Seo (2003) suggests might be helpful to address problematic emotions that accompany learning and change. Finally, the roles and processes of continuous improvement may be able to enhance organizational learning by helping to balance exploration of new and potentially productive ideas and exploitation of current effective practices.

Avoiding Vicious Circles and Creating Virtuous Ones

Michael Masuch (1985) observed that organizations under stress can get caught in vicious circles of action and reaction that can lead to underperformance, stagnation, and eventual failure. According to Masuch, vicious circles are spiraling processes, "like Merton's famous 'tragic circle of self-fulfilling prophecy'" (p. 17). Once set in motion, a decline in one element will cause similar declines in others. Once a critical threshold is reached, "nothing can stop the contracting circles" (p. 18). And once caught in a vicious circle, human actors are likely to "continue on a path of action that leads further and further away from the desired state of affairs" (p. 23). Masuch argues that vicious circles can increase threat-rigidity or threat-anxiety loops in which the actual danger is aggravated by anxiety-inflated thinking and decision making.

Masuch's observations are similar to those made by Martin Landau (1973) some years earlier (see also Hambrick & D'Aveni, 1988). Landau argued that organizations operate on the basis of "patterned meanings" of stimuli learned by their members. These meanings, sometimes referred to as codes or schemas, regulate responses to what is encountered and which signals are received by organizations from their environments. They permit organizations to sense, interpret, and act in response to those encounters and signals. Landau contends that to many persons meanings are "no more than stereotypes," reinforced by how well they justify stability and persistence in organizational operations.

The consequence is a vicious circle that leads to a "radical restriction" of our range of attention, of our horizon of thought, of the number of things we are prepared to see; and instead of the habit of discounting, adherence to rules displaces results in the judgment of performance (Landau, 1973, p. 536). This can have terrible consequences for organizations. According to Landau, when organizations finally get around to thinking about problems and failures, "*post hoc* all too often becomes *post mortem*" (p. 537).

Jenny Rudolph and Nelson Repenning (2002) observe that major disasters in organizations do not typically have "proportionally large causes." Small events can connect in unexpected ways to create "disproportionate and disastrous effects." Charles Perrow (1984) has suggested that as organizational technologies become increasingly complex and interconnected with other systems, the likelihood of chain reactions increases substantially. That is, one problem can reverberate through the entire system and trigger "a cascade of malfunctions and breakdowns, greatly increase[ing] the chance [that] minor, every day events will lead to major disasters . . ." (p. 1). He continues that a "novelty-induced crisis" can result from an interruption that an organization does not fully comprehend and for which the organization lacks an appropriate response. A series of such interruptions can overwhelm an organization's capacity for information processing, lead to bad decisions, and trigger a vicious circle of declining performance. When interruptions come in rapid succession, their "accumulating stock" can lead to narrowing of perceptions, less use of relevant knowledge, and poorer strategic decisions, all of which limit the ability of the organization to realize that it is in crisis and handle it effectively (p. 25). An organization may not recognize the impending disaster until it is too late. Its response can unknowingly and inadvertently push it over the edge. The situation is analogous to the assembly line scenes in Charlie Chaplan's movie *Modern Times* and the "Candy Factory" episode of the popular television show *I Love Lucy*.

Continuous improvement may help prevent an organization from getting stuck in periods of low performance and getting caught in vicious circles. By continuously examining their own operations, performance, and outcomes and by continuously looking for ways to improve, organizations may be able to avoid the accumulation problems and missteps that lead to downward spirals. Indeed, the processes of continuous improvement build organizational routines that can reduce such possibilities. Vicious circles can be anticipated and avoided by proactive learning or be discovered "in time" by alert organizational members (Masuch, 1985). In addition, continuous improvement can be a way to promote the opposite of vicious circles: virtuous circles, or expanding circles as Masuch (1985) calls them. Expanding or virtuous circles have a different dynamic—a self-perpetuating spiral of growth and improvement.

A COUNTER LOGIC

The logic of continuous improvement is countered by revolutionary or "punctuated equilibrium" theories of organizational change. At issue is the basic premise of continuous improvement that small, incremental changes can add up to fundamental changes in organizations and organizational processes. Small, incremental changes may be sufficient for organizations to make minor adaptations to changes in their environments and make minor improvements in their operations and outcomes. But can those changes be strong enough to overcome powerful sources of inertia that preserve organizational structures, cultures, and core functions? To a number of organizational theorists, the answer is "no." According to Burke (2008), for example, overcoming inertia is difficult, if not impossible without "a discontinuous jolt to the system" (p. 70). He continues that "organizational change does occur with continuous attention and effort, but it is unlikely that fundamental change in the deep structure of the organization would happen" (p. 70, see also Weick & Quinn, 1999).

The "punctuated equilibrium" perspective on organizational change emerged in the mid-1980s and early 1990s largely through the work of Michael Tushman, Elaine Romanelli, and their colleagues, and through the work of Connie Gersick. Tushman, Newman, and Romanelli (1986; see also Tushman & Romanelli, 1985) argue that organizations generally operate in two types of alternating periods: convergence and reorientation. Convergence is an ongoing process defined by incremental changes, such as fine-tuning and minor incremental adjustments to changes in environments. According to Tushman and his colleagues (1985, 1986), these incremental adjustments are "ten-percent change[s]" that are generally compatible with prevailing organizational structures, systems, and processes (p. 34). Change occurs during periods of convergence; the overall system adapts, but it is not transformed. When such adjustments improve an organization's "fit" with its environment, convergence is thought to improve organizational effectiveness. It can help an organization execute its strategy successfully and reinforce its values, operations, and working relationships. At the same time, however, increased effectiveness may strengthen inner sources of organizational stability. Organizations tend to persist at what they think makes them effective, making it increasingly difficult to make major changes when necessary.

Tushman and his colleagues (1986) tell us that historical research shows that most successful companies are able to continue in phases of convergence, maintaining a "workable equilibrium" with their environments over a number of years. At the same time, they are able to engage in phases of reorientation, that is "sharp, widespread change" (p. 29) when their performance falls, when their environments shift substantially, and when maintaining a workable equilibrium through more incremental adjustments is impossible. Such "frame-breaking change" could counter inertial tendencies and renew and revitalize the organization (p. 36). Periods of reorientation tend to be relatively short, compared to periods of convergence, and they involve intense activity designed to make major changes in organizational structures, strategies, and work processes. Most reorientations bring change to the entire organization or at least have implications for the whole organization. These periods of reorientation are followed by longer periods of convergence during which incremental changes are made to solidify and reinforce major changes. Tushman and his colleagues warn that not all reorientations are successful. However, they contend that if an organization is performing poorly and if the environment changes substantially, organizational reorientation may be the only way to improve organizational performance and effectiveness and, perhaps, ensure survival.

Gersick (1991) elaborated this reasoning further:

Gradualist paradigms imply that systems can "accept" virtually any change, any time, [and] as long as it is small enough, big changes result from the insensible accumulation of small ones. In contrast, punctuated equilibrium suggests that, for most systems' histories, there are limits beyond which change is actively prevented, rather than always potential but merely suppressed because no adaptive advantage would accrue. (p. 12)

Using different labels than Tushman and his colleagues, Gersick (1991) contends that organizations alternate between equilibrium periods and revolutionary periods. But even more so than Tushman and his colleagues, Gersick emphasizes the importance of inertia and deep structure in organizational change. It is a question of the kinds and intensities of change necessary for organizational inertia to be disrupted and for fundamental changes to occur in organizational structures, cultures, and core operations.

Gersick (1991) argues that during periods of equilibrium, an organization's "basic organization and activity patterns stay the same" (p. 18). During these long periods, the organization is focused on maintaining these patterns. It may make incremental refinements in and adaptations to these patterns to "compensate for internal or external perturbations," but it does so without changing its "deep structures." Inertia maintains the organization's equilibrium leaving its deep structure intact as incremental adjustments are made. There come times, however, when severe internal or external changes or declining levels of performance make equilibrium untenable. It is then that organizations enter revolutionary periods of change.

According to Gersick (1991), revolutionary periods are necessary to disrupt and alter deep structures and bring about fundamental changes in organizations. She argues that as long as deep structures remain intact, they generate inertia "first to prevent the [organization] from generating alternatives outside its own boundaries, then to pull any deviations that do occur back into line" (p. 19). In order to bring about fundamental change, deep structures must first be dismantled, "leaving the system temporarily disorganized, in order for any fundamental changes to be accomplished" (p. 19). Then, the organization can be reassembled in a new configuration and operate according to a new set of rules. Gersick reasons that dismantling old deep structures frees organizational members to search for "symmetry-breaking information in new fields and perceive material that they already knew in new ways" (p. 29). However, if a "new order" does not take shape and is not established relatively quickly, old forces may reemerge and revolutionary periods may "end quickly by default" (p. 29). Gersick does not assume that revolutionary periods lead inevitably to organizational improvement. They tend be very disruptive and make an organization vulnerable until changes can be put into place. Revolutionary periods may vary in how much they benefit or harm an organization; indeed, these transitions may leave organizations weakened and worse off than during equilibrium periods that preceded them.

Not much empirical research has been conducted to validate punctuated equilibrium as a theory of organizational change. However, the abundant work on organizational inertia, persistence, and resistance to change lend substantial credibility to the idea (e.g., Burke, 2008; Weick & Quinn, 1999). And a few case studies illustrate and provide general support for it. In one such study of microcomputer companies, Romanelli and Tushman (1994) found that during a relatively short three-year period, organizational transformations occurred as would be predicted by the theory. Fundamental organizational transformations happened in short, discontinuous bursts. These changes were triggered by major changes in internal and external environments and performance crises. In between, these companies made small incremental changes that did not accumulate to produce transformations.

Another example of research illustrating punctuated equilibrium is Barbara Gold's (1999) case study of an elementary school. This study documented the school's history across a 23-year period to see if that history reflected elements of punctuated equilibrium theory. Gold concluded that the theory described well the dynamics of change at the school: "As the theory predicted, organizational failure produced punctuations that resulted in new leadership that introduced changes altering the organizational deep structure, followed by an equilibrium period" (p. 210). The school experienced two such sequences during the period covered by the study.

While punctuated equilibrium may describe organizational change as it occurs typically and naturally, the theory is not clear that this is how change inevitably occurs. The theory places a great deal of emphasis on organizational inertia and the power of deep structures to maintain organizational stability. One might interpret punctuated equilibrium as a view of organizational change "at the extremes." At one extreme is fine-tuning and minor adjustments to maintain steady states and fits with external environments. At the other extreme is dismantling, revolutionary change required to remake an organization when small change will no longer do. Minor adaptations and steady states are thought to be desirable conditions of organizations. Disorienting, destructive upheaval is assumed to be undesirable yet at times unavoidable. To exaggerate a bit, the theory paints change in organizational life as all or (almost) nothing. It is equilibrium or revolution. The theory does not leave much room for change between.

Tushman and O'Reilly (1996) suggest some middle ground with the idea of the "ambidextrous organization." Their argument, developed with examples from the semiconductor and watch manufacturing industries, is consistent with that of punctuated equilibrium. To remain successful over long periods, managers and organizations must be able to implement *both* incremental and revolutionary change. The idea of the ambidextrous organization emphasizes the importance of strategy and agency in organizational change in managing incremental and revolutionary changes effectively, as well as the transitions between them. Moreover, the idea of the ambidextrous organization points to the prospect that organizations can be designed and managed in ways to moderate the extremes, to make incremental adaptive changes more strategic and potent and to make revolutionary change less frequent, less disorienting, and less disruptive.

This takes us back to the idea of continuous improvement as an organizational orientation, a strategic organizational process, and a dynamic organizational capability. It takes us back to the basic logic of continuous improvement as a means of managing environmental uncertainty and change, as a means of becoming better and better at enacting organizational vision and core values and at improving organizational performance and outcomes. This logic suggests that continuous improvement is likely to reduce the need for and the costs of major organizational change. It may help organizations counter tendencies toward rigidity when under stress and toward unproductive imitation of other organizations. It may help organizations engage in productive organizational learning. And continuous improvement may help organizations avoid vicious circles and pursue virtuous ones instead. Indeed, the idea of continuous improvement may be an answer to the inevitable question that arises from theories of revolutionary change: What new organizational forms should come as the result of fundamental change? That is, if the old form no longer works and is to be reconstructed through radical change, what new form should be put in its place? This question is broached by Murphy and Meyers (2007) who contend that continuous improvement may be the best organizational form to follow from the radical change strategy of "school turnaround."

QUESTIONS FOR STUDY, REFLECTION, AND ACTION

1. Compare and contrast the meaning of continuous improvement as the following.
   - A set of values and beliefs
   - A strategic organizational process
   - An organizational property
   - A "means" and an "end"

2. Beyond the "comprehensive" definitions described in the chapter, how might these different ways of thinking be synthesized into one concept of a continuously improving school organization?

3. Compare the improvement processes at your school with the common characteristics of different definitions of continuous improvement. How are they similar and how are they different?

4. How credible is the logic that continuous strategic incremental changes can add up to fundamental changes in schools? Under what conditions is this logic most likely to "work"? How likely is this logic to work in your school? What conditions would need to be present for it to work in your school?

5. Compare the logic of continuous improvement to the logic of a punctuated equilibrium perspective on organizational change. What are the relative strengths and weaknesses of each in improving schools in general? In improving your school in particular?

6. What is the idea of the "ambidextrous organization" and how applicable is it to thinking about the long-term improvement of schools in general? Of your school in particular?

Evidence of the Effectiveness of Continuous Improvement

3

The most effective strategies of major enterprises tend to emerge step by step from an iterative process in which the organization probes the future, experiments, and learns from a series of partial (incremental) commitments rather than through global formation of total strategies.

—James Quinn, 1980[11]

This chapter focuses on empirical evidence of the effectiveness of continuous improvement. What does research tell us about the outcomes of continuous improvement? What evidence is there that continuous improvement helps organizations generally and schools in particular increase their effectiveness especially as they face rapidly changing environments and uncertain futures? This chapter addresses these questions drawing on evidence from the education literature and from the more extensive literatures on non-education organizations.[11]

This chapter is divided into two major sections. The first section focuses on evidence from research on non-education organizations that include businesses and industries, nonprofit organizations, and government agencies. In this section, three types of studies are considered: (a) research on high-performing organizations and evidence that continuous improvement or similar processes have played a role in long-term organizational performance, (b) research on the role of continuous improvement in improving and innovating organizations, and (c) research specifically focused on continuous improvement processes themselves. The second major section focuses on evidence found in studies of schools and school districts. These studies come from the effective schools literature, literature on large-scale school reform initiatives, and literature on various continuous school improvement processes.

As will become clear as this chapter progresses, there is substantial consistency among findings across organizational sectors and types, including schools. The collective evidence points to a number of positive outcomes associated with continuous improvement or continuous improvement-like processes. Overall, this evidence indicates that continuous improvement is associated with high performance and organizational improvement across time. It indicates that continuous improvement helps organizations adapt to changes in their environments, reduces the need to make radical change, and moderates the stresses and costs of radical change when it has to be made. This evidence also indicates that continuous improvement helps organizations develop the capacity for creativity and innovation even in uncertain and rapidly changing environments.

A few initial observations are in order. First, the evidence on the outcomes of continuous improvement is hardly a well-organized body of knowledge. It comes from different types of studies of many different types of organizations. There are a number of problems across individual studies that range from lack of conceptual clarity and methodological rigor to variation in the processes under investigation. And there is substantially more evidence on the outcomes of continuous improvement from studies of non-education organizations than from studies of schools and school districts. Despite these limitations, the consistency of evidence of positive outcomes coupled with the absence of evidence of negative outcomes creates reasonable confidence in general conclusions about the effectiveness of continuous improvement.

Second, a number of individual studies are discussed in this chapter in detail to provide concrete descriptions of continuous improvement processes and supporting organizational factors found to be related to organizational performance, improvement, and innovation. Few detailed descriptions of continuous improvement practice exist in the education and non-education literatures. So while we will get to the matter of practice in Chapter 4, this chapter provides an advance organizer for that discussion.

EVIDENCE FROM STUDIES OF NON-EDUCATION ORGANIZATIONS

As noted earlier, evidence on the effectiveness of continuous improvement in non-education organizations comes from three types of studies. The first type consists of studies of high-performing organizations. The second consists of studies of improving and innovating organizations. The third consists of studies of continuous improvement processes themselves. The first two types of studies ask the question: What organizational processes and characteristics are associated with long-term high performance, improvement, and innovation? We look to these studies to see if processes of continuous improvement appear among factors found to contribute significantly to these outcomes. We look to studies focusing specifically on continuous improvement processes for more direct evidence of outcomes.

Studies of High-Performing Organizations

Since the early 1980s, there have been a number of studies of high-performing organizations that speak to the effectiveness of continuous improvement. Most of these studies have been of businesses and industries, but a number have been of nonprofit organizations and government agencies. A look at this research indicates that processes of continuous improvement contribute significantly to high organizational performance across time. These processes are not readily apparent or are weak in comparatively low-performing organizations. These general findings are consistent across private and public sectors and across for-profit and nonprofit sectors. They are also consistent across different organizational types that have been studied.

One of the earliest studies of high-performing organizations that identified processes of continuous improvement as a contributing factor to success is James Quinn's (1980) investigation of how major corporations make strategic changes to sustain their performance across time. Quinn suspected that conventional formal planning and management strategies of the day were only part of the explanation of why successful companies were able to sustain their performance. Quinn found that managers of these companies made small adjustments to sustain high performance through processes that neither formal strategic planning paradigms nor practices explained adequately. According to Quinn, these managers "*consciously* and *proactively* moved [their companies] forward *incrementally*" (p. x, emphasis in the original). They guided streams of actions and events strategically to make small cumulative adjustments and improvements. They "blended processes together to improve both the quality of decisions and the effectiveness of their implementation" (p. 16). Quinn observed that in the hands of skillful managers and executives, such "logical incrementalism" was an intentional way of "improving and integrating the analytical and behavioral aspects of strategy formulation" (p. 17). Quinn concluded the following:

> The most effective strategies of major enterprises tend to emerge step by step from an iterative process in which the organization probes the future, experiments, and learns from a series of partial (incremental) commitments rather than through global formulation of total strategies. Good managers are aware of this process and they consciously intervene in it. They use it to improve the information available for decisions and to build the psychological identification essential to successful strategies. (p. 58)

Shortly following Quinn's work, Thomas Peters and Robert Waterman (1982) published their well-known study of high-performing organizations, *In Search of Excellence.* The focus of this study is how big companies "stay alive, well, and innovative" (p. 22). The most well-known findings of this study were a number of attributes "clearly visible and quite distinctive" in these "excellent" companies. These attributes include (a) a bias for action; (b) being close to the customer; (c) autonomy and entrepreneurship; (d) productivity through people; (e) being hands-on and value driven; (f) "sticking to the knitting"; (g) simple form and lean staff; and (h) simultaneous loose and tight properties, pushing autonomy down with tight central control over core values. Above all, the study found these companies marked by an intensity stemming from a strong system of beliefs that guided action.

Soon after their release, Peters and Waterman's (1982) findings were called into question largely because a number of the "excellent" companies they studied began to falter, some rather significantly. But this critique tended to overlook less publicized aspects of the study. In their findings, Peters and Waterman argue that the marketplace is continuously evolving and that if excellent companies want to sustain their performance adaptation would be critical. They observe that few companies are able to adapt successfully for extended periods of time. Almost prophetically, they acknowledge that while the companies in their study "had a long run—a much longer and more successful than most," many would probably not stay "buoyant forever" (p. 110).

This is because few companies had developed processes of what Peters and Waterman (1982) call "intentionally seeded evolution." The idea, they observe, had only recently become a concern of management theorists. However, they saw that the very top companies in their study had developed and were using a number of devices and management strategies "to stave off calcification" (p. 111). Perhaps because of a lack of attention and a language to describe it at the time, few companies could articulate what they were doing in this regard.

Peters and Waterman (1982) found that these companies had adopted a range of routines that, guided by a tight values system, systemically called for regular assessments of external demands from customers and competitors and assessments of internal capacity to meet those demands. These routines encouraged experimentation and supported internal competition of new ideas. They also established comprehensive channels of communication across the organization and used those channels to ensure regular exchange of important information, quicken feedback about performance, and promote the diffusion of new ideas. Such routines pushed these companies toward expansion and innovation. They stood in contrast to routines of other "excellent" companies that aimed to promote and sustain performance through control and constraint.

A few years after the publication of *In Search of Excellence,* Jim Collins and Jerry Porras (1994) began a five-year study of "truly exceptional companies" and what made them so. The findings of this study would become the basis of their best-selling book *Built to Last.* Collins and Porras were not interested in studying specific management practices or "the incessant barrage of management buzzwords and fads of the day" (p. xxiii). Instead, they sought to document enduring principles of organization and management that distinguish outstanding companies from other companies across time, even generally successful ones. Collins and Porras focused on what they called "visionary" for-profit companies. They wanted to study companies that were more than successful and more than enduring. They wanted to study companies that distinguished themselves as strong and resilient performers across long periods of time, companies that constituted "a very special and elite breed of institutions" (p. 2).

This study produced a number of key findings. Here are but a few. Visionary companies were unlikely to have started fast with a "great idea." Instead, they often got off to a slow start and worked steadily to "win the long race" (p. 7). High-profile charismatic visionary leadership was not required for long-term success of visionary companies. Indeed, it could be a detriment. Leaders of visionary companies were more likely to concentrate on building enduring institutions than on being a great individual leader. Visionary companies pursued a variety of objectives, of which making money was only one and not necessarily the primary one. However, visionary companies were guided consistently across time by a core ideology—a set of core values and ideals, a sense of purpose beyond just making money. Collins and Porras (1994) found that there was no "right" set of core values associated with being a visionary company. The content of a company's ideology was less important than "how deeply that company believes its ideology and how consistently it lives, breathes, and expresses it in all that it does" (p. 8). In visionary companies, this core ideology was vigorously preserved across time, changing seldom if ever. It served as a basis for setting demanding work standards, hiring and terminating personnel, and aligning all parts of the organization.

In addition, Collins and Porras (1994) found that while adhering to and preserving their core ideology, these visionary companies never sat still. They strategically and judiciously adopted and pursued what are called Big Hairy Audacious Goals (BHAGs) to "stimulate progress and blast past the comparison companies at crucial points in history" (p. 9). Of particular relevance here, these companies also had histories of constant experimentation, trial and error initiatives, and opportunistic pursuit of productive "accidents." They kept a primary focus on beating themselves. Collins and Porras found the following:

> The critical question asked by a visionary company is not, "How well are we doing?" or "How well do we have to perform in order to meet and competition?" For these companies the critical question is, *"How can we do better tomorrow than we did today?"* They institutionalize this question as a way of life—a habit of mind and action. Superb execution and performance naturally come to the visionary companies not so much as an end goal but as the residual result of a never-ending cycle of self-stimulated improvement and investment for the future. There is no ultimate finish line in a highly visionary company. There is no "having made it." (pp. 185–186, emphasis in the original)

Collins and Porras (1994) observed that while "continuous improvement" became a management catchphrase in the 1980s, the concept had been commonplace in visionary companies for decades, indeed more than a century in some cases. They concluded that their findings clearly reveal the concept of continuous improvement as a distinguishing characteristic of high-performing visionary companies. Collins and Porras were careful to say that in these companies, continuous improvement did not exist as a separate program or a specific management strategy. Rather, continuous improvement functioned as "an institutionalized habit—a disciplined way of life—ingrained into the fabric of the organization" (p. 188). It was executed and reinforced through routines and mechanisms that continually created discontent with the status quo and linked to ongoing efforts not simply to do well in the short-term but also to build for long-term success. This meant ongoing and aggressive investment in their own capacity to perform—in physical and material resources; in research and development; in developing human capital through recruitment, training, and professional development; and in adopting new and innovative technologies and industry practices consistent their core values. Collins and Porras found little evidence of these properties and practices in the histories of comparison companies.

Collins and Porras' findings are echoed in a more recent study of high organizational performance by Paul Light (2005). Light set out to identify lessons about what organizations can do to "achieve and sustain high performance in a turbulent world" through an analysis of research conducted during the past 60 years by the RAND Corporation. From this "knowledge base," Light identified four "powerful" predictors, or pillars as he calls them, of high organizational performance in uncertain times: (a) alertness, (b) agility, (c) adaptability, and (d) alignment of organizational design and activity with organizational purpose. To be alert, high performing organizations continuously and rigorously monitor their external environments, their internal capacities and processes, and how they are doing at any particular point in time. They adopt "robust, adaptive" plans against a variety of possible futures (plural) and accept the "inevitability" of surprise. Light found that to be agile, high-performing organizations "organize for lightening." They recruit workforces for maximum flexibility, train for change, set "just-beyond-possible" goals, and provide organizational members authority to "think lean" and act independently on almost every aspect of their work.

To be adaptive, high-performing organizations constantly challenge prevailing wisdom by creating freedom for their employees to learn and imagine new things and by aggregating and creating productive tension among various sources of expertise through teams and networks. They use "futures tense" and multiple measures of performance and productivity to avoid complacency and cheating, and they invite and cultivate intuition. Light (2005) indicates that adaptability is not a synonym for innovation. Rather, it is "the ability to rapidly adjust strategies and tactics to meet changes in the environment" (p. 109). Finally, Light found that to be aligned with purpose, high-performing organizations "lead to mission." They are clear about and constantly communicate their core values and purposes. They use images and stories to reinforce those values and purposes. They test everything they do against them. These organizations grow and groom their leaders from the inside. They anticipate threats from the inside and outside through careful study and they ignore irrelevant issues that distract them and impede their ability to perpetuate their values and achieve their goals.

Spanning these four pillars, Light (2005) constructs an image of organization that can be "robust" as uncertainty rages. According to this image, high performance requires more than a strategy that will succeed in a variety of scenarios. According to Light,

> It also requires an organization that is among the first to sense a change in probabilities across the range of possible futures; among the fastest to deploy resources against threats, surprises, and opportunities; among the most creative in forging a presence in the evolving future; and among the very best in moving as a whole into whatever the ever-evolving future holds. In a word, such organizations are robust. They are alert to change, agile in deployment, adaptive in practice and product, and aligned in purpose. (pp. ix–x)

A key question for Light (2005) was not whether there is one best organizational system. Instead, the question was how to make a given system better. Simply stated, robust organizations assume that surprises and downturns are inevitable. They watch for signals that a given future is coming true. And they take action to hedge against threats and vulnerabilities, while shaping the future to their advantage. Quoting Gary Hamel and Liisa Välikangas, Light concludes the following:

> The goal is a strategy that is forever morphing, forever conforming itself to emerging opportunities and incipient trends. The goal is a company that is constantly making its future rather than defending its past. (p. 98)

Light's (2005) findings about the management of change echo the findings of Collins and Porras's (1994) study. Light speaks about duration, motivation, and intensity as "velocity of change," and targets, goals, and participants as "vectors of change." He found that while RAND does not have an "official" stance on organizations, their performance, or change, its "knowledge base" clearly favors longer-term, thinking-based, and continuous incremental change over "the radical, disruptive change currently in vogue" (p. 212). Light indicates that while RAND recognizes that occasions exist when radical change is necessary, particularly when internal and external threats to performance are high, its researchers and reports generally favor process change over whole-organization reform, employee-centered change over leader-driven change, and a goal of steady growth over the pursuit of breakthrough innovation. He argues that RAND researchers and reports are not unwilling to recommend radial, disruptive change. But most of their recommendations tend to support more pragmatic incremental change. In essence, Light concludes, RAND believes in a long-haul philosophy of change. Organizations that are designed for continuous change are more likely to be able to perform well across long periods of time in contexts of increasing uncertainty. Organizations that lock themselves into an immutable plan face "a near-certain guarantee of failure" (p. 226).

Collins and Porras (1994) and Light (2005) contend that their findings are applicable to organizations outside the business world. In the introduction to the paperback edition of *Built to Last*, Collins and Porras (2002) write that they have come to believe that their work is not about business—"this is not a business book"—but it is about "enduring, great human institutions of *any* type" (p. xvii, emphasis in the original). They argue the following:

> Conceptually, we see little difference between for-profit visionary companies and nonprofit visionary companies. Both face the need to transcend dependence on any single leader or great idea. Both depend on a timeless set of core values and an enduring purpose beyond just making money. Both need to change in response to a changing world, while simultaneously preserving their core values and purpose. . . . [T]he essence of what it takes to build an enduring, great institution does not vary. (p. xviii)

Light (2005) makes a similar argument. The findings of his analysis of the RAND knowledge base are derived from study of different organizational sectors and many different types of organizations, from corporations to government agencies, from the military to community social service organizations, from industries to schools. The pillars of high-performance, the image of a robust organization in uncertain times, the lessons on continuous change were identified as common strengths across studies of different organizational types and thus, presumably, apply across organizational types.[12]

More direct evidence can be found in two other studies by Light (2002, 2004) on nonprofit organizations. Like the *Four Pillars* study, these two proceeded from the problem of nonprofit performance in times of increasing uncertainty and threat. In the first of these studies, *Pathways to Nonprofit Excellence*, Light (2002) focused on "preferred states of organizational being." By this, Light means organizational design principles and processes associated with high nonprofit performance. This was a survey of national opinion leaders and executive directors of high performing nonprofits about sources of high nonprofit performance.

These experts pointed to several common principles or "preferred states" they believed led to high nonprofit performance. Among them are several that are consistent with the concept of continuous improvement. One preferred state is aggressive interaction with the outside world. High-performing nonprofits are seen to face the outside world, "exposing themselves to the winds of change, competition, and turbulence" (p. 46). Another is leadership and other organizational processes driven by mission. Yet another is an imperative to promote collaboration and push authority downward in the organization to encourage experimentation and improvement. Still another concerns the importance of internal management systems and processes, particularly planning. While management systems and planning were clearly important to the experts in this study, their take on planning was different from more traditional perspectives. A number of experts emphasized that planning had to be regular, flexible, and frequent. Light (2002) quotes one executive director who explained the idea this way:

> The world is changing rapidly, so I think the idea of a strategic plan lasting for five years doesn't work anymore. . . . I think the old fashioned way of doing strategic planning isn't going to be very effective anymore with things changing so rapidly (p. 99). Consistent with the concept of continuous improvement, this executive concluded, "I'm just one of those people that (sic) looks at a strategic plan as a rolling plan." (p. 99)

In his own conclusion, Light (2002) summarized the expert opinion he gathered by painting a picture of an organization designed for continuous improvement:

> Having started the journey to higher performance, a nonprofit-like organization keeps the pressure on no matter where it happens to be in the journey. It updates its strategic plan regularly, invests in staff training, continues to evaluate and measure its performance, modernizes its systems, and continues to exploit opportunities. Regardless of the competition, or lack thereof, nonprofit-like organizations constantly raise the bar on their own performance. They do not look for the pressure to improve, but to their own mission. (p. 131)

In the second of the two studies, *Sustaining Nonprofit Performance,* Light (2004) examined the relationship between organizational capacity and organizational effectiveness through national surveys and historical case studies of high-performing nonprofit organizations. He was interested in "testing" the logic that the development and presence of organizational capacity relate to effective organizational operations and to positive programmatic outcomes, and then that operational and programmatic effectiveness relates to public confidence, discretionary giving, and voluntarism, each a critical source of nonprofit vitality and survival. In addition, and most relevant to our focus on continuous improvement, Light was interested in learning how the development of nonprofit organizational capacity contributes to high performance across time. In this study, organizational capacity encompassed "virtually everything an organization uses to achieve its mission, from desks and chairs to programs and people" (p. 15). More specifically it referred to the knowledge, skills, and commitment of staff and volunteers; the quality of leadership; information and technology; fiscal and material resources; and the organization's infrastructure and management systems, among other things. Light viewed this capacity at once as an "output" of basic organizational activities such as fundraising, organizing work, developing personnel, managing budgets and evaluation programs, and an "input" to program implementation and impact. Capacity can be both developed and expended through organizational activity and in interaction with the environment.

Light (2004) found evidence of a positive relationship between nonprofit capacity and effectiveness, and he found evidence of a positive relationship between nonprofit effectiveness, or perceived effectiveness, and public confidence and voluntary giving of time and money. Having found evidence of these relationships, Light turned his attention to how the development of capacity may help nonprofit organizations achieve and sustain effectiveness across time. He introduced a model of organizational capacity development called the "Spiral of Sustainable Excellence." This spiral has five landings or stages of development. Movement from one landing to another, up the spiral toward stronger and stronger capacity and higher levels of performance, is consistent with notions of continuous improvement. According to this model, organizations that reach the top two landings—the robust nonprofit and the reflective nonprofit—are engaging in organizational processes synonymous with continuous improvement and possess other aspects of capacity that promote those processes.

A picture of these processes emerges from Light's (2004) cases of high-performing nonprofits. These organizations share a number of common features. They clearly understand that change happens; none are certain about what the future might hold. The success of these organizations across time depends in large part on "asking the right questions, addressing potential threats, and choosing the right strategies" for the time and situation in which they find themselves (p. 140). This means "picking the right improvement effort at the right time" (p. 139). These organizations have the capacity not simply to withstand inevitable uncertainty but to exploit it. They prepare for uncertainty by hedging. This means developing willingness and exercising the capacity to think and act in futures (plural) tense that in turn requires agility and adaptability. Looking across this sample of high-performing nonprofits, Light sees the following:

> Even as they protect themselves against uncertainty . . . , [these organizations] continue to challenge and inspire themselves. . . . They [invest] in renewal even during good times. They do not take success for granted or assume that their organization is working well just because they do not hear any complaints. (pp. 144, 145)

These nonprofits do not assume that they will remain high performing in the future. They have developed capacities that help them react well to "inevitable surprises and disappointments" but also help them shape the future.

Light (2004) focuses on one aspect of capacity that distinguishes more highly developed nonprofits from less highly developed ones—strategic planning. All of the high-performing nonprofits in the study had strategic plans. What distinguished more from less highly developed nonprofits was how strategic planning was defined and pursued. For the most highly developed nonprofits, strategic planning was much like a process of continuous improvement. It was often a part of everyday organizational life, a way of thinking within the organization. It involved many or all organizational members across levels. It was ongoing. It was grounded in information and analysis of internal and external factors. And it was focused on improving performance and on improving the organizational capacities that drive performance.

Light's (2004) general conclusion is that nonprofit organizations will substantially limit their potential for high and sustained levels of performance if they fail to continuously develop their capacity to perform and improve their effectiveness. He argued the following:

> [N]onprofits are spending too much time fixing leaky pipes and broken windows, while jumping at available funds, and not enough doing the kind of continuous improvement [his words] that prevents crises and emergencies in the first place. (p. 175)

This is not to say that leaky pipes and broken windows need not be fixed nor does it mean that opportunities for available funding should not be carefully considered and possibly exploited.

Light's (2004) point is that organizations, here nonprofits, that fixate on the present and on the small problems to the neglect of the future and building their broader capacity to effectively engage it will soon be in trouble. At the beginning of this study, Light observed that any organization, "no matter how moribund and inefficient," can be effective for a time: "All it needs are extraordinary employees who are willing to put up with old computers, stress, and burnout. . . . The trick is both to achieve and to sustain effectiveness over time." (p. 22). The solution is the ongoing development—the continuous improvement—of organizational capacity and performance.

Studies of Improving and Innovating Organizations

Additional evidence on continuous improvement comes from research on improving and innovating organizations. As found in the research on high performing organizations, continuous improvement is among a number of factors found to contribute to organizational improvement and innovation. The discussion later features several studies that follow from or are directly related to studies discussed before.

On the first page of *Good to Great,* Jim Collins (2001) tells the story of a dinner conversation with a group of "thought leaders" gathered for a discussion of organizational performance. The conversation took place shortly after the publication of *Built to Last* (Collins & Porras, 2002). Collins reports one corporate executive saying, "You know, Jim, we love *Built to Last.* . . . Unfortunately, it's useless." The executive explained, "The companies you wrote about were, for the most part, always great. They never had to turn themselves from good companies into great companies. . . . [W]hat about the vast majority of companies that wake up partway through life and realize that they're good but not great?" (p. 1). That question plunged Collins and his research team into a second five-year study to address the issue of whether a good company can become a great company and, if so, how. Like the objective in the *Built to Last* study, the objective for *Good to Great* (2001) was to search for "timeless, universal answers that can be applied by any organization" (p. 5). It was a comparative study of companies that "made the leap from good results to great results and sustained those results for at least 15 years" beyond key transition points (p. 3).

Collins (2001) found that going from good to great was a long, transformational process of "buildup followed by breakthrough" (p. 12). In companies that made the transformation, this process generally followed three broad stages. The first stage focused on the development of "disciplined people." This meant developing what Collins refers to as *Level 5 Leadership*, that is, executive leadership that is a blend of personal humility, professional will, and ferocious, unwavering resolve to produce results for the company and make it great. It also meant getting the right people into the organization and into the right places in the organization and getting the wrong people out. Once the right people were in place, the organization could employ them as a key resource to figure out and enact its vision and strategy.

The second stage focused on "disciplined thought." With the right leadership and people in place, companies that transformed from good to great systematically "confronted the brutal facts" about themselves and about the world around them. They created cultures where people throughout the company could be heard. They "lead with questions" and engaged in systematic dialog and debate; they conducted "autopsies" of failure "without blame"; and they developed "red-flag mechanisms" to ensure that important information could not be ignored. A second element of this stage, one that extends through all stages and becomes the motor driving all organizational activity is the "Hedgehog Concept." The Hedgehog Concept refers to the core purpose and value of the organization. It is the "one big thing" that the organization does better than anyone else. It is the focus of the company that both grounds and propels all that the company does. Good-to-great companies find and embrace such singularity of purpose, and they pursue that purpose with "dogged determination."

The third stage focused on "disciplined action." Collins (2001) found that good-to-great companies required their people to "adhere to a consistent system" but at the same time gave people substantial "freedom and responsibility to work within the framework of that system" (p. 142). He found that in these companies, "the single most important form of discipline for sustained results [was] fanatical adherence to the Hedgehog concept and the willingness to shun opportunities that fall outside [of it]" (p. 142). In these companies, it was just as important to decide what things to stop doing and what opportunities to bypass as it was to decide what to do. These companies consistently relied on their sense of core purpose and value to make such decisions. This resolve resembles the idea of "sticking to the knitting," shown by Peters and Waterman (1982) to be associated with high performance in their study. But the "knitting" that Collins (2001) emphasizes is not programs, strategies, technologies, organizational structures, or operational processes. In good-to-great companies, those things were treated as flexible, provisional, and expendable. Instead, among good-to-great companies, the "knitting" is the pursuit of core purposes and values. The second element of "disciplined action" is technology. Good-to-great companies were often pioneers in the application of "carefully selected" technologies (p. 13). They were constantly assessing new technologies and using the Hedgehog concept to determine what technologies to avoid and which to pursue and apply. Good-to-great companies never used technology as the primary means of "igniting transformation" (p. 13). Instead, they used it as an "accelerator of momentum" (p. 162). Collins concludes, "Great companies respond [to technological change] with thoughtfulness and creativity, driven by a compulsion to turn unrealized potential into results; mediocre companies react and lurch about, motivated by fear of being left behind" (p. 162).

Collins (2001) found that all three of these stages were important in the companies he studied. These stages functioned in symbiotic relationship: "It is the combination of all of the pieces working together in an integrated package *consistently and over time*" that makes all the difference (p. 213, emphasis in the original). Without them all at work, it was unlikely that a good organization would become great, or if it did, it was unlikely to continue to function as a great organization for long.

According to Collins (2001), the overall process of going from good to great, of moving through the stages, resembles putting a flywheel in motion. In good-to-great companies, transformations never happened all at once.

> There was no single defining action, no grant program, no killer innovation, no solitary luck break, no miracle moment. Rather, the process resembled relentlessly pushing a giant heavy flywheel in one direction, turn upon turn, building momentum until a point of breakthrough, and beyond. (p. 14)

In good-to-great companies, it was a process of "persistent pushing in a consistent direction over a long period of time and eventually hitting a breakthrough" (Collins, 2001, p. 186). Taken together, the stages of good to great, coupled with the flywheel concept, resemble closely the concept of continuous improvement. The histories of these companies provide evidence of how focused, disciplined, strategic, systematic, and incremental push to improvement across time can add up, even exponentially, to high sustained performance.[13]

Collins (2005) took on the issue of the applicability of his findings to organizations outside the "business world" in a follow-up, self-published monograph titled *Good to Great and the Social Sectors*. He argued that the principles of *Good to Great* are applicable to any type of organization, and he provided some preliminary evidence that they are applicable to organizations in the social sectors. In order to "test" this argument, Collins sought critical feedback on good-to-great principles from 100 social sector leaders.[14] According to these leaders, good-to-great principles are applicable to organizations in the social sectors. And they may be more applicable there than in the business world.

For instance, because of the complex governance and diffuse power structures that characterize many social service organizations (recall the discussion of governance and control of schools in Chapter 1), there may be even greater need for Level 5 Leadership for organizational success and greatness than directive, self-interested leadership. Because financial and other tangible rewards are more difficult to come by, it may be even more important in social service organizations to attract and retain self-motivated, self-disciplined people who are devoted to and driven primarily by an organization's core purpose and values. Because of growing competition and the scarcity of resources in the social sectors (also recall discussion of school funding in Chapter 1), achieving "greatness" may hinge even more on the Hedgehog Concept, requiring "deeper and more penetrating insight and rigorous clarity than your average business entity" into core purpose and values (p. 20). Because of increased uncertainty, declining resources, and growing accountability, greatness in the social sectors may depend even more on "disciplined thought" and "disciplined action," to use evidence to constantly track progress, raise questions and challenge assumptions, to "confront the brutal facts" about one's own organization and the environment, and to demonstrate an organization's value.

Finally, the leaders Collins (2005) interviewed saw the concept of the flywheel at work in going from good to great in the social sectors. Getting to greatness was viewed as a transformational process that took place incrementally across time. Great social sector organizations were seen to focus doggedly on core purposes and values to build initial results. Those initial results attracted resources and commitment that in turn helped to further develop a strong organization. Organizational strength led to better results that attracted even greater resources and commitment, and so on and so on (pp. 23–24). Collins concluded from these interviews that in the social sectors as well as the business world, "Greatness . . . is largely a matter of conscious choice and discipline" (p. 31). From the perspectives of sector leaders, great social service organizations cling to their core purposes and values but at the same time are never complacent. Through endless assessment, experimentation, and adaptation, they continuously challenge themselves and seek improvement in strategies and operational processes to better achieve those core purposes and values.

Evidence of the role of continuous improvement in innovating organizations outside the corporate world can be found in another study by Paul Light (1998). This was a five-year investigation of how nonprofit organizations and government agencies increased their chances of becoming innovative and sustaining their "innovativeness" across time. Light defined *innovation* as "an act that challenges the prevailing wisdom as it creates public value" (p. xvi). An innovating organization was defined as one that is "structured and led to make such innovation more natural and frequent" (p. xvi).

In this study, Light (1998) focused on several organizational features consistent with the concept of continuous improvement. These features were associated with an organization's ability to innovate and to sustain innovativeness across time. Because Light found substantial variation in specific practices among the organizations that he studied—there is "no one true path to innovating" (p. 238)—he framed these features (along with other findings) as "preferred states of being" rather than absolutes. Among the most consistent features of these organizations was a clear understanding that they operated in turbulent and uncertain contexts. These organizations saw that their environments were not always predictable, and the resources they needed for survival and success were no sure things. They understood that to survive and even prosper they had to "stay young," to constantly "renew themselves or face extinction" (p. 126).

One of the most important things that these organizations did was to face their outside worlds squarely and work hard to anticipate, adapt, stay ahead, and provide value before the environment demanded it. Even as they viewed their environments as unpredictable, these organizations thought of those same environments as contexts to be "managed, exploited, even manipulated" (Light, 1998, p. 14). These organizations saw their long-term success in terms of constant adjustment—both reactive and anticipatory—aligning their structures, systems, and leadership with their environments but also working to align their environments with themselves. "They are ecologists of a sort," Light wrote, "who work both to create and nurture the conditions in which they can succeed" (p. 28).

To that end, these organizations developed structures and processes that allowed them to constantly monitor their environments, track the results of their programs and services, monitor their own operations, identify and diagnose problems by raising questions and challenging prevailing assumptions, and experiment with new ideas. While turbulence and uncertainty of their environments required them to constantly paddle, they developed the structures and processes to be able to "pull out of the white water and reflect on ways to change course" (Light, 1998, p. 68).

These nonprofits and government agencies were able to anticipate shocks from their environments, shocks that might have otherwise surprised them and put them in a reactive and potentially costly position. They had developed a sense of heightened alertness and an ability to notice and adjust to subtle changes before the need to adjust reached a level that might compromise their ability to innovate. These capacities for anticipation and adaptation were linked to the fact that these organizations tended to be well managed. According to Light (1998), high operational performance may be a necessary if insufficient prerequisite for innovativeness. What is important to the discussion of continuous improvement is that these organizations understood that their innovativeness concerned not only the programs and services they delivered. They understood that innovation applied to their organizational operations as well.

These findings are similar to those of other studies of nonprofit organizations that have worked with schools to promote school improvement. In a review of empirical literature about these organizations, Thomas Corcoran and I (Smylie & Corcoran, 2009) found that success in working with schools and school districts could be explained in large part by these organizations' "strategic capacity" (p. 16). Strategic capacity has several dimensions. The first is the capacity for assessment and analysis, that is, the ability to identify and define problems effectively and to access accurately contexts and organizational capacities for engaging and implementing change. This also involves an organization's capacity for self-analysis and the ability to develop new capacity for meeting new demands for service. A second dimension is the ability of the organization to establish a match between the type of service it provides and the needs, interests, and demands of the contexts in which it works. These contexts can include schools, school districts, the policy environment, and funding agencies. Another dimension is the ability of the organization to adapt to changes in the needs, interests, and priorities of schools, school systems, policy environments, and funders. Being able to adapt services to such changes requires a substantial amount of flexibility in organizational functions and processes.

These general findings are illustrated in a number of studies that examine how such organizations promote implementation of education reform initiatives at the school and district levels (see Smylie & Corcoran, 2009). In one such study, Datnow, Hubbard, & Mehan (2002) examined design teams whose job it was to promote the adoption and implementation of comprehensive reform models in schools. These design teams represented a number of different reform models, for example, Achievement Via Individual Determination (AVID), Coalition of Essential Schools, the Comer School Development Program, New American Schools, and Success for All. The focus of their research was on the design team as an organization.

This study found that the design teams that experienced the most success working with schools (success meaning school implementation and sustainability of reform models) reflected a number of the properties and processes of continuous improvement. Indeed, the most successful design teams were those that were able to adapt and respond successfully to changing demands from (a) "scaling up," that is, from growing numbers of schools and school districts adopting their models; (b) policy conflicts, resource limitations, and other constraints imposed by adopting schools and school districts; (c) local school and district politics; and (d) changing market forces, such as competition for resources from other reform organizations. Successful design teams frequently changed their organizational forms and processes, even their reform models, as they worked with schools and school districts. Datnow and her colleagues (2002) concluded, "Whether design teams (and their associated reforms) were founded five or twenty years ago, we have found that they are constantly evolving" (p. 91). Some of the successful design teams in the study described themselves as being in a "state of continual learning, progressively refining their model[s] and their approach[es] to working with schools" (p. 92). One member of a successful design team captured the essence of it: "We're always moving" (p. 92).

Studies of Continuous Improvement Processes

Many of the claims about the benefits of continuous improvement are based on anecdotal reports or second-hand evidence. It is common to find references in the literature to "well known" success stories of continuous improvement, to companies that, in the words of Lillrank and his colleagues (1998), have "committed themselves wholeheartedly to a continuous improvement culture, . . . made fundamental changes in their managerial philosophies and practices, and continuously improved company performance" (p. 48). Usually, these stories are told with little supporting evidence. Likewise, plenty of claims exist about the failure of continuous improvement (see Lillrank et al., 1998). These claims are also largely anecdotal. They assert that many organizations have tried to implement continuous improvement processes and that relatively few have achieved significant change or results accorded with initial expectations (e.g., Krishnan, Shani, Grant, & Baer, 1993; Nohria, 1996; Torbert, 1992). These claims of failure are also made with little supporting evidence.

However, when we examine empirical studies that focus specifically on continuous improvement processes, we find an overall pattern of positive outcomes. One of the general findings of this empirical literature is that these processes are associated with an organization's ability to adapt to changing environments, especially rapidly changing environments. These processes are associated with an organization's ability to engage effectively in strategic change and to respond successfully to swiftly shifting markets and competitive conditions. For example, Shona Brown and Kathleen Eisenhardt (1997) found in their research that processes of continuous improvement helped computer companies engage in the rapid continuous change and product innovation required in their highly competitive markets. These processes helped them perform well and compete effectively across long periods of time.

Violina Rindova and Suresh Kotha (2001) made similar findings in their case studies of two Internet companies, Yahoo! and Excite. Their research provides additional evidence of the importance of continuous improvement processes in companies that have been successful across time in turbulent environments. These case studies describe how these companies "repeatedly changed their function and form to respond to shifting market and competitive conditions. They continuously redefined what they were and what they offered . . ." (p. 1272). They were able to do so by engaging in a process they call "continuous morphing." Rindova and Kotha found that two organizational mechanisms were associated with continuous morphing. The first were dynamic capabilities consisting of emergent learning processes and organizing principles. The second was strategic flexibility. By using these mechanisms, these companies were able to sustain competitive advantage by the continuous and comprehensive adaptation and redefinition of their products and services, changes in the deployment of resources and capacities for production, and the creation of new resources and capacities.

Robert Burgelman (1991) also found that firms he studied that were relatively successful for a decade or more tended to have active, ongoing, adaptive internal change processes. In these organizations, change activity would be as frequently self-initiated as induced from the outside. Those companies with regular strategic adaptive processes were contrasted with failing companies that tended to have no established change processes or that employed irregular and "hyperactive" processes (i.e., excessive and vacillating) that restricted their ability to adapt effectively to changing environments (see Hambrick & D'Aveni, 1988). Dean, Carlisle, & Baden-Fuller (1999) also found that processes of continuous improvement helped the water industry in the United Kingdom adapt to its changing regulatory environment and even improve its performance in that changing and challenging context. Quinn's (1980) case studies of major corporations made similar findings.

These and other studies have found that continuous improvement processes are associated with product innovation, something that is often necessary for organizations to prosper in volatile and competitive environments. This was one of several findings from Brown and Eisenhardt's (1997) study of computer companies. Taina Savolainen (1991) made a similar finding in 15-year longitudinal case studies of two Finnish manufacturing companies. Those case studies documented a positive relationship between the adoption and implementation of new ideas and practices and patterns of managerial thinking and organizational processes consistent with continuous improvement.

Other studies have found that processes of continuous improvement can increase the probability of successful organizational adaptation and change in the future. The presence of these processes can reduce the chances that organizations might become stagnant with age. This finding is well illustrated in Amburgey, Keppy, & Barnett's (1993) study of more than 1,000 newspaper organizations in Finland. This study showed that the presence of these processes and previous changes and environment adaptations achieved through them established change routines and precedent that made future change and adaptation "normal" and more likely to be achieved. It also illustrated another general finding, that processes of continuous improvement can reduce the disruption of major episodic change and risks posed by such disruption. By engaging in ongoing, incremental change and adaptation, the need for major change among these newspaper companies was reduced. This study showed that when organizations must engage in major change, the processes of and precedent with continuous improvement tend to lower internal resistance to major change and limit the "damage" such changes exact on an organization's ties to its environment, especially an organization's relationships with other organizations on which it depends. Dean and her colleagues (1999) made a similar finding in their study of the U.K. water industry, that continuous improvement processes reduce the "costs" of major episodic change.

Another finding of this body of research is that continuous improvement processes reduce the chance of "recidivism" or backsliding after a change is introduced. Several studies suggest that backsliding is more likely after major disruptive changes than after incremental changes generally associated with continuous improvement. In one study, Susan Fox-Wolfgramm and her colleagues (1998) examined processes by which banks "interacted with" and responded to their policy environments, focusing particularly on regulation. Noting that organizations have "biographies that affect how they respond to change" (p. 89), they found a relationship between the strategic orientations that were reflected in banks' organizational biographies and their ability to successfully adapt to changing regulatory environments and sustain, even improve their performance. One orientation was associated with what Fox-Wolfgramm and her colleagues called "prospector" banks; another was associated with what they called "defender" banks. Prospector banks were dynamic organizations with broad product lines that focused on innovation and market opportunities. They emphasized creativity over efficiency. Prospectors were found to adapt to their environments by using high levels of scanning to identify opportunities for developing new products or markets critical to their success. Structurally, prospector banks were "organic," with low formalization and specialization and high levels of decentralization. Compared with prospectors, defender banks were less dynamic and more focused on promoting efficiency in their existing operations. They were more rigid organizationally, more mechanistic than adaptive, and more formalized, centralized, and specialized than prospectors.

Fox-Wolfgramm and her colleagues (1998) found that prospector banks were more responsive to changes in their environments and more open to change. Their strategic orientations served as "interpretive schema" through which environmental change could be processed and acted upon. Change was easier in prospector banks because they were oriented toward and organized for it. Once changes were made, prospector banks were more likely than defender banks to sustain them. Prospector banks' identities as "changing organizations" allowed for ongoing adaptation without challenging or changing the organization's core identity and values; indeed their core identities and values embodied change. The plasticity of prospector banks helped them absorb major changes more easily and supported, even promoted, ongoing adaptation without backsliding. On the other hand, because of their tendency to resist incremental change, defender banks were more likely to need to make "intensive" punctuated changes. These major changes were more likely to conflict with defender banks' identities, values, and strategic orientations and thus were more difficult to sustain.

EVIDENCE FROM STUDIES OF SCHOOLS AND SCHOOL DISTRICTS

As noted at the beginning of this chapter, relatively few empirical studies of the outcomes of continuous improvement have been conducted in schools and school districts. And relatively few studies of school effectiveness or school improvement are designed to reveal continuous improvement or similar processes "at work." In this section, we examine several studies that shed light on the outcomes of continuous improvement in schools. Consistent with findings about the outcomes of continuous improvement in non-education organizations, the overall evidence about the outcomes of continuous improvement in schools is positive.

Studies of Effective and Improving Schools

Most studies of effective schools, that is, schools that perform well academically across time, focus on organizational characteristics related to high performance. For the most part, these characteristics are considered static qualities (Reynolds, 1999; Teddlie & Reynolds, 2000). Few studies of academically effective schools examine how these characteristics may have developed and few studies document processes that have helped schools to attain and sustain success across time.

Of the few effective schools studies that shed light of such processes, Susan Rosenholtz's (1989) research stands out as particularly instructive. Her study, which focused on 78 elementary schools in Tennessee, sought to identify organizational features that distinguished schools considered "learning enriched" from schools considered "learning impoverished." The designation of learning enriched and learning impoverished referred to qualities of schools as workplaces for teachers. Those schools considered learning enriched were characterized by strong expectations and ongoing opportunities for continuous teacher learning and improvement in classroom instruction. Those schools considered learning impoverished lacked such expectations and opportunities.

Rosenholtz's (1989) study found that teachers' views of their own practice were substantially different in learning enriched schools and in learning impoverished schools. In the latter schools, teachers tended to think that excellence in teaching was something that could be attained in a particular amount of time, and that once attained, the problem became one of maintenance. In these schools, there was not the dynamic concept of teaching excellence found in the former schools, where teachers tended to think that excellence in teaching could never be fully achieved. The objective in these former schools was continuous learning and improvement. In addition, Rosenholtz's data indicated that students performed better on standardized tests of academic achievement in schools that for their teachers were learning enriched than in schools that were learning impoverished.

There are only a few studies in the school improvement literature that document school improvement across time and that also identify organizational or leadership processes that might explain that improvement. In one of these studies, Karen Louis and Matthew Miles (1990) examined five urban high schools and their efforts to improve. The objective of this research was to identify organizational and leadership processes associated with improvement across time. The study began with the premise that "tomorrow won't be the same as today" (p. 14). Louis and Miles reasoned that "demands for change bombarding us [now] are just the beginning. . . . Nowhere are these pressures for massive change and adaptation more evident than in urban districts where the gap between expectations and performing often seems the widest." (pp. 14, 15). The overarching finding of their study was that creating more effective schools in this context required significantly different patterns of organization and leadership at the school level. Rather than a "bureaucratic" model of schools, they identified an "adaptive" model of school organization and leadership that was much more conducive to improvement in rapidly changing contexts. This model allowed schools to be "planful" and not simply reactive to external pressures and crises. The underlying theme was the imperative for constant learning and evolution, driven by a clear vision of what the school was to accomplish, to continuously improve the basic functioning of the school.

One important feature of this adaptive model was the use of what Louis and Miles (1990) called "evolutionary planning." Evolutionary planning reflects the qualities of continuous improvement. It involves "coherent, intelligent adaptation based on direct experience with what is working toward the [school's] vision and what isn't. It's not living 'a day at a time,' but through a stream of examined experiences." (p. 32). Louis and Miles explained evolutionary planning this way:

> If rational planning is like blueprinting, evolutionary planning is more like taking a journey. There is a general destination, but many twists and turns as unexpected events occur along the way. (p. 193)

Key to evolutionary planning is a set of actions that promoted change. These actions included continuous monitoring of the external environment, with particular attention to identifying potential problems and resources, and repeated efforts to prevent or address actual problems that might interfere with the schools' improvement activities. Principals of improving schools constantly searched for, confronted, and acknowledged serious problems when they first appeared and acted decisively to solve them. They were opportunistic, looking for ways to do things more effectively before problems presented themselves. They were not captured by formal planning processes (although improving schools used combinations of various formal planning processes). Rather, they were able to experiment and innovate within the parameters of their schools' visions. These principals were able to generate what Louis and Miles call "inspirational themes" for improvement that motivate and galvanize faculty, and then engage the school in "reflection on the relationship between action and improvement" (p. 215). Good evolutionary planning involved careful and regular monitoring of improvement activity and it involved the discipline to live with ambiguity and stave off the tendency to reach premature closure (p. 292).

Additional evidence of organizational and leadership processes related to school improvement comes from a multi-year study of the Chicago Annenberg Challenge (Smylie & Wenzel, 2003).[15] This study found that high-performing and improving schools possessed many of the properties and processes that characterize continuous improvement. These schools possessed an orientation not only toward improving student learning but also toward making the school organization better, in particular improving the organizational capacity to improve. High performing and improving schools focused on continually developing strategic combinations of capacities related to particular improvement objectives. So for example, if an improvement objective was instructional, these schools might also focus on the concurrent development of teacher capacity and structural coherence and efficiencies. A second thing that characterized high-performing and improving schools was the idiosyncratic combination of change strategies employed and adapted across time to align with the school's progress, the development of its capacity, and changing external conditions. Each high-performing and improving school exhibited different patterns of strategies reflecting ongoing assessment of external demands, internal capacity, and change objectives sought. A third thing that characterized these schools was that they engaged in constant, opportunistic, and strategic search for resources. It was not the amount of resources that mattered. Indeed, some of the low-performing and non-improving schools in the study had no difficulty obtaining resources. It was the "intelligent" acquisition and use of flexible combinations of human, fiscal, material, and even political resources that distinguished the groups of schools. And as part of developing resources, high performing and improving schools worked to develop and flexibly deploy leadership across the organization not simply within particular formal roles. The strategic cultivation of leadership work across the school organization in anticipation of and in response to opportunities for improvement distinguished high performing and improving schools from others.

Studies of Continuous Improvement Processes

There are few studies that focus on the outcomes of specific processes of continuous improvement in schools and school districts. One such study is the five-year evaluation of the Bay Area School Reform Collaborative (BASRC) (Copland, 2003; McLaughlin & Mitra, 2003; McLaughlin & Talbert, 2000, 2002).[16] At the heart of BASRC's vision and strategy was a Cycle of Inquiry. This cycle is described in detail in Chapter 4, and a vignette of a school employing it is presented in Chapter 6. As a prelude to this more detailed discussion, it is enough to say here that the Cycle represents a logic and process of continuous school improvement. It begins with using data to identify problems and areas for improvement. It proceeds to identify gaps between current performance and performance objectives and then to set goals and a work plan to close the gap between the two. The work plan is to be implemented and analyzed, and the findings fed back into the cycle for continuous improvement. The Cycle is to involve the entire school organization, and it is to focus primarily on the improvement of instruction and student learning. The logic of the Cycle is that through collective continuous inquiry schools will be able to develop professional community and capacity for instructional improvement that will in turn lead to more effective teaching and stronger student learning. As Milbrey McLaughlin and Dana Mitra (2003) described it, "the Cycle of Inquiry would permit schools to build both the processes and the knowledge base for continuous improvement" (p. 5).

The BASRC evaluation found evidence to support this logic of continuous improvement. According to McLaughlin and Mitra (2003, see also McLaughlin & Talbert, 2002), the Cycle helped schools develop their capacity for inquiry and evidence-based decision making. Teachers reported becoming more conversant with the idea of continuous inquiry and what it means. Faculty conversations shifted to focus more on data and connections between student outcomes and classroom practices. Faculties developed from being merely reactive to problems to being more proactive to make things happen before problems arose. This evaluation also found positive relationships between maturity in use of the Cycle of Inquiry and development of faculty norms that support innovation and mutual support for improving practice. These norms included collective problem solving and commitment to the learning of all students. This evaluation also found a positive relationship between the development of inquiry practices and how much a school's faculty shared responsibility for school improvement and student success. It found a positive relationship between the development of shared leadership and practices that in turn sustained continuous inquiry and improvement (see Copland, 2003).

Analyses of student achievement data indicate that during the course of the evaluation, schools using the Cycle of Inquiry made significantly greater improvement in their students' performance on standardized tests of basic skills achievement than did comparison schools (McLaughlin & Mitra, 2003; McLaughlin & Talbert, 2000, 2002). BASRC schools serving the largest proportions of low-income students, English language learners, and African American students outperformed matched comparison schools. BASRC schools serving moderate and low proportions of these student groups also made greater gains than comparison schools. In addition, BASRC high schools made significant progress in narrowing within-school achievement gaps between economically advantaged and disadvantaged students.

In other study, Sharon Kruse (2001) examined the development and outcomes of continuous improvement processes used by planning teams in three school districts. These teams were composed of representatives from different school buildings, central office personnel, community members, and external consultants whose responsibility it was to guide the teams in the development and implementation of a "comprehensive, continuous improvement planning process" (p. 364). The continuous improvement process here focused on creating new structures and systems to effect ongoing change. The process model had six elements: (a) revision of mission, vision, and beliefs concerning student learning; (b) identification of goals for students and student learning; (c) identification of performance requirements for what must take place for goals to be achieved; (d) identification of performance standards that attend to measurable outcomes of implementation; (e) strategies or development activities to achieve goals according to standards; and (f) assessment of strategies and outcomes.

Kruse (2001) found that the implementation of this process across several years led to a number of positive outcomes. It fostered collaboration among educators for the improvement of student learning. This collaboration involved the growth of internal expertise, trust, and respect among staff. It sharpened the focus and increased the use of data-driven decisions and use of external resources for learning, planning, and decision making. The process engendered a greater sense of purpose and meaning related to discussion and choices concerning student achievement. Overall, the process generated new organizational capacity and fostered more focused and better-considered decisions with regard to improving student learning.

There are several studies of organizational learning processes in schools that reflect processes of continuous improvement and these studies provide additional evidence of their efficacy. In one such study, Halia Silins, William Mulford, and Silja Zarins (2002) explored the relationship of organizational learning in Australian high schools to student participation in and engagement in school. This study also examined the relationship of organizational learning to a number of other outcomes, including leadership and teachers' work.[17] Silins and his colleagues found that organizational learning as defined in the study was directly and positively predictive of the quality of teachers' classroom work, measured as students' liking of the ways in which teachers instruct them, the variety of instructional activities, the organization of classes, teachers' expectations that students do their best work, and the intellectual challenge of classroom instructional activity. Teachers' work exerted a direct influence on student participation and engagement. Organizational learning was found to have a statistically significant positive indirect effect on student participation and engagement through teachers' work and through participative patterns of school leadership.

Other evidence of outcomes of continuous improvement processes, also framed in terms of organizational learning, can be found in historical case studies of schools in Ontario Canada and New York State conducted by Corrie Giles and Andy Hargreaves (2006; Hargreaves, 2003). One of these cases, the most positive one, is portrayed in a vignette of continuous improvement "in action" in Chapter 6. This case and evidence of outcomes at this school are discussed there. So too can other vignettes in that chapter speak to the issue of the effectiveness of continuous improvement in schools.

SUMMARY

In summation, research on organizations across sectors and of different types—schools and non-education organizations alike—points to the contribution of continuous improvement to high organizational performance and improvement across time. It points to the potential of continuous improvement to help organizations be more adaptive to changing environments, to reduce the need to make radical change, and to moderate the stresses and costs of significant changes when they need to be made. In addition, the research suggests that continuous improvement may help develop organizational capacity for creativity, invention, and self-initiated improvement, all of which help organizations perform at high levels as the face uncertainty and turbulence in their environments.

The strength of the evidence of positive outcomes comes from its consistency across studies. Whether from non-education organizations or schools and school districts, whether derived from studies of high-performing organizations or improving and innovating organizations, or whether derived from studies of continuous improvement processes per se, the evidence points in the same general positive and promising directions.

QUESTIONS FOR STUDY, REFLECTION, AND ACTION

1. How would you describe the quality of existing evidence on the effectiveness of continuous improvement? What are the strengths and weaknesses of the evidence overall? How confident can we be of the overall evidence about the effectiveness of continuous improvement?

2. Compare the findings of effectiveness from research on schools and school districts with findings from research on non-education organizations. How similar and different are findings across studies of different types of organizations? Overall, how do the findings add up to a set of general conclusions about the effectiveness of continuous improvement?

3. What evidence exists in your school and school district about the relative effectiveness of different approaches to school improvement? How do the overall findings of research about the effectiveness of continuous improvement relate to the evidence you see around you?

4. This book takes the position that there are lessons from non-education organizations that can help promote understanding and the practice of continuous improvement in schools (see Preface). Do you agree with this position? Why or why not? How far do you think one can and should go in applying knowledge from non-education organizations to schools and school districts? What limitations or cautions do you think are appropriate?

5. How would you determine if continuous improvement was working in your school? How might you assess its implementation and effectiveness?

Processes of Continuous Improvement

4

Virtuous Circle. n. A condition in which a favorable circumstance or result gives rise to another that subsequently supports the first.

—American Heritage Dictionary (2006)

Will the circle be unbroken, bye and bye Lord, bye and bye. There's a better home a waiting in the sky, Lord, in the sky.

—Traditional

Myriad management strategies and techniques can be used to carry out the processes of continuous improvement. Among them are strategies for decision making, strategic planning and other planning techniques, techniques for gaining participation, and methodologies and tools for data collection and analysis. Also among them are strategies for training and professional development and systems of incentives and accountability to motivate participation and accomplishment. The literature on such strategies is vast, as evidenced by the voluminous body of work in the fields of organization development (e.g., Cummings & Worley, 2005) and of the implementation of new programs, policies, and practices (e.g., Honig, 2006; Odden, 1991). This chapter focuses more generally on process models of continuous improvement, attending particularly to those models developed for and used by schools and school districts. These models represent particular "theories-of-action" about how continuous improvement takes place.

INTRODUCTORY CONSIDERATIONS

Before taking a look at these models, a few considerations are in order. First, the literature is clear that the success of any particular process of continuous improvement depends on the quality of its implementation. And implementation depends in no small part on the organizational context in which the process is enacted. As Chapter 5 will explain in some detail, particular elements of organizational design can promote or impede the implementation and effectiveness of continuous improvement processes in schools, as well as the implementation of initiatives that emanate from them. These elements include a school's norms, values, and culture; human capital and its development; the organization of people and work; systems of reward and accountability; fiscal and physical resources; internal management systems; and leadership among others. This makes attending to the organizational design of schools an important aspect of the practice of continuous improvement.

Second, as noted in Chapter 2, the literature suggests that most organizations engaged in continuous improvement rarely adhere to only one model or to one particular set of strategies and techniques. Depending on their circumstances, most organizations find that single approaches will not help them address all the issues they confront. Therefore, they turn to combinations or "hybrids" of several approaches that to them make the most sense. These combinations vary according to organizational mission and core values, organizational context and capacity, the particulars of external environments, and the resources on which an organization can draw. These combinations of strategies and techniques may change over time as situations demand. Most organizations, particularly those considered successful in continuous improvement, operate from a contingency perspective. As Nadia Bhuiyan and Amit Baghel (2005) observe

> To overcome the weaknesses of one program or another . . . companies have merged different continuous improvement initiatives together, resulting in a combined continuous improvement program that is more far reaching than any one individually. (p. 765)

This leads to a third consideration, also raised in Chapter 2. The organization and management literature indicates that it is wise to think about models and strategies in terms of equifinality. Recall that equifinality is a concept that means that the same goal can be attained from different starting points and by following different paths (Burke, 2008). Equifinality means that there is no one best practice, no one formula or "recipe." Different organizations, in different contexts, with different goals may follow different paths to successful continuous improvement (General Accounting Office, 1994; Hopkins, 2001; Lillrank et al., 1998; Savolainen, 1991). However, the literature is also clear that not all methods of continuous improvement may be equally effective. There are certain principles, elements, and qualities of continuous improvement processes that increase the likelihood that they will be successful.

A fourth consideration is the danger of goal displacement. Goal displacement is a phenomenon whereby an initial objective is replaced by another, typically when "means become ends-in-themselves that displace the original goals" (Blau & Scott, 1962, p. 229). A common instance of goal displacement is when the successful implementation of a policy or a practice becomes viewed as the end to be achieved rather than the objective that was to be achieved through the implementation of that policy or practice. In the classroom, goal displacement may occur when the completion of assignments becomes the goal rather than the student learning that is to be achieved through those assignments. With regard to continuous improvement, goal displacement can occur when successful implementation of processes or specific strategies becomes the outcome sought (or settled for) rather than the improvements in organizational outcomes they are intended to achieve.

Finally, the literature on continuous improvement raises questions about the best "location" for continuous improvement processes in an organization. This is the issue of the most effective relationship between continuous improvement processes and the central operations or core technology of the organization. Should continuous improvement processes be part of the core, or should these processes operate outside of and parallel to the core? Should continuous improvement be part of everyday activity or something "extra"? This issue is explored at the end of this chapter.

THE BASIC PROCESS MODEL

One of the earliest process models of continuous improvement was developed by Walter A. Shewhart in 1939. This model was created to provide a means to identify and address problems of quality control in industrial organizations. Referred to as the "Shewhart Cycle," this model is generally acknowledged as the foundation for subsequent continuous improvement processes (Choi, 1995). Indeed, most continuous improvement models seen today in the business and management and the education literatures are variations of the Shewhart Cycle.

The Shewhart Cycle has four basic steps. In its original presentation (Shewhart, 1939, cited in Deming, 2000), these steps are described as "Plan-Do-Check-Act" (see Figure 1). The first step—*Plan*—involves addressing questions of goals, deciding what changes might be needed to meet those goals, and assessing the availability of data to determine if changes achieve their objectives. It also involves developing plans for a particular change or a test run of something new and deciding how observations of putting the change or test in place would be used. The second step—*Do*—concerns carrying out the change or test decided upon. Preference was given to starting off "on a small scale." The third step—*Check*—calls for observing the effects of the change or test. The fourth step—*Act*—is a bit of a misnomer. It refers to studying what was observed and determining what can be learned and predicted from those observations for what to do next. This fourth step leads back to the first, and the cycle repeats into the future.

Figure 1   The Shewhart Cycle

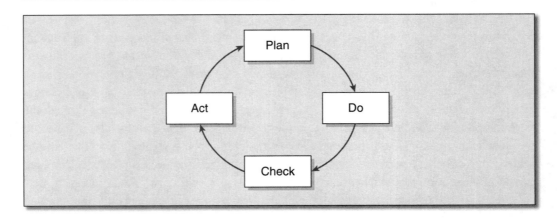

According to Ty Choi (1995), the basic logic of this process is that incremental improvement occurs through "the endless churning" of the cycle (p. 614). Furthermore, he contends,

> As the Shewhart cycle continues, members collect data on how the change processes are unfolding, evaluate the data, and gain knowledge. . . . The incremental progression of changes is governed by the knowledge gained from each previous change cycle. . . . Only when such data are analyzed and the analysis is converted to action, will the organization begin to reap the benefits of continuous improvement. (p. 614)

The logic and elements of the Shewhart Cycle are reflected in models and methods of quality control found in the industrial management literature of the 1960s. For example, George Box and Norman Draper (1969) presented their method of Evolutionary Operation as a "continuous investigative routine" (p. 5) that established a process in which "*useful ideas* are continually forthcoming" (p. 16, emphasis in the original). While not acknowledging Shewhart specifically, Box and Draper's model included all the elements of the Shewhart Cycle—collecting data, identifying problems, generating new ideas, planning, acting, and studying results for the future.

In the 1980s, the Shewhart Cycle appeared prominently in the work of W. Edward Deming. In his book *Out of Crisis,* Deming (2000) specifically refers to the Shewhart Cycle as a useful and effective method to achieve continual improvement in quality. He presents a figure of the cycle and describes its steps much in the way that they are described in Shewhart's original work. With magnanimity, Deming tells his readers that after his work in Japan promoting quality management, Shewhart's cycle was popularly and mistakenly renamed the "Deming Cycle." Deming is clear that the cycle is Shewhart's and not his own.

The logic and steps of the Shewhart Cycle maintained their prominence largely through Deming's writing and through the broader quality movement that swept through business and industry and other sectors, including education, during the 1980s and 1990s (Bhuiyan & Baghel, 2005; Choi, 1995). Shewhart's ideas are at the center of a number of contemporary management systems such as the Balanced Scorecard and Six Sigma (e.g., Harry & Schroeder, 2006; Kaplan & Norton, 1996). They are embodied in and promoted through the widely recognized Malcolm Baldrige National Quality Award Program. Established in 1987, the Baldrige program seeks to promote awareness of the importance of quality improvement to the national economy, recognize organizations that have made substantial improvements in products, services, and overall competitive performance, and foster sharing of best-practices information among organizations in the United States (Karathanos & Karathanos, 1996). The program reaches across organizational sectors.

Elements of the Shewhart Cycle are readily identifiable in the Baldrige criteria for educational organizations (Baldrige National Quality Program, 2006). While not laid out in specific steps, the basic ideas of Plan-Do-Check-Act can be seen in the criteria's core values and concepts. One of the core values and concepts—*management by fact*—points directly to the importance of developing "critical data and information about key processes and results" and means of analysis to extract "larger meaning from data and information" to support evaluation, decision making, and improvement. It points to the establishment of "a comprehensive and integrated fact-based system" for data collection, analysis and reflection, planning, and implementation that, according to the logic of the criteria, will promote continuous improvement and high performance over time.

EARLY APPLICATIONS TO SCHOOLS

The earliest applications of this basic process model of continuous improvement to schools can be traced to the mid-1960s. The focus at the time was on promoting educational improvement through school self-renewal. Introduced as the concept of self-design in Chapter 2, self-renewal is a "theory" of change based on the premise that schools, or any organization for that matter, have an inherent capacity for improvement. In schools, that capacity is underutilized in large part because it is underdeveloped, because schools lack the realization that they possess it, and because schools lack the means to activate and employ it effectively.

One early process model associated with promoting the self-renewal of schools was published by Goodwin Watson in a 1967 report prepared for the National Training Laboratories. The report, *Toward a Conceptual Architecture of a Self-Renewing School,* laid out ten steps to successfully "realize a program of continuous self-renewal." As described in the opening to the report, these steps include the following:

1. Sensing possible areas and needs for improvement

2. Determining items that merit further investigation

3. Diagnosing specific needs through some form of research and development

4. Inventing or generating remedies by wide personnel participation

5. Weighing resultant solution proposals

6. Deciding on the course to follow

7. Introducing the chosen innovation into the system

8. Operating the innovation on a trial basis

9. Evaluating the innovation both continuously and periodically through an objective agency

10. Revising the innovation to improve its effectiveness

About the same time that Watson published his report, John Goodlad and his colleagues began a multi-year project called the *Study of Educational Change and School Improvement* (SECSI) (Bentzen, 1974; Goodlad, 1975). This project was sponsored by the Institute for Development of Educational Activities (I/D/E/A) and sought to promote and study the process of self-renewal in 18 elementary schools in southern California. It was developed around a simple process model that represented "the set of behaviors by which all staffs carry out the business of the school—the process by which they consider change or reject it" (Bentzen, 1974, p. 19). This model collapsed a number of the steps in Watson's model into four steps that reflected, in a somewhat different order, the basic elements of the Shewhart Cycle. It was called the DDAE Process, an acronym identifying each step of the model.

The first step was *Dialogue* about what was to be done. Dialogue might include the identification of problems, goals to be achieved, alternative strategies and resources that might be required to achieve those goals. The second step was *Decision Making*. Whether by the principal, groups of teachers, or consensus, this step would identify and select a course of action among viable alternatives. The third step, *Action*, meant to implement that course, be it by an individual or a group, be it by reason or intuition. The fourth step in the process was *Evaluation*. In this step, action and outcomes intended and unintended would be assessed. The findings of such assessment would provide the focus for new dialogue and the process would begin again.

During late 1960s and into the 1970s, attention to other change strategies in schools increased. Many were adopted from business settings. They included general strategies of self-development and renewal associated with organization development (see Fullan, Miles, & Taylor, 1980; see also Cummings & Worley, 2005). In the 1980s and 1990s came an increase in the application of strategies associated with total quality management, along with various forms of strategic planning and development planning (e.g., Bostingl, 1996; Bryson, 1995; Hargreaves & Hopkins, 1994; Sallis, 2002). Also during this period, attention began to shift away from processes of organizational development toward strategies or techniques to implement specific programs and policies effectively (e.g., Fullan, 1992; Odden, 1991).

CONTEMPORARY PROCESS MODELS

In the late 1990s, more systematic models of continuous improvement began to emerge. These contemporary models share many of the same elements. Most are variations on a common theme. And they have much in common with earlier generations of models. This section presents a sample of six contemporary models of continuous improvement for schools. These models are generally representative of the range of models found in the education literature. The particular models discussed here were selected because they are among the most "prominent" on the education landscape, readily available to schools and promoted by national professional education organizations, prominent school improvement consultants, and major school reform initiatives.[18] They include the following:

- Lawrence Lezotte and Kathleen McKee's (2002, 2006) *The Effective Schools Continuous Improvement Process*
- The National Study of School Evaluation's (NSSE) model of *Breakthrough School Improvement* (AdvancED, n.d.a, b; North Central Association, 2004)
- The San Francisco Bay Area School Reform Collaborative's *Cycle of Inquiry* (Copland, 2003; McLaughlin & Mitra, 2003)
- Allison Zumda, Robert Kuklis, and Everett Kline's (2004) *Six Steps of Continuous Improvement*
- The National Education Association's KEYS for Excellence in Your School *Continuous School Improvement Model* (KEYS-CSI) (2008)
- Willis Hawley and Gary Sykes's (2007) *Model of Continuous Improvement*

The KEYS-CSI model was informed a great deal by the initial work of Hawley and Sykes on their model. The final versions of the two models contain some important differences so both will be discussed. Before we begin this review, it is important to look at a key feature that extends beyond the processes of continuous improvement depicted in these models—how these models define "improvement."

Defining Improvement

Most contemporary process models of continuous improvement are tied to a particular conception of an effective school. They define *improvement* not simply by gains in student learning but also by the development of particular aspects of school organization conducive to organizational effectiveness in general and to effective teaching and learning in particular. Earlier models of continuous improvement tended to be "generic" or "content free." They were not anchored in a particular conception of organizational effectiveness that continuous improvement was to promote, other than perhaps greater student academic performance. Most conceptions of school effectiveness tied to contemporary models of continuous improvement are derived from the effective schools literature. And they tend to focus on many of the same elements. Several examples from the models discussed in this section, with acknowledged oversimplification, will illustrate.

Lezotte and McKee (2002, 2006) link their model of continuous improvement closely to "the correlates of effective schools." They distinguish between a "first generation" correlate, which represents what the original effective schools research found to be the "minimum standards of a particular characteristic that a school must meet to be effective," and a "second generation" of each correlate that incorporates subsequent research findings into our understanding of the original correlates (p. 279). These correlates include (a) a safe and orderly environment, (b) a climate of high expectations for success, (c) instructional leadership, (d) clear and focused mission, (e) opportunity for students to learn and student time on task, (f) frequent monitoring of student progress, and (g) supportive home-school relations.

The North Central Association's (NCA) accreditation process links the National Study of School Evaluation's Breakthrough School Improvement model to the NCA's standards of effective schools through the latter's school accreditation process. Grounded in a concept of effective schools similar to that of Lezotte and McKee, these standards are articulated in NCA's accreditation materials as follows (AdvancED, n.d.a, b):

Standard 1: Vision and Purpose. The school establishes and communicates a shared purpose and direction for improving the performance of students and the effectiveness of the school.

Standard 2: Governance and Leadership. The school provides governance and leadership that promote student performance and school effectiveness.

Standard 3: Teaching and Learning. The school provides research-based curriculum and instructional methods that facilitate achievement for all students.

Standard 4: Documenting and Using Results. The school enacts a comprehensive assessment system that monitors and documents performance and uses these results to improve student performance and school effectiveness.

Standard 5: Resources and Support Systems. The school has resources necessary to support its vision and purpose and to ensure achievement for all students.

Standard 6: Stakeholder Communication and Relationships. The school fosters effective communication and relationships with and among its stakeholders.

Standard 7: Commitment to Continuous Improvement. The school establishes, implements, and monitors a continuous process of improvement that focuses on student performance.

In a third example, the National Education Association's (NEA) KEYS-CSI Model is grounded in six categories of "keys" or indicators of school quality drawn from the effective schools research and other related research (Hawley with Rollie, 2007; NEA, 2008). These categories include (a) shared understanding and commitment to high goals for student learning among all members of a school community; (b) open communication and collaborative problem solving among school staff and between home and school; (c) continuous assessment for teaching and learning and use of assessment in decision making; (d) personal and professional learning of teachers; (e) resources to support teaching and learning, including a safe environment and sufficient space, instructional materials, and student support services; and (f) quality curriculum and instruction.

The basic idea of linking models of continuous improvement to conceptions of effective schools is to provide direction and guidance for improvement efforts. As discussed in Chapter 2, improvement is not about any change per se. It is about change in a particular valued direction. What better direction than toward those aspects of school organization believed to be associated with high levels of student performance? At the same time that such guidance may be helpful, tying processes of continuous improvement to models of effective school organization raises several issues.

Models or concepts of effective schools identify different, often discrete characteristics of school organization that are related (or purportedly relate) positively to high levels of student academic achievement. They do not constitute models or theories of school organizational development. The two are different. A model of school development represents a theory about how a school might progress from an underdeveloped and ineffective state to a developed and presumably more effective state. Such a model might articulate differences between high and low qualities or the presence, absence, or intensity of characteristics and conditions of schools associated with different types or levels of student performance. Such a model would suggest how student performance might improve (or decline) as the presence and qualities of different elements of school organization strengthen (or weaken). A model or theory of school development might also specify how improvement in one or more elements of school organization might relate systemically to improvement in other elements. This might suggest which changes in particular aspects of school organization would likely precede others or would be most conducive to evoking change in others, leading to the general improvement of the entire organization and its performance (see Burke, 2008).

Few models of school organization development exist in the education literature. Perhaps contextual variations and the concept of equifinality obviate the need for them. Still, it is important to be able to distinguish between "static" conceptions of school organizational effectiveness and "dynamic" conceptions of school organizational development that suggest points of leverage that some elements may have over others. Such models of school organizational development could be useful to persons engaged in processes of continuous improvement. These school development models could aid "theorizing" and "strategizing" about how to promote change in particular schools, decide what steps might be taken first and second, now and later, and provide some reason for doing so.

In addition, models of effective school organization consist of characteristics and conditions that research associates with the effectiveness of *today's* schools. As argued in Chapter 1, today's conceptions of effective schools may not be conducive to success in a future of rapid change, increasing demands, and growing uncertainty. We may not know now what schools that function effectively in this future might look like or what they might be doing. That is one of the reasons advanced for why schools and other organizations need to be organized around processes of continuous improvement—to discover, to innovate, to evolve into more effective but now unknown organizational forms. This is not to argue that current conceptions of effective school organization are not useful. This is not to say that they should be abandoned in favor of a directionless, "content free" improvement process. Nor is this to say that the elements of organizational design conducive to continuous improvement do not give some sense of what that future school organization might look like. It is to say that current conceptions of effective school organization need to be held provisional and made problematic. These conceptions should be tested through processes of continuous improvement. The challenge for schools may be to seek what is valuable from current conceptions of effective schools and at the same time avoid entrapment by conceptions of organization and organizational effectiveness that may not work so well in an uncertain future.

Examples of Models

We now turn to several examples of contemporary process models of continuous school improvement. Each contains basic elements that can be traced back to earlier more generic process models. Each is explicit about or strongly implies the need to involve the entire school community in different aspects of the improvement process. Each emphasizes the importance of school-level administrative leadership. And each points to the value of engaging teachers and other members of school communities in leadership of continuous improvement. Finally, each suggests that processes of continuous improvement should be routinized, integrated into the core operations of schools, and reflected in school organizational culture. These and other organizational matters are explored later.

These models share many of the same characteristics. They also differ in several ways. Some include steps, contain emphases, and provide substantive elaborations that others do not. Their starting points and orders of steps also vary. The question is whether these variations matter. Recalling the concept of equifinality, the answer may be "it depends." It may depend on the particular school, its needs and objectives, its capacity for improvement, its environment, and myriad other factors. There are good arguments that some variations may be more important than others. These arguments will be explored at the end of this chapter. The potential importance of these variations is good reason to examine each process model separately.

Few models of continuous improvement described in the education literature have been documented "in action" or evaluated systematically, including those selected for this chapter. Most claim to be "data-based" or derived from research. One can look to the history of models of continuous improvement applied to schools and argue that contemporary versions are indeed derived from research or based on "the literature." However, it is ironic that so little empirical evidence has been gathered to test the general efficacy of models that themselves place a premium on data collection and assessment.[19]

Lezotte and McKee's "The Effective Schools Continuous Improvement Process"

We begin with this model because its developers, school effectiveness consultants Lezotte and McKee (2002, 2006), trace its ancestry directly to Shewhart's Plan-Do-Check-Act Cycle. They refer to their model as a "modified version" of that cycle. Their rationale for modifying the cycle is twofold. First, they contend accommodations need to be made because schools and school districts are "existing" systems and "somewhere on the journey" to their missions. Unless they are new, schools do not begin the cycle on a blank slate. The model must be applicable in the context of changing environments and the ongoing production of new knowledge. Second, they want to discourage educators from jumping right into planning without first laying the proper foundation.

Following this logic, Lezotte and McKee's process model proceeds from three "antecedent" activities, which can be considered the true first step of the model. These activities require constant attention as the steps of the process model are followed. One activity is to establish and then nurture the process itself. This means developing the inclusive and collaborative working relationships among school personnel that will be required for the continuous improvement process to be successfully engaged. A second activity is to clarify the school's mission and core beliefs and values. Mission and core beliefs and values are the anchors of the process. Following from this is the identification of "essential student learning" that will also guide the continuous improvement process.

Lezotte and McKee's continuous improvement model has four steps: *Study-Reflect-Plan-Do* (see Figure 2). *Study* focuses on the problems that schools may be experiencing. Properly executed, study generates descriptions of problems and hypotheses as to what may be the "root causes" of these problems. *Reflect* focuses on learning. It directs a school's attention to what it is learning through the identification, description, and generation of hypotheses about problems. This step also involves "external scanning" to explore research literature and the practices of others that relate to the school's situation and to alternative solutions to its problems. This search prepares the school to move to the next step—*Plan*. This third step involves selecting solutions and developing action plans to implement them. In this step, training needs are identified, time lines are set, and strategies are developed for monitoring implementation and evaluating the overall effectiveness of the plans.

Figure 2   Lezotte and McKee's "The Effective Schools Continuous Improvement Process"

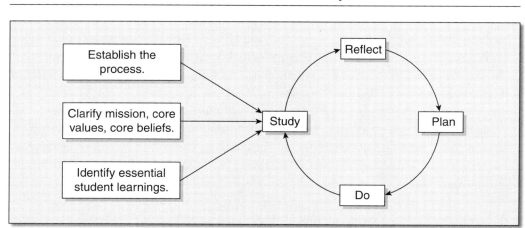

Finally, *Do* is the implementation of the plan and the collection of implementation and evaluation data. These data provide the opportunity to identify new problems and the cycle begins again.

Lezotte and McKee contend that in many cases, substantial preparation needs to occur to enter this cycle. Such preparation is important for the long-term sustainability of the process. While preparation and organizational capacity for continuous improvement are the subjects of Chapters 5 and 7 it is important to note here the importance of leadership. Lezotte and McKee argue that leadership, especially principal or other top administrative leadership, is crucial to the long-term success of the process. In order to be effective, leadership must create a common vision and language and set a tone for the entire continuous improvement process. Leadership must clarify the school's mission and core beliefs and values to give direction to the process and it must identify essential goals for student learning. Leadership must also establish the inclusive and collaborative working relationships among school personnel (and perhaps others who may join in) on which the process depends.

National Study of School Evaluation's "Breakthrough School Improvement" Model

A second contemporary model of continuous improvement comes from the National Study of School Evaluation and is associated with the NCA (2004; AdvancED, n.d.a, b). This model was designed to help manage a school's or school district's improvement process and meet planning requirements for NCA accreditation. It consists of a four-step cycle of activity with each part containing several "key actions" (see Figure 3). The process is supported by materials (i.e., data collection instruments, rubrics, and computer software) provided by NCA and its parent organization AdvancED, as well as by external leaders and external teams organized and dispatched by NCA who perform both formative and summative functions.

The process begins with establishing a vision for the school. This step involves four key actions. The first is to examine research-based factors related to student performance. The second is to determine the core beliefs and values of the school. The third is to develop a shared vision to focus school improvement efforts. And the fourth is to determine specific expectations for student learning. These key actions set the stage for the second step of the cycle—developing a descriptive school profile that forms a baseline analysis for goal setting and planning. This step involves four key actions focused largely on data collection and assessment of the current status of the school. These actions include developing current data-based descriptions of three crucial areas: (a) students and their performance, (b) school organization and effectiveness, and (c) the school in its community context. The last action is initial assessment of these descriptions to determine target areas for improvement.

The third step in the process is a systematic step of planning and implementation. Five key actions are associated with this step. These actions include using the school profile to identify gaps between expectations for student performance and current levels of performance, setting improvement goals, determining appropriate interventions, developing action plans, and implementing, monitoring, and adjusting those interventions. The fourth step focuses on evaluating results. Four key actions are associated with this step. The first is identifying measures to determine the outcomes of interventions and action plans. The second and third are to employ those measures to document and analyze student performance results and the success of interventions. The last key action is to communicate and use these results for further improvement. The cycle begins again as this last

Figure 3 National Study of School Evaluation's Model of "Breakthrough School Improvement"

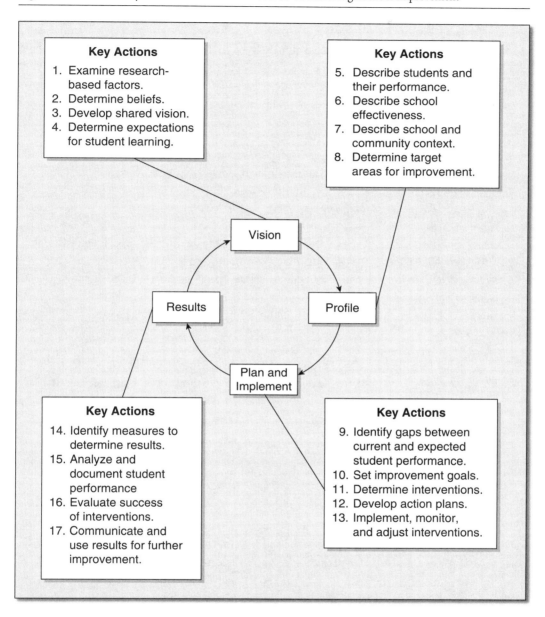

activity generates data to re-examine the school's vision and expectations for student learning (the first step) and update the descriptive profile of the school (the second step) for ongoing planning and implementation (the third step).

Bay Area School Reform Collaborative's "Cycle of Inquiry"

A third model of continuous improvement is the Bay Area School Reform Collaborative's (BASRC) "Cycle of Inquiry" (Copland, 2003; McLaughlin & Mitra, 2003). Recalling the discussion of BASRC in Chapter 3, the Collaborative was established in the San Francisco area as one of a group of six Challenges founded and funded in the mid-1990s by the Annenberg Foundation to promote large-scale school improvement. Central to BASRC's vision and theory of change was a model of continuous improvement called the Cycle of Inquiry. According to Michael Copland (2003), the cycle was an effort to "embed structures and processes at the level of the school that promote the sustained pursuit of shared enterprise—namely improving student learning—through work that is at once the province of groups and individuals" (p. 380). He continued with the following:

> The cycle of inquiry is intended to help schools pose, investigate, and respond to questions about politics and practices. . . . [It] aims to inform schools about the degree to which they are actually accomplishing what they think they should be in terms of a focused reform effort and consequences for students. (p. 380)

The logic of the cycle goes farther. The cycle is intended to develop the capacity of a school for inquiry and problem solving. This capacity can support more frequent and effective use of the cycle that would continue to build capacity that could further enable inquiry, problem solving, and yet more capacity development, and so on.

Milbrey McLaughlin and Joan Talbert (2000) summarized the general phases of the inquiry cycle as follows:

> [T]he school initially identifies a problem with student achievement, develops a focused effort in response, sets measurable goals, develops a concrete action plan, takes action, and collects and analyzes evidence of progress. . . . [T]his analysis of the relationship between action and results then feeds into revision of the problem statement, effort, and goals. (p. 12)

Copland (2003) expanded this general description to identify six specific steps and sub-steps (see Figure 4). The cycle begins with using data to identify problems and particular academic areas as foci for improvement. It then moves to a second step of refining foci for improvement by identifying gaps between expectations for student learning (e.g., standards) and student performance and identifying potential causes of those gaps. The third step involves the identification of measurable goals for improvement in student performance and in instructional practice. These goals can be defined at the school level, the grade level, or the department level. They can also be defined in terms of or in relation to student learning standards. This leads to a fourth step of developing a concrete work plan at both the school level and at relevant grade and department levels. This work plan would include the selection of evidence-based strategies for implementation, timelines, budgets, management and decision making, among other things. It might also include strategies for introducing cycles of inquiry at grade and department levels of school organization. The next step is to take action and implement the work plan. The final step is to collect, analyze, and reflect on data that will allow the school to gauge progress in achieving its objectives for change and will provide new evidence that can be used in returning to the first step of the cycle—identifying problems and focal areas for ongoing improvement.

Figure 4 The Bay Area School Reform Collaborative's "Cycle of Inquiry"

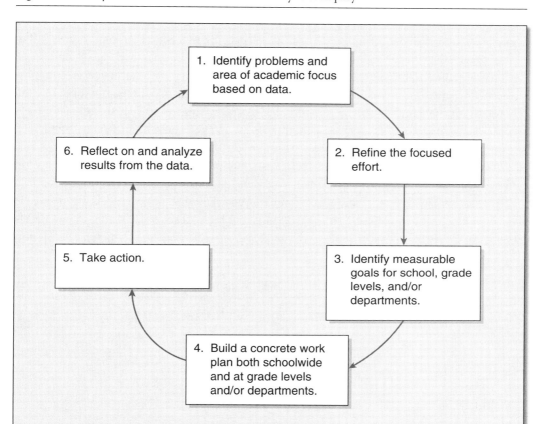

While the primary focus of the cycle is on improving student achievement, the foci on particular problems, planning, and action can extend to any aspect of teaching and learning and school organization considered relevant to achieving improvement goals. These elements can concern teacher professional learning and development, improving teacher "professional community," extending opportunities for leadership through the school organization, strengthening relationships between school and parents, and so on. What matters is how developing these elements relates to improving student learning.

Like the two examples of models presented earlier, BASRC's Cycle of Inquiry does not assume that schools have the capacity to enact the cycle successfully, at least initially. Therefore, the Collaborative developed a system of supports, mostly focused on developing the knowledge and skills teachers and principals need to initiate and manage the cycle. These supports were available to schools through Collaborative staff and schools' district offices. The objective was to provide ongoing professional development to help school staff ask questions and understand problems well, develop conceptual frameworks to guide cycles of inquiry, and construct standards and benchmarks against which to measure progress toward achieving improvement goals (Copland, 2003). The objective was also to develop the knowledge, skills, and levels of confidence required for school staffs to make the cycle a regular part of teachers' professional repertoire and a school's core operating processes.

Zumda and Colleagues' "Six Steps of Continuous Improvement"

A fourth example of a contemporary process model of continuous improvement is "Six Steps of Continuous Improvement." This model was developed by two education consultants of the Association for Supervision and Curriculum Development (ASCD) and a retired school administrator, and was published by ASCD (Zumda et al., 2004). The stated purpose of the model is not to provide an "off-the-shelf-solution" to the problem of school improvement but rather to "prescribe the end result" of school improvement—a model of a "competent system" (p. 17). Accordingly, a competent system links together systems thinking, vision and core beliefs, collegiality, continuous improvement, and accountability. An "incompetent system" fails to link these things together; it fails to cultivate among school personnel a common sense of purpose and bring them into collective improvement activity. A competent system must also be "personalized to local context" (p. 3).

The first step in this model consists of identifying and clarifying the core beliefs that define the school's culture (see Figure 5). According to Zumda and her colleagues (2004), these core beliefs either drive support for the status quo or the need to change the status quo. The second step is to

Figure 5   Zumda and colleagues' "Six Steps of Continuous Improvement"

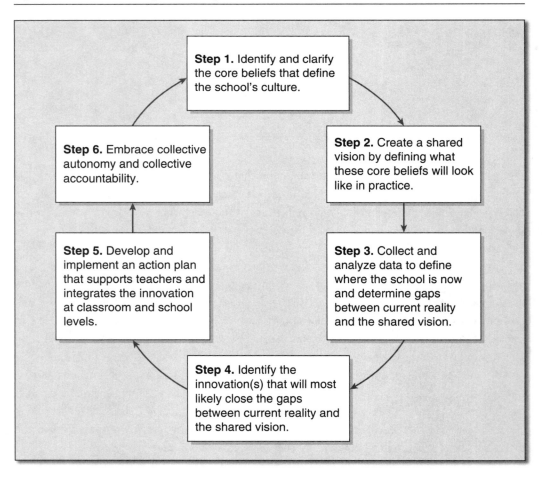

create a shared vision by defining what core beliefs should look like in practice. This is a narrative description of what is seen and heard in every part of the school community when the school's core beliefs truly inform its practices. The third step is to collect and analyze data—accurate and detailed—to define where the school is currently and to determine the gaps between the current state and the shared vision. Data collection and analysis are expected to lead to "rich conversations" among teachers and administrators about the meaning of the data and to "honest assessments" of teaching and learning. By identifying gaps, school personnel gain clarity on what they need to do to achieve the vision.

The fourth step is to identify the changes, and the initiatives to achieve them, that will close the gaps between the current reality and the vision. As part of this step, school personnel need to have the opportunity to learn what the changes entail and what impact those changes will have on them individually and collectively. They must be able to see what those changes might look like in practice. The fifth step is to develop and implement an action plan that supports teachers through the change process and integrates changes within each classroom and through the school. These action plans would likely include strategies for the professional learning and development of teachers and other staff members. They may also include provisions for reallocating resources. At this step, leaders need to be responsive to particular concerns of staff and but still hold staff accountable to ensure that the changes succeed. The sixth and final step is to "embrace collective autonomy" to close the gaps between the current reality and the shared vision and "embrace collective accountability" to establish responsibility for closing those gaps.

Zumda and her colleagues (2004) contend that this process will function best at the school level when there exists a partnership between schools and their central offices. Central office can support school-level continuous improvement processes by providing, among other things, information and data to schools, professional development opportunities for school personnel, and change facilitators who can bring expertise to the school and can serve as liaisons between schools and their districts.

NEA's "KEYS-Continuous School Improvement Model"

The Keys to Excellence in Your Schools (KEYS) is a comprehensive, data-driven program for supporting local continuous school improvement. Developed by the NEA, it is the result of a 15-year collaboration among educators, school and district administrators, parents, researchers, and business and community leaders. It is one of the most widely used school improvement processes in the country. According to the NEA, in mid-2009, this program was being used by nearly 1,750 schools, in 300 school districts, in 42 states and the Virgin Islands.

The KEYS program consists of a number of interconnected parts. One is a survey and data reporting process by which schools can assess themselves on measures of 42 indicators organized around six keys of school quality (outlined earlier in this chapter). Another part is a comprehensive array of resources to help schools use these self-assessments to identify problems, set goals, and plan for school improvement. A third part is a multi-step model of continuous school improvement that frames and guides these efforts (NEA, 2008).

The KEYS-Continuous School Improvement (CSI) model consists of eight sequential steps (see Figure 6). The first step is preparing the entire school community for the CSI process. This involves introducing the school community to the theory and practice of continuous school improvement, introducing the community to the KEYS survey and its importance of school improvement, and securing commitments from all relevant stakeholders for engaging in continuous improvement. The second step is collecting and organizing different types of data that may be needed to make important decisions. This step includes administration of the KEYS survey and collection of other data related to student learning and engagement; student characteristics that might relate to differences in student performance; school programs, curricula, and policies that might affect student learning; and perceptions of faculty, students, and families. The third step is to identify "priority" goals for student learning and to develop a consensus on ways to know whether those goals are achieved. This step also includes preliminary analyses of KEYS survey data to begin to identify strengths and weaknesses in the key areas of school organizational quality. The fourth step focuses on continued assessment of data. Here, analyses of KEYS survey data continue, but the focus expands to include collective analysis of student performance across the school and across academic subjects. The primary purpose of this step is to identify specific priorities for school improvement to achieve goals for student learning.

The fifth step of the model is developing strategies to address the priorities and goals set in earlier steps. This step involves framing problems and considering possible sources or causes of these problems. It also involves considering alternative strategies for addressing those problems and identifying evidence to assess the potential effectiveness and feasibility of implementing the most promising of them. From this analysis, specific courses of action are selected and a plan of action is developed. The sixth step, professional development, involves five tasks. These include

Figure 6 National Education Association's "KEYS-Continuous School Improvement (CSI) Model"

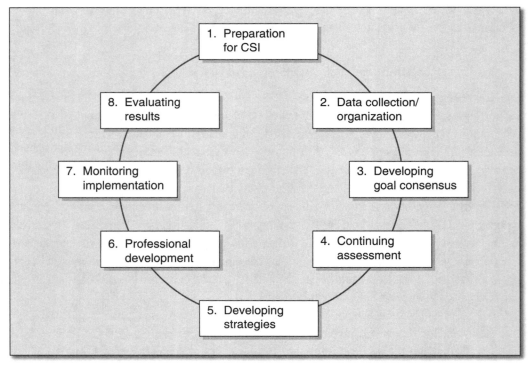

(a) determining what professional development experiences might need to be provided given the school's priorities and goals for improvement; (b) designing specific professional development programs and activities; (c) identifying resources needed and how they can be secured; (d) integrating professional development with the more comprehensive plan for school improvement; and (e) implementing and evaluating the effectiveness of these professional development strategies. The seventh step involves monitoring the implementation of improvement strategies. The CSI cycle ends with formal evaluation of and action research related to the school's improvement efforts. The findings of these inquiries are to feed back into the goal and priority setting process and the cycle repeats.

Several features of this model are particularly important. It specifies that schools begin with attention to goals, assessments, and the larger issue of "evidence." According to KEYS-CSI materials (NEA, 2008), reliance on evidence is the basis for forward progress. The model emphasizes that schools need to gather a wide range of evidence, particularly about student learning, and to use it at various points in the improvement process to inform decision making. Another important feature is a collaborative culture that supports the continuous improvement process. While the KEYS-CSI model considers these features important "capacities" for successful continuous school improvement, it does not assume that these capacities exist in all schools. Indeed, the model anticipates that schools may need to direct continuous improvement efforts toward the development of these capacities that, in turn, will support subsequent improvement efforts.

The Hawley-Sykes Model of Continuous Improvement

Hawley and Sykes's (2007) model is a four-phase cycle of school improvement (see Figure 7). Each phase contains a number of activities that would need to be adapted to particular contexts. It is beyond the scope of this summary to describe these activities fully. Like NEA's KEYS-CSI model, Hawley and Sykes identify evidence and a collaborative school culture as crucial features of the model. Also like the KEYS-CSI model, Hawley and Sykes indicate that continuous improvement should be engaged by the entire school community and that its processes should be integrated into the school's core functions and routines.

Phase 1 of the model concerns the development of consensus on goals and assessments of students' learning and performance. It calls on schools to clarify their core values related to student learning and from those values to set specific goals for student learning. Recognizing that schools are not able to "do it all at once," nor perhaps should they, this phase also involves identifying a set of high priority objectives. Then, a viable consensus on those learning goals and objectives should be obtained. This consensus should be tied to agreement on how progress toward goals and priority objectives will be measured and assessed. Deciding on how to measure and assess progress makes goals and objectives "operational." While perhaps more difficult to obtain consensus on goals and objectives defined in concrete terms than in vague abstract terms, once obtained that consensus is likely to be more meaningful. These decisions should become part of the "public, objective, collective practice" of the whole school community (Hawley & Sykes, 2007, p. 157). They should also be accompanied by a shared vision for instruction that is grounded in research on teaching and learning. Finally, this phase can be engaged over a long period of time, shifting from goals and priority objectives in one area to goals and priority objectives in another, even as other phases of the

Figure 7 Hawley and Sykes's "Four-Phase Cycle of Continuous Improvement"

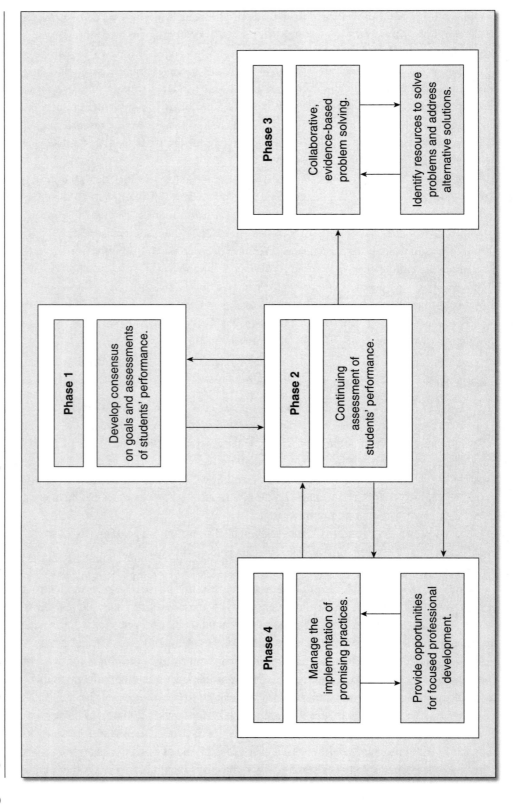

model are underway. Hawley and Sykes recognize that achieving complete agreement on these matters is probably unrealistic; however, some level of agreement among "substantial numbers" of teachers and other stakeholders with engagement of those who dissent is necessary.

Developing consensus on goals and assessments initiates the improvement process. The next phase propels it forward. Phase 2 is an "injunction to continuously assess" student performance (Hawley & Sykes, 2007, p. 159). Hawley and Sykes suggest that particular methods and tools of assessment are numerous and will vary from school to school. Successful schools are likely to develop complementary sets of formal and informal assessments. What matters is how particular assessments embody the basic principles of evidence-based decision making. The first principle is that assessment must be aligned with the school's goals and objectives. The second is that information from assessment must be supplied in a timely and transparent manner so that it can be used in teachers' and other staff members' work. The third principle is that assessment must be public and collective. The objective is to make assessment a "central, driving force in the school, moving front and center" (p. 160). It can then function as a guide and a lever for improvement. This phase can provide feedback to the first phase of the cycle by identifying areas for new goal development. It also sets the stage for Phase 3 by providing evidence of gaps between goals and learning outcomes.

Phase 3 of the cycle is collaborative, evidence-based problem solving. This phase has four dimensions. The first is to engage the whole school community in a collaborative process of problem solving. Collaboration can develop shared understanding of problems, increase access to a broader range of ideas, mobilize the school to respond to problems, and enhance the legitimacy of the process. A school may need to develop conditions that are conducive to collaborative problem solving and may need to develop staff members' knowledge and skills to engage productively in decision making processes. According to Hawley and Sykes (2007), this agenda can be served simultaneously with work directly related to improving student academic performance. Phase 3 also involves problem framing, the task of coming to agreement on the definition of the problem and the nature or likely sources of the problem. After problem framing, this phase calls on the school community to identify "promising" practices and programs to address the problem. This will likely involve examining research and other evidence on the effectiveness of different strategies and on the likelihood that those strategies are "promising" for addressing the particular problem in the context of the school. From this analysis, school leaders engage the whole school community in the process of selecting the strategy they wish to adopt. To decide, the school community is to consider evidence and the "fit" of the strategy to the problem and how it was framed, the context of the school and implications for implementation, and the resources required to enact the strategy successfully.

Phase 4 involves moving from adoption to implementation and dealing with the problems of implementation. Here Hawley and Sykes (2007) point to the importance of providing teachers the opportunities for professional development, driven by analysis of student learning needs and the improvement process. They also point to the importance of strategic and flexible leadership to manage the implementation process and to create conditions in schools conducive to "steady, problem-focused learning on the part of teachers" (p. 169). Phase 4 is informed by Phase 2, the continuing assessment of student performance, which can provide information for guiding the implementation process. What is accomplished through the implementation of new programs and practices becomes the focus again of Phase 2 assessment, and the cycle resumes again.

COMMON PROPERTIES

Looking across this group of process models we can see a number of common properties. Some common properties can be called *essential elements* that define steps in the process of continuous improvement. Others can be called *key qualities* that will increase the likelihood that the process will be successful. These qualities are not given the same emphasis across all the models discussed in the previous section, but they have a theoretical and intuitive sensibility to them. They are also consistent with current thinking about the concept and theory of continuous improvement discussed in Chapter 2 and evidence presented in Chapter 3.

Essential Elements

This chapter began with an observation that most historical and contemporary models of continuous improvement are variations of the Shewhart Cycle. The six models just reviewed are good examples. To oversimplify, the basic features of these models boil down to the following elements or steps.

1. Get your vision and core values clear.

2. Determine where you are with respect to your vision and values, using evidence to identify differences and assess likely reasons for those differences.

3. Set goals and objectives for addressing these differences.

4. Identify strategies to achieve these goals and objectives and develop plans for implementing them (including developing resources that will be needed).

5. Implement these strategies.

6. Assess their implementation and outcomes, feed this information back into the first and second steps, and begin the cycle again.

We can add the point made before, that the foci of assessment should not be limited to problem identification (second step) or the implementation and outcomes of strategy to address those problems (sixth step). Assessment should also focus on the continuous improvement cycle itself. We can also add the importance of using assessments to define goals and objectives for improvement in concrete, operational terms. A school should not be limited in setting goals and objectives by the measures available to it. That is, it should not let limitations of assessment systems limit the goals and objectives it sets. Measures and assessment systems can be obtained or developed for a wide range of outcomes. However, the process of clarifying and agreeing on goals and objectives can only succeed when those goals and objectives are specific enough to convey to everyone what they really mean and what will be required to achieve them. That may be a tall order to fill. However, as Richard Cyert and James March (1959) observed many years ago, "nonoperational objectives are consistent with virtually any set of objectives." Meaning it is much easier to get people to agree to vague abstract notions but those notions probably won't take you very far.

This review of models indicates that enacting a cycle of continuous improvement requires myriad "enabling" strategies that bring each element to life. It also suggests that these strategies might vary without seriously compromising the integrity of the overall continuous improvement process. What may be more important to the success of continuous improvement than a particular set of enabling strategies (so long as there are adequate ones in place) are particular qualities that should infuse the process.

Key Qualities

One key quality that can be derived from the models discussed in this chapter is readiness of people and the school organization to support the process of continuous improvement. Several models refer to the importance of preparing teachers and other staff members for the dynamics of inquiry and assessment, or developing the knowledge, skills, and collaborative working relationships that are conducive to problem identification, goals setting, and decision making. Chapter 5 will explore this subject farther.

A second key quality is the focus of the mission, vision, and core values. For schools and school districts, that focus should be centrally and primarily on student learning and development. All the rest, including goals for school operation and improvement, follows. Hawley and Sykes (2007) expressed it this way:

> As a first order of business, schools continuously engage in the process of clarifying their *core values*—those matters that call forth their deepest passions, commitments, and caring responses. Values come first and foremost, even before their technical representation in learning goals, standards, and assessments. (pp. 155–156)

For Hawley and Sykes (2007), clarification of core values provides the foundation on which consensus can be developed around goals for student learning and school improvement. This does not mean that a school's vision and values cannot or should not have other dimensions. It means that student learning is primary and that other things are secondary and instrumental to it. It may be that values concerning student learning cannot be realized without also valuing and attending to other matters, such as teacher workplace conditions and opportunities for teacher learning and professional development.

A third key quality that is highlighted in several models is the primacy of data. This can be thought about in several ways. One is the extent to which the collection, assembly, and analysis of data (regardless of source) and the reflection and interpretation that convert data to evidence (Knapp, Swinnerton, Copland, & Monpas-Huber, 2006) permeate the entire process of continuous improvement. This includes clarifying vision and values, assessing current practice and performance, setting goals for improvement, and so forth, including assessing the continuous improvement process itself. A second way to think about data is in terms of quality. Hawley and Sykes (2007) and others cited earlier remind us that not all data are equal. Data can vary considerably in their technical quality (i.e., validity and reliability), relevance to the subjects at hand, and usefulness. Usefulness can mean whether data can be understood by those who need to work with them and the extent to which data may suggest particular courses of action. A third way to think about data is in terms of the value and weight they are given in the process of continuous improvement. Giving high quality data primary rather than provisional status will likely enhance the success of continuous improvement.

A fourth quality that can be seen from this review of models is that the process of continuous improvement should apply to the whole school. Recall the discussion of this matter in Chapter 2 and Chapter 3. This means that the entire school should participate in the process of continuous improvement. Of course, it is unreasonable to think that every member of a school community can or should be involved in every aspect of the continuous improvement process all the time. However, what can and should be expected is that in some way and at some time every member be involved. Whole school also means that in order to be successful the "reach" of continuous improvement should extend to any and every aspect of the school—its organization, its people, and its practices. Nothing should be off limits to assess or address in the interest of student learning.

A fifth quality that can be derived from this review concerns the "place" of continuous improvement practice in the school organization. As suggested earlier in this chapter, processes of continuous improvement should be integrated into schools' core operations. However, the literature indicates that organizations have a choice in where they will "locate" these processes. Location has consequences depending on the type of organization and the nature of the work it performs.

Bhuiyan and Baghel (2005) observe that continuous improvement processes can be "located" in organizations in two general ways. The first is through parallel structures of programs and practices and the other is through integrated structures. Parallel structures make continuous improvement a process separate from the basic operations of an organization. It is "something else" that the organization does in addition to its core functions. This does not suggest that there is no substantive or operational relationship between continuous improvement processes and core organizational activity. It means that they are distinguishable and exist independently. Integrated structures merge continuous improvement processes with core organizational functions so that the former become part of the latter. Continuous improvement processes are not "added on." They become seamless parts of what the organization does.

Paul Lillrank and his colleagues (2001) argue that the relative effectiveness of parallel and integrated structures depends in large part on the nature and structure of work an organization performs (see also Lindberg & Berger, 1997; Mitki et al., 1997). If work is highly standardized, parallel structures may be sufficient for the effective implementation of continuous improvement processes. However, where work is nonstandardized, where it is decentralized, where a certain amount of discretion is required for it to be performed effectively, and where continuous improvement processes cannot reasonably be controlled centrally, those processes should be integrated into the core operations of the organization. Where central coordination and control are weak, the integrity and coherence of continuous improvement processes can be developed and maintained more effectively if they are integrated into the routines of regular work. This logic applies well to schools, where goals can be vague, where work is nonroutine, where teachers require a good bit of autonomy and discretion to teach children effectively, and where coordination and control may require some "loose-coupling" in order to preserve such autonomy and discretion (e.g., Lipsky, 1980; Weick, 1976; Weick & McDaniel, 1989). This logic is consistent with the models described earlier in this chapter that suggest that continuous improvement is likely to be much more effective if integrated into the core functions of the school.

QUESTIONS FOR STUDY, REFLECTION, AND ACTION

1. How does the concept of equifinality compare to the concept of *best practice* as you understand them? What are the implications of both concepts in planning and implementing continuous improvement processes in your school or school district?

2. What are your school's mission, core values, and vision for the future? With regard to student learning and development? With regard to the school as an organization? What roles do mission, vision, and core values now play in guiding improvement efforts at your school? How might your school's vision and core values be developed and expressed to guide continuous improvement effectively?

3. Compare and contrast the six contemporary process models discussed in the chapter. What are their primary characteristics and qualities? How are they similar and different and what are their relative strengths and weaknesses? Which might be a good "fit" for your school? Why?

4. How might a process model of continuous improvement be used to assess itself? In other words, how might a process of continuous improvement be turned on itself to continuously examine and improve its implementation and effectiveness?

5. What are the relative strengths and weaknesses of parallel and integrated "locations" of continuous improvement processes in school organization? Which might be the most conducive to making continuous improvement an organization-wide endeavor in your school? Why?

Organizational Design for Continuous Improvement 5

It is the pervading law of all things organic and inorganic, of all things physical and metaphysical, of all things human and all things super-human, of all true manifestations of the head, of the heart, of the soul, that the life is recognizable in its expression, that form ever follows function.

—Louis Henri Sullivan, 1886

Form follows function—that has been misunderstood. Form and function should be one, joined in a spiritual union.

—Frank Lloyd Wright, n.d.

Form and function. In modern architecture and design, the two are inextricably intertwined. The familiar rendering of the relationship, attributed to American architect Louis Henri Sullivan, is "form follows function." In principle, this means that the shape of a building or an object should be predicated on its intended purpose. For Sullivan and other modern architects of the period, the idea was a normative and practical imperative. In the early 1900s, when new technologies, aesthetics, and economic forces were developing rapidly and challenging conventions, it signaled a return to basics. It called for considering the structure and logic of a building in terms of its functional requirements—what it is supposed to do and how it is supposed to do it—rather than by traditional forms or aesthetic styles of the day that would not work well any more. Architect Frank Lloyd Wright saw the relationship another way. According to Wright, form and function are one in the same. One does not necessarily drive the other. They are an organic whole.

More later on Wright's perspective in relation to continuous improvement. The point now is that Sullivan, Wright, and other modern architects were wrestling with an issue that has been central to organization theory since its inception as a field of study (Hatch, 2006). That issue is how the design of organizations—their structures, operations, and configurations of resources—relates to organizational performance and effectiveness. In a nutshell, organization theory and related research are clear—organization design matters and it matters a lot. How organizations are designed has much to do with how well they function. Different aspects of design can promote or impede organizational activity and the attainment of organizational goals. Whether an organization's design functions in one way or another depends a great deal on the congruence between the organization's design and its goals and core operations (Burns & Stalker, 1994; Mintzberg, 1979; Scott, 2002). That is, what matters is how the organization's form supports its function. And as recent analyses of the bureaucratic organization of schools suggest (e.g., Ogawa, Crowson, & Goldring, 1999; Rowan, 1990), organizations are not always designed with optimal function in mind.

For this reason, organizational design is seen as very important to the function and success of continuous improvement. Organization design can play a significant role in supporting or constraining an organization's processes of improvement. As Nadler, Gerstein, & Shaw (1992) observed, "How a firm organizes its efforts can be a source of tremendous advantage, particularly in times where premiums are placed on flexibility, adaptation, and the management of change" (p. 3). If organizations are going to function in a manner consistent with continuous improvement, their form must be consistent with and facilitative of that function. Therefore, organizational design is as much a part of the practice of continuous improvement as processes and strategies.

How might organization design matter to continuous improvement? First, it is very difficult, if not impossible, to implement the continuous improvement processes discussed in Chapter 4 in an organization that is not designed to support them (Kerber & Buono, 2005; Lillrank et al., 2001). Absent certain elements of organizational design, these processes are difficult to initiate, and once put in place, they are unlikely to gain much traction. As Paul Lillrank and his colleagues (1998) put it, without particular organizational supports, continuous improvement processes are likely to function as little more than transient management practices destined to marginalization and failure.

Second, the chances of achieving continuous improvement outcomes would be slim if organizations are not designed for change. Edward Lawler and Christopher Worley (2006) contend that most organizations are designed to achieve and sustain stability. This is a point made specifically about schools in Chapter 1. According to Lawler and Worley, persistence and lack of meaningful improvement are problems of organization design that not even the best management techniques, operating processes, or leadership are likely to overcome. Unless continuous improvement also attends to organizational design, or redesign, it will be very difficult to achieve ongoing improvement no matter what change processes may be in place.

INTRODUCTORY CONSIDERATIONS

In his writing on the characteristics of continuously innovating and high-performing nonprofit organizations, Paul Light (1998, 2002) argues that is it important to think about organizational design as "preferred states of organizational being." Recall from Chapter 3 that Light refers to preferred states as conditions that "favor" particular qualities or objectives rather than absolute characteristics. Light makes two arguments for thinking this way. First, there are so many contingencies that it would be extremely difficult if not impossible (and wrong-headed) to ascribe specific design features across different organizations and organizational contexts. Second, existing empirical research simply does not provide evidence to justify such claims. Rather, existing research provides enough evidence to support situational variation in organizational design.

Lillrank and his colleagues (1998, 2001) also argue that there is probably no one best way to design an organization for continuous improvement. Depending on the organization and the context, different ways of organizing will have different strengths and weaknesses. This is the concept of equifinality applied to organization design. Lillrank and his colleagues' (1998) argument does not mean that any way of organizing will do. Like Light, they think in terms of variations on particular requirements for continuous improvement.

Another consideration is that the literature strongly suggests that various organizational design elements are most conducive to continuous improvement when they function as mutually-reinforcing systems (Kerber & Buono, 2005; Lillrank et al., 1998; Nadler et al., 1992). This means thinking about design elements together not separately. Certain elements may be necessary but insufficient to support continuous improvement processes without the presence of other elements.

It is also important to note that organizations cannot only be thought of in terms of their formal elements but also in terms of their informal elements (e.g., Hatch, 2006; Weick, 1979). There is the organization as formally construed and the informal organization of social and power relationships that functions within a formal structure and sometimes in conflict with it. Often, the informal aspects of organization are most influential on the thinking and behavior of organizational participants. While very little of the literature on organizational design for continuous improvement focuses on the informal aspects of organization, it is worth noting that to be most effective, the formal and the informal aspects of organization should be aligned and function in mutually reinforcing manner.

A final consideration is that organizational design elements should not be considered static and unchangeable. Instead, they should be thought of as dynamic qualities of organization that are themselves subject to change. As argued in Chapter 2 and Chapter 4, continuous improvement processes operate in dynamic interaction with their organizational contexts. At the same time that organizational contexts support continuous improvement processes, those contexts are always subject to scrutiny and improvement through those processes. This is Frank Lloyd Wright's notion, introduced at the beginning of this chapter—that in fact, form and function are one.

TEN ELEMENTS OF ORGANIZATIONAL DESIGN FOR CONTINUOUS IMPROVEMENT

We now examine 10 elements of organizational design that are shown in the research literature to support continuous improvement. Put another way, these are design elements for constructing a continuously improving organization. Much like the research on the outcomes of continuous improvement discussed in Chapter 3, the research on organizational design for continuous improvement has been conducted primarily in non-education organizations, particularly in businesses and industries. There are fewer studies of organizational design for continuous improvement in nonprofit organizations and government agencies. And there are even fewer studies in schools.

Like the research on outcomes, the research on organizational design for continuous improvement is remarkably consistent in its findings across public and private sectors and among different types of organizations. Many of the design features found to be conducive to continuous improvement in business and industry and in nonprofit organizations and government agencies have also been found to be conducive to continuous improvement in schools. Of course, these features would probably look different in an elementary school as they would in a paper mill, an automobile parts manufacturing plant, or a maximum security prison. But in principle and in function, the design features found to be conducive to continuous improvement in non-education settings appear to be quite similar to those features found to support continuous improvement in schools.

The elements of organizational design examined here are not mutually exclusive. As will become apparent quickly, there are considerable overlaps among them. This helps us think about these elements as a system. These 10 elements are not presented in any particularly meaningful order. There is no implication of a sequence that is most conducive to a continuously improving organization. Nor is there any implication of primary or secondary value among them. They are all important. That said, it is worth drawing attention to two overarching elements. The first is the organization's norms, values, and culture. This element of organization creates a context for everything else. The second is leadership. Leadership plays a significant role in directing and developing most all aspects of organizational design and in supporting processes of continuous improvement. The nature of leadership may change over time as continuous improvement proceeds and as different organizational members may come to perform "leadership work" of continuous improvement. However, as the literature suggests in one form or another, leadership remains important throughout.

Norms, Values, and a Culture for Continuous Improvement

Virtually every study that has examined the relationship between organizational design and continuous improvement emphasizes the importance of organizational norms, values, and culture to ground and guide continuous improvement. The research finds that organizations that are successful in continuous improvement have made continuous improvement a defining element of their cultures, their identities, and their goals. In these organizations—be they businesses, industries, nonprofit organizations, government agencies, or schools—continuous improvement is an expected and valued aspect of organizational life. Continuous improvement is not a "tack-on." It is an organizational property, part of the organization's definition.

According to Ty Choi (1995), continuous improvement "is" the work culture of a continuously improving organization. For continuous improvement to be successful, "the work culture must include norms for change and creativity rather than for stability and rigid conformance" (p. 613). Choi argues that the culture of a continuously improving organization is a process culture not a results-oriented culture. Not that specific goals and accomplishments are unimportant. Rather, the culture of a continuously improving organization would frame accomplishments as provisional and as subject to further improvement. While maintaining consistency with the core values and identity of the organization, one accomplishment leads to another—the work is never done.

Others have suggested that specific norms and values are particularly conducive to continuous improvement. For instance, in his exposition of "footnotes to organizational change," James March (1981) made the case for the importance of norms of playfulness, foolishness, experimentation, and risk taking. He argued that these norms may be hard to justify, but they are crucial to promote creativity and innovativeness required for organizations to continuously adapt to their environments. Indeed, they provide a productive counter-balance to or "dialectic" with more rational, conventional, and "sensible" norms and processes of organizational change such as strategic planning and decision making.

Robert Burgelman (1991) also highlighted the role of norms of experimentation, creativity, and foolishness in successful continuous organizational change. Like March, he saw a crucial dynamic between individual-level "entrepreneurship" that is promoted by these norms and organizational-level strategic intent and decision making. Based on his reading of the research at the time and his use of Intel, the computer chip manufacturing company, as a focal case study, Burgelman reasoned that separately, neither individual entrepreneurship nor organizational strategic intent is sufficient for ongoing organizational change and survival: "Both are needed *simultaneously*" (p. 256, emphasis in the original). He observed that the ability to maintain these different elements concurrently seemed missing in the failing corporations studied by Donald Hambrick and Richard D'Aveni (1988). Those failing firms operated either in an inactive or hyperactive mode. They lacked the ability to engage in strategic change promoted by broader organizational-level intent and decision making or they vacillated according to unguided and ungrounded individual initiative. The point to be drawn from this analysis is that organizations may use individual-level foolishness, playfulness, and experimentation to enhance organizational-level adaptation and survival. Such norms may promote creativity and challenge and extend the "boundaries of capabilities" of the organization. They grant permission for, indeed encourage "bottom-up internal experimentation and selection processes" that increase organizational ability to exploit opportunity.

The role of norms in promoting ongoing adaptation and opportunistic change is also illustrated in Susan Fox-Wolfgramm and her colleagues' (1998) research on organizational adaptation in the banking industry. Recall from Chapter 3 that their research focused on longitudinal case studies of two banks and their responses to federal regulation. Fox-Wolfgramm and her colleagues found that these two banks exhibited very different "process patterns and change tracks in response to institutional pressures for change" (p. 102). In large part, these differences were attributed to "strategic orientations" that reflected differences in norms and values. One bank operated from a "defender" orientation. Its responses to external demands for change were consistent with a punctuated-equilibrium theory of change—long periods of inaction and resistance followed by short bursts of upheaval (see Burke, 2008; Gersick, 1991). However, unlike what punctuated-equilibrium theory would suggest, short bursts of upheaval were not followed by periods of convergence during which organizational operations aligned with external demands. Instead, upheavals were followed by recidivism whereby the bank became disenchanted with changes it adopted and "drop[ped] the 'disguise' over time so that it could resume being its familiar self" (p. 113).

In contrast, the second bank operated from a "prospector" orientation. This bank was always on the lookout for new opportunities and ways to adapt to new demands. However, this bank was not open to any and all change. While opportunistic, it pursued change consistent with its core values and identity. When confronted with demands of the new regulation, it was initially slow to respond but later adopted behavioral and interpretive changes not only consistent with regulatory demands but also within its normative-identity framework. These changes were incorporated slowly into the organization, and unlike the defender bank, this bank experienced little backsliding.

The importance of norms, values, and culture to continuous improvement can also be seen in several studies of nonprofit organizations and government agencies. In his *Sustaining Innovation* project, Paul Light (1998) found that nonprofit organizations and government agencies that became innovative and sustained their "innovativeness" over time had cultivated and reinforced a culture to guide the "innovating organizational life." This culture was grounded in norms of honesty, rigor, trust, and faith. Light explained their importance this way:

> If the organization cannot trust its employees or itself, if it cannot be honest and truthful, if it has no interest in rigor, and if it has little faith, the organization simply cannot succeed. If it is honest, trustworthy, rigorous, and faithful, it cannot fail. It will know when to innovate and when to stop. (p. 244)

In a later study, *Sustaining Nonprofit Performance,* Light (2004) found that nonprofit organizations that achieve a level of sustained high performance kept their norms and core values at the fore. Key among them was organizational mission or purpose. All else—organizations structures, capacities, and operational processes—proceeded from and were designed to support them. In that study, Light also found that nonprofit organizations that were able to sustain strong performance over time had cultures that placed high value on risk taking, experimentation, and openness to new ideas. Staff members of these nonprofits were generally comfortable within these cultures, perhaps because these organizations also placed emphasis on norms of fairness in decision making and trust in interpersonal relations. These nonprofits were trusted to "do the right thing" in maintaining their mission and core values and in handling internal problems.

Research on continuous improvement in schools similarly emphasizes the importance of such norms, values, and cultures. For example, Rosenholtz (1989) found substantial differences between the norms, values, and cultures of schools that were considered "learning enriched" for teachers—that promoted continuous improvement in instruction and that achieved high student performance—and the norms, values, and cultures of schools that were considered "learning impoverished" for teachers and did not promote or achieve these other things. The former schools were characterized by strong norms for continuous teacher learning and instructional improvement and high expectations for student learning. These schools were also defined by norms of sharing, joint problem solving, and collaboration. In these cultures, teaching was a collective enterprise of mutual responsibility for student learning, not individualistic and private work. In the latter schools, such workplace cultures did not exist.

Several studies of schoolwide inquiry processes make similar findings. In one of these studies, Lew Allen and Emily Calhoun (1998) examined school organizational factors that contributed to the success of ongoing collaborative action research projects. They found that engagement in these action research projects and efforts to achieve continuous improvement through them were associated with the degree of shared understanding and value held by schools of the inquiry and improvement process. The greater the understanding and held value, the greater the engagement and effort. Schools that were more successful with these projects had organizational cultures conducive to continuous improvement. Those that were organized around norms of collaboration, experimentation, and public examination of practice were more successful than schools organized around norms of privacy, individualism, and isolation. Bruce King's (2002) study of schoolwide inquiry and improvement processes made similar findings.

Two other studies of schoolwide inquiry and continuous improvement processes provide yet additional evidence. Both focused on BASRC's Collaborative's Cycle of Inquiry. In one of these studies,

Copland (2003) found successful implementation of the Cycle to be associated with associated with supportive school organizational cultures. These cultures placed high value on "collaboration, trust, professional learning, and reciprocal accountability" (p. 379). Kiley Walsh's (2003) study found that BASRC schools that made the greatest progress improving student academic achievement and closing achievement gaps cultivated a shared norm of equity for accomplishing these objectives.

Finally, several studies have found that school culture can have an important effect on the use of data, an important element of continuous improvement (see Knapp et al., 2006). In their analysis of data-driven decision making in education, Marsh, Pane, & Hamilton (2006) found that data use is more prevalent in schools with norms of openness and collaboration. Collective examination of data tends to be "constrained" in schools characterized by beliefs that teaching is a private and individual enterprise. Similarly, Jeffrey Wayman, Steve Midgeley, and Sam Stringfield (2006) found that the success of collaborative teams and data-based decision making in schools is a function of establishing a common and accepted understanding and value of teaching, learning, and measurement of learning. Such understanding serves as a normative framework to guide these teams and keep students and data on student learning at the heart of team work.

Human Capital

A second element of organization design for continuous improvement is human capital and means for its development. Human capital refers to the knowledge, skills, commitments, attitudes, and attributes of individuals and groups that contribute to their ability and willingness to do productive work. Ty Choi (1995) is unequivocal about the importance of human capital to continuous improvement:

> To work, [continuous improvement] relies on the knowledge and ideas of people in the organization. . . . The ideas for change most appropriately and naturally arise from workers who are most familiar with the operation and who are going to stay at the job. . . . The success of [continuous improvement] depends on a well-trained, well-disciplined workforce that is willing to undertake incremental yet incessant changes, rather than through an emotionally charged workforce that soon grows tired of change and becomes disillusioned. (p. 614)

Also important is the ability of an organization to develop its human capital for continuous improvement. According to Choi, organizational participants need to be "continually trained and developed," particularly in the methods of improvement "that will facilitate the formulation of new ideas for improvement" (p. 614). To this, we might add that organizations need to develop their human capital to put those ideas into place and enhance the overall effectiveness of the organization.

A number of studies provide evidence of the importance of human capital and its development to continuous improvement. In its analysis of applicants for the Malcolm Baldrige National Quality Award, the General Accounting Office (1994) found a set of common features that distinguished companies with the most improved performance from companies with the least improved performance. One of these features was employee capacity for engaging in continuous improvement processes and for implementing the improvements that resulted from those processes. Also distinguishing were opportunities for employee training to be involved in efforts to continuously improve organizational performance.

Alastair Bain's (1998) comparative case studies of a computer services company and a day nursery in the United Kingdom and a maximum security prison in Australia, Lillrank and his associates' (1998, 2001) case studies of businesses, and research conducted under the auspices of the Continuous Improvement Research for Competitive Advantage (CIRCA) project at the University of Brighton in the United Kingdom (Bessant & Francis, 1999) all point to the importance of knowledge, skills, and attitudes needed to engage in processes of continuous improvement and to commit to and enact the improvements that emerge. If these resources are absent or weak, then it is important that the organization develop them. R. Krishnan and his colleagues' (1993) case study of a telecommunications company points to more specific aspects of development. In that study, success in continuous improvement was tied to the company's provision of learning opportunities to its employees, not just to develop individual skills needed for job performance and the enactment of improvements but also for promoting communication, commitment, and "the psychological and social conditions for organizational learning" (p. 18–19).

Light's (1998) *Sustaining Innovation* project found that innovating nonprofit organizations and government agencies aggressively sought to develop demographic, professional, and intellectual diversity among their employees. The logic was that a wide range of perspectives would increase the odds of generating new and good ideas for innovation. Light's (2004) later study of nonprofit organizations that used continuous improvement-like processes to sustain high performance of long periods of time found that all had adequate staffing relative to their missions, programs, and operations. Not only were there sufficient numbers of personnel, but also staff members possessed or were able to develop the knowledge and skills necessary for continuous improvement and high performance.

Walsh's (2003) study of BASRC schools found that successful use of the Cycle of Inquiry was associated with teachers' ability to use data and with professional development opportunities to help teachers improve classroom instruction (see also McLaughlin & Mitra, 2003). Marsh and her colleagues (2006) also identified staff capacity and support as key factors in data use and data-driven decision making. They refer to teachers' level of preparation and skills to formulate questions; analyze, interpret, and use data to identify problems; and develop solutions that address those problems. They also refer to schools' and districts' capacity to provide teachers with learning opportunities to develop their technical and inquiry skills and to provide support from individuals who are skilled at data use and who can make data more interpretable and useable.

Organization of People and Work

A third, important element of organizational design for continuous improvement is the organization of people and their work. Research points to many different ways in which roles, relationships, and tasks can be configured to support continuous improvement. What is common across different configurations are a number of features, including structured flexibility, interdependence, and "bounded" autonomy that promote communication, learning, joint problem solving, experimentation, and change.

Bain's (1998) case studies attribute success in continuous improvement in part to structured individual and group task interdependencies. Such linkages promoted communication and reflection on individual and organizational performance. They also promoted a sense of "awareness" of the organization as a whole, its problems, and demands and opportunities it encounters. These linkages contributed to continuous learning and the ability of individuals and the organization to change. They weakened maladaptive social defenses that would impede individual and organizational learning and in turn compromise continuous improvement.

The importance of structured interdependencies can also be seen in Rick Delbridge and Harry Barton's (2002) study of manufacturing plants in the United States and United Kingdom. This study focused on the importance of teams and problem-solving groups to individual and organizational learning and to continuous improvement. Delbridge and Barton found no one particular configuration of teams or groups to be effective. Depending on the organization and context, these teams or groups could be large or small, functional or cross-functional, ad hoc or permanent. What seemed important was that the team or group structure provide for the free flow of information within and among teams or groups and throughout the organization. Also important was the flow of information from external sources into the organization and into teams and groups. Particularly salient was information from customers and from inter-organizational relationships and activities that provided sources of learning and impetus for improvement. In plants where there was little infusion of external information, exchange and problem solving tended to be reactive, focused on the mundane, and constrained by existing ideas and routine ways of thinking.

Another study that points to the importance of the organization of people and work to continuous improvement is Shona Brown and Kathleen Eisenhardt's (1997) comparative analysis of U.S. firms in the fast-paced computer industry. The purpose of this study was to identify organizational elements that distinguish relatively successful firms where change is "frequent, relentless, and even endemic" from relatively less successful firms where change is "rare, risky, and episodic" (p. 2). Brown and Eisenhardt found that three organizational "properties" distinguished the former group from the latter. One of these elements—the systematic use of low-cost probes to explore the future—will be discussed later. The two other elements pertain more directly to the organization of people and work.

The first element that distinguished more from less successful firms was what Brown and Eisenhardt call dynamic "semi-structures." Semi-structures make formal work roles flexible and fluid. Instead of being standardized or prescribed, the work process is only loosely articulated, and there are few rules governing practice. Work is infused with substantial amount of autonomy and there is the expectation and opportunity for the exercise of discretion and improvisation in practice. What provides direction, coherence, and accountability to work is the articulation of particular responsibilities that need to be performed and somehow linked to clear organizational values, priorities, and expectations for performance and achievement. In more successful firms, these values, priorities, and expectations were reinforced by extensive systems of interaction and communication. The "what" of the organization and the work was highly articulated and strongly enforced. The "who" and the "how" were much less structured and much more flexible. In contrast, less successful firms lacked well-defined priorities. Responsibilities were often unclear, and work was likely to be "over-prescribed" to the point of constraining flexibility and experimentation. While there was often communication within groups, communication across groups was particularly low.

A second aspect of structuring work that Brown and Eisenhardt (1997) found associated with more successful firms was the ability to link present and future work together with "rhythmic, time-paced transition processes" (p. 1). Such processes created an expectation for continuous improvement and set a pace for change. They also created some order to and continuity in the work. Brown and Eisenhardt describe this "structuring" of work transitions using the analogy of Tarzan. These firms "swing on the current vine, look ahead for the next, and make the switch between the two" (p. 7). In the more successful firms, the switch was choreographed, predictable, and almost seamless. Structuring was continually fine-tuned in response to and in anticipation of rhythms of change in the environment. In the less successful firms, linking past and future work was usually an afterthought. There were no predictable intervals between present and future and transitions to future work were often haphazard. Movement from present to future was often reactive and failed to keep pace with environmental changes, placing these firms at competitive disadvantage and often leaving them unprepared to meet new challenges.

Communication channels and opportunities for interaction are other important structural elements identified in this research as conducive to continuous improvement. As indicated before, communication of information and exchange of ideas are crucial to the organization of people and work for continuous improvement. The logic is that continuous improvement depends substantially on the free flow of information into and throughout the organization as well as the open exchange of ideas and the opportunities for learning across all parts of the organization. This points to the superiority of network-oriented communication structures over hierarchically oriented "silo" structures in different parts of an organization that are largely disconnected from each other (Kerber & Buono, 2005).

Bain's (1998) comparative case studies found that in addition to designing task interdependencies and promoting communication, it was also important to create spaces and specific occasions—events, activities, projects—for information sharing and for the development and exchange of ideas. It was not enough to depend on the structure of work to promote the communication required for continuous improvement. Additional opportunities had to be created for individual and collective reflection and learning and for developing an awareness of the whole organization across the organization.

Mitki and colleagues' (1997) longitudinal case study of a U.S.–Israeli paper mill also identified structural opportunities for communication and exchange as crucial for continuous improvement. Success of continuous improvement was attributed in large part to individual and group learning that took place in the mill and that learning was attributed to structures and processes that "facilitate knowledge and concepts acquisition, skills and tolls attainment, and competency development" (p. 442). In particular, Mitki and his colleagues pointed to the importance of structured channels of communication linking organizational levels and members and of arenas for dialogue, exchange of ideas, information processing, and problem solving.

Light (1998) found that similar internal structural design elements played a key role in the long-term innovativeness of nonprofit organizations. These elements were used to encourage interaction, experimentation, and creativity, to act together as an "instrument for innovation" (p. 98). He found, "what matters is not so much whether an organization looks like a pyramid or a blimp but how many people touch an idea going up or a message going down" (pp. 17–18). Innovating nonprofit organizations tended to "stay thin." They minimized layers of management, used self-managed teams, decentralized decision making, and emphasized organization-wide communication. These innovating organizations created structures to "prime the organization for innovation." They reduced barriers to internal collaboration through role development, task assignment, and joint work. In addition, they created time and opportunity for experimentation as well as a marketplace for the honest and rigorous evaluation of new ideas.

Light's (2002, 2004) studies of high-performing nonprofits emphasized the importance of similar design elements. The nonprofit experts he interviewed identified flat, team-oriented structures with few barriers between operating units as particularly conducive to sustaining high performance. They also pointed to the importance of collaborative work structures. However these structures were configured, they shared two common features. The first was open channels of communication that linked all parts of the organization. It was important that all employees had access to important information from the organization's environment and from its internal operations. Information had to flow freely from top to bottom, from bottom to top, and among organizational units. The second common feature was that personnel were likely to work in teams. Teams provided opportunities for exchange of information and ideas, collaboration, joint problem solving, and learning.

Several studies emphasize the importance of the organization of people and work to the success of continuous improvement or similar processes in schools. For example, in research on the implementation of the DDEA model of continuous organizational self-renewal, Mary Bentzen (1974) found that higher levels of implementation were associated with formal and informal staffing arrangements—roles and relationships, task assignments, and staff groupings—that promoted exchange of ideas and information and that promoted common understanding about what was going on in the school, both good and bad.[20] King's (2002) later research also emphasized the importance of open channels of communication and regular, structured opportunities for teachers and administrators to exchange ideas and collaborate to the success of schoolwide inquiry and continuous improvement processes. Walsh's (2003) study of BASRC schools pointed to the importance of structured opportunities for teachers to share and discuss data and to collaborate with each other to develop strategies to address problems revealed by those data. In a final example, Marsh and her colleagues (2006) found that data use in improvement processes was associated with the structure of instruction, particularly the organization and pacing of curricula. Data use was more extensive and more effective in schools where curricula allowed for flexibility to alter instruction when analyses of data reveal problems. In other schools, pressure to "stay on" curriculum, particularly in the context of mandated curriculum with pacing plans, acted as a deterrent to data use for ongoing instructional improvement.

Distribution of Authority and Influence

A fourth element of organizational design for continuous improvement is the distribution of authority and influence. Interestingly, there are relatively few studies that directly address this element in the context of continuous improvement. Some insights can be gleaned from research on internal management systems and leadership that will be discussed shortly. The few studies that do directly address it indicate that continuous improvement may be best served if authority and influence are diffused throughout the organization rather than lodged in a particular location, position, or role, say "at the top." Bain's (1998) comparative case studies tell us that continuous improvement may be promoted through the distribution of authority and responsibility for it across roles and levels of the organization. Taina Savolainen (1991) made a similar finding about the distribution of authority and influence in longitudinal case studies of two construction materials manufacturing companies in Finland. These cases also highlighted the importance of executive management. Savolainen found that sufficient and authoritative "position-bound" support and influence from the top of the organization was a "necessary condition" for continuous improvement to be successful.

These findings, along with those concerning the organization of people and work, suggest that the distribution of authority and influence for continuous improvement is not a "zero-sum" proposition. The work of continuous improvement is organizationwide. To be successful, it requires that persons throughout the organization have authority to collect and disseminate information, identify problems, challenge assumptions, and experiment with alternative solutions. The development of expertise about the environment and about organizational processes contributes little to continuous improvement unless that expertise is accompanied with the authority to influence others. At the same time, successful continuous improvement is not a "free-for-all." It needs to be cultivated and guided as a systematic process across the organization. It needs to be informed by perspectives that take the whole organization into account not only those parts occupied by different members. It also needs to be informed by views of the environment broader than those that may come from individual members' partial knowledge of it. And successful continuous improvement relies upon advocacy and the ability to address "attitudinal and structural opposition" wherever it may surface (Savolainen, 1991, p. 1218)—thus, the need to ensure sufficient authority and influence from the top to inform and guide the process.

Light's (1998) research found that the most innovative and innovating nonprofits tended to push authority down to the lowest levels of the organization, creating potential for influence from the bottom to the top of the organization, not simply from the top down. They also adopted more inclusive and participative democratic processes of decision making. His studies of high performing nonprofits also found evidence of the importance of pushing authority downward in the organization and to authorizing staff to make routine decisions on their own (Light, 2002, 2004). Another finding regarding the distribution of authority and influence was a "structural preference" among high performing nonprofits for decentralization of decision making and for delegation of routine decisions to frontline employees. This preference moved a good amount of decision making closest to the sources of problems and increased the likelihood of more effective decisions.

Several other studies made similar findings about the distribution of authority and influence and continuous improvement in schools. Bentzen's (1974) early study linked the use and quality of the DDEA process to how power and influence was distributed among staff members. Higher use of the process was associated with wider staff participation in school-level decision making. Copland's (2003) study of BASRC schools found that successful implementation of the Cycle of Inquiry was more likely to occur in schools with collective decision making. In these schools authority and influence was shared among administrators and teachers in such a way that both were involved in joint identification of problems and solutions. We will return to Copland's research and to this subject later when we discuss leadership for continuous improvement. Wayman and his colleagues (2006) also pointed to a relationship between the distribution of authority and influence and the success of data-based team decision making. Those teams that were the most successful ensured that teachers and professional staff were given a voice in the process alongside of school administrators and central office staff. Such participation spread authority and influence down to the school level. It helped to build school-level support for data-driven decision making at the team level and provided valuable professional insight and feedback that informed teamwork.

Relational Trust

A fifth element of organizational design for continuous improvement is relational trust. Carrie Leanna and Bruce Barry (2000) observe in their analysis of stability and change in organizational life that "increasingly fluid work settings elevate the importance of trust as a basis for worker self-management and self-organization" (p. 758). The trust that organizational members have in one another and trust that they have in the organization as a whole enables problem identification and analysis, experimentation and risk taking, and change. Trust helps to mitigate the uncertainty and fear of challenging prevailing ways of thinking and doing (Yong & Wilkinson, 1999). According to Leanna and Barry, the problem is that change that is too rapid, frequent, or unpredictable may threaten or undermine trust. This presents a paradox of sorts—trust is needed for change but change has the potential to erode trust and make future change more difficult to achieve. As Leanna and Barry contend, trust is most readily developed from sources of stability and predictability. But those sources do not necessarily have to be associated with lack of change. Trust can be developed and sustained through processes that produce change, so long as those processes are predictable, are perceived as legitimate, and serve the interests of organizational members. That is, the processes themselves must be trustworthy. Therefore, it is possible to see trust as an important source of support for processes of continuous improvement. It is also possible to see these processes, if developed and enacted as predictable and stable meta-routines, as means to develop and strengthen trust as a source of support for ongoing change.

Bain's (1998) case studies suggest that trust is a crucial factor in confronting and dismantling social-psychological defenses that impede individual and organizational learning and continuous improvement. According to Bain, all organizations have defenses that may be seen in their structures, operating procedures, information systems, cultures, work roles, and in the "gap between what the organization says it is doing and what it is actually doing" (p. 413). These defenses are constructed and enforced socially, and they operate to mitigate individual and collective psychological anxiety associated with difficult work, risk, and uncertainty. They provide a source of stability by helping organizational members make meaning of what they experience in their work, the problems they confront, and the ways to address those problems. Often these defenses are maladaptive, reinforcing prevailing ways of thinking and behaving when learning and change would be more productive. Dismantling such defenses in order to promote continuous improvement could be disruptive and threatening. It would expose organizational members anew to risks and uncertainties associated with their work and to new risks and uncertainties associated with change. It is difficult to see how such an effort might succeed without a substantial amount of trust.

Hyun-Jung Lee's (2004) study of a Korean high-tech multi-national manufacturing company suggests that the relationship of trust to continuous improvement may be a bit more complicated than its presence or absence or its intensity. In that study, trust was defined as the "willingness of a party to be vulnerable to the actions of another party based on the expectation that the other party will perform a particular action important to the trustee or irrespective of the ability to monitor or control that other party" (p. 625). Based on data collected from nearly 500 shop floor workers in this company, Lee found no direct relationship between levels of trust and continuous improvement efforts. However, employees' identification with the organization—that is the extent to which employees saw the organization's values and interests as aligned with their own and organizational development linked to their own personal growth and development—was positively related to continuous improvement efforts. Organizational identification mediated the relationship between trust and continuous improvement efforts. In other words, for trust to operate as a source of support for continuous improvement, employees also had to feel a sense of organizational identification—that the organization was operating in a manner consistent with their best interests.

Studies of continuous improvement or similar processes in schools also identify trust as an important aspect of organizational support. Bentzen's (1974) study of the DDEA process found that its implementation was associated positively with mutual trust and respect among principals and teachers. It was also associated with staff members' commitment and willingness to attend to the process of self-renewal. In high-use schools, there was greater respect among teachers and principals of each other's professional competence. In these schools, there was stronger commitment and higher value placed on the goal of continuous improvement and the DDEA process as a means to achieve it. In their later research on ongoing collaborative action research projects, Allen and Calhoun (1998) found that schools with higher levels of trust among teachers and between teachers and administrators were more successful in these projects than schools with lower levels of trust. And King's (2002) study of continuous improvement in schools found that particular qualities of teachers' professional relationships contributed to the success of these processes. Along with shared commitment and collaboration, trust provided support for inquiry and improvement efforts which, in turn, promoted greater trust, shared commitment, and collaboration in mutually reinforcing ways.

Accountability and Reward Systems

A sixth element of organizational design for continuous improvement is accountability and reward systems. Several studies indicate that continuous improvement is more likely to be successful if organizational accountability and reward systems are designed to support and promote it. While it seems axiomatic that what gets inspected and rewarded is what gets attended to, it is not always the case that accountability and reward systems are aligned with organizational priorities. When such alignment is not tight, it is unlikely that organizational priorities will be achieved while those things that people are held accountable and are rewarded for will be pursued.

Research conducted through the CIRCA project at the University of Brighton in the United Kingdom supports this general logic (Bessant and Francis, 1999). Among the key "mechanisms" identified in this work to support continuous organizational improvement is the "development of an appropriate reward and recognition system" (p. 1107). From their longitudinal case studies, Lillrank and his colleagues (2001) also identified reward systems as a "generic design requirement" for continuous improvement. Nothing in the research identifies specific rewards that are more effective than others in promoting continuous improvement. What "works" depends on what may be motivational to organizational members and what is motivational to members of one organization may not be as motivational to members of another. The point is that reward systems need to be tailored and targeted appropriately. They need to be aligned with what is valued and is to be promoted. In the case of continuous improvement, the research implies that "appropriate" reward systems should aim to promote the integrity and effectiveness of the process, the implementation of changes that result from that process, and overall organizational performance and goal attainment in the context of continuous improvement.

Light (1998) also found that nonprofit organizations that sustained their "innovativeness" over long periods of time developed reward systems and allocated extra resources to encourage experimentation and risk taking. At least two studies of schools made similar findings. King's (2002) research on schoolwide inquiry processes found that regular monitoring and maintaining accountability for these processes was important to their success. While accountability and the feedback and facilitation that followed from it were important, King found that administrative leadership did not script these processes nor direct them toward any predetermined ends. They were dynamic and responsive to where inquiry processes were taking the schools. Marsh and her colleagues (2006) made a similar finding that systems of teacher rewards and sanctions designed to promote data use were associated with data use in schools. These systems were tied to accountability policies for student academic performance. They were found to "drive" school staff toward data use by tapping into teachers' internal motivation to help students and by applying external pressure to improve student performance.

Capacity for Data Analysis

A seventh element of organizational design for continuous improvement is capacity for data analysis. Capacity for data analysis refers to the ability of a school or other organization to collect, obtain, analyze, interpret, and use data to promote its mission and core values, to pursue particular goals, and to inform processes of continuous improvement. Such capacity is a key feature of the process models of continuous improvement discussed in Chapter 4 (see also Lawler & Worley, 2006).

Most research on continuous improvement in schools considers data capacity in terms of the knowledge and skills of individual teachers and administrative leaders to work with data and to use them effectively in decision making and in individual and organizational learning. Very little attention is paid to the organizational structures and capacities of schools or school districts needed to generate the types of data that are most conducive to continuous improvement. Data that seem most conducive to continuous improvement focus on students and student learning, are accessible by the people who need to use them, are of high technical high quality (and are perceived by organizational members to be that way), and are relevant, regularly collected, and timely to the problems and opportunities that present themselves. Processes of continuous improvement, such as those discussed in Chapter 4, suggest that beyond the capacity to collect data on students and student learning, it is also important for schools and school districts to have the capacity to generate data about organizational design, operational processes, and what is going on in their internal and external environments.

In much of the literature, the existence of good data is largely assumed. Even those sources that focus on processes of data generation forego much consideration of organizational structures and resources needed to support them (e.g., Leithwood et al., 2001). This is an important gap in our thinking about organizational design for continuous improvement. Much of continuous improvement depends on the generation and use of data. If the capacity for use is present but the capacity for generating timely and useful data is absent, it is unlikely that efforts to achieve continuous improvement will be very successful (Marsh et al., 2006).

Fiscal and Physical Resources

An eighth element of organizational design for continuous improvement concerns fiscal and physical resources. Included in this discussion is the very important resource of time. The literature from business and industry is clear that processes of continuous improvement and the changes generated by them cannot be done well "on the cheap." They require appropriate, sufficient, and sustained levels of fiscal and physical resources. Often, they require resources beyond those needed for general organizational operations. The specific types and amounts of resources needed for continuous improvement will vary considerably across organizations. But as Kenneth Kerber and Anthony Buono (2005) observe, what is appropriate and sufficient will certainly involve more than financial support. What is appropriate and sufficient may also include operational support (see following discussion about management systems), time, space, and "mind share," the latter referring to intellectual resources discussed earlier as human capital. In the context of total quality management, Josephine Yong and Adrian Wilkinson (1999) also point to the importance of adequate time, physical and fiscal resources, as well as human capital and internal management systems to support continuous improvement.

Kerber and Buono's (2005) argument for the importance of resources goes farther than the dictum that "change is resource-hungry." They contend that if organizational members feel overwhelmed and distracted by other pressures and impediments, including lack of resources for the work they are presently performing, it is less likely that they will engage in change processes and enact improvements that emanate from those processes. In such context, efforts to promote continuous improvement will likely struggle and fail. March (1981) suggested that in order for organizations to engage successfully in ongoing improvement they need to develop and maintain a certain amount of "slack" in their resources. Slack refers to a cushion or a surplus that can be allocated to the unexpected. March argued that resource slack is important because it helps to support an organization's search for problems and opportunities. It provides protection and support for experimentation, risk taking, and foolishness that may lead to improvement and innovation. Slack may be costly to an organization in the short term, but it is likely to be advantageous in the long-term, particularly in the context of continuous improvement.

Lillrank and his colleagues' case studies (1998, 2001) provide additional evidence of the importance of resources dedicated to ongoing change processes. As noted earlier, specific resource requirements are likely to vary considerably across organizations, but Lillrank and his colleagues take note of the importance of time, facilities, and physical equipment. Most likely their emphasis on these particular resources has to do with the types of organizations that they studied. These cases also point to the importance of slack. A common finding across these cases was the benefit of having enough appropriate resources to support continuous improvement efforts and to "unfreeze" these organizations to support unanticipated changes that result.

Findings from the CIRCA project also point to the importance of accumulating slack to support continuous improvement (Bessant & Francis, 1999). The reasoning is similar to that of Lillrank and his colleagues (1998). Not only do continuous improvement processes require particular fiscal and physical resources, but also how these processes develop and the improvements they generate are often unpredictable. Therefore, organizations need to create resource slack and, one might add, creatively manage that slack in the service of continuous improvement.

King (2002) and Marsh and her colleagues (2006) all found evidence of the importance of resources for the improvement processes they investigated. King emphasized the importance of adequate funding and the availability of external expertise to support those processes. He also emphasized the importance of time as a resource, in his case study, release time for teachers from classroom instruction, days set aside for teacher professional development, and extended time during the school day for teachers and administrators to work together. Marsh and her colleagues found that the ability of schools and districts to allocate and protect time for teachers and administrators to examine and reflect regularly on data was a "critical for effective data-driven decision making" (p. 9).

Internal Management Systems

A ninth element of organizational design for continuous improvement consists of internal management systems. Beyond advocacy and guidance of the process, management systems need to support the day-in-and-day-out work of continuous improvement. Delbridge and Barton's (2002) case studies of manufacturing plants emphasize the importance of assigning personnel the direct responsibility to manage continuous improvement processes. Savolainen's (1991) study of manufacturing companies also emphasizes the importance of management systems to support the implementation of these processes. Continuous improvement does not simply happen through the activity of individual organizational members or by virtue of leadership that promotes it. It must be coordinated and managed on an ongoing basis (see also Yong & Wilkinson, 1999).

Several studies identify specific elements of management systems that support continuous improvement. The CIRCA project identified the need for management systems to receive and respond to ideas that develop in different parts of the organization (Bessant and Francis, 1999). Management systems need to conduct and coordinate flows of information and exchanges of ideas and to link flows and exchanges to processes of problem identification, experimentation, and improvement. As discussed earlier, Brown and Eisenhardt's (1997) study of computer firms emphasized the importance an organization's ability to manage the orderly transition between current and future projects. Also, among the organizational features that supported continuous improvement in the more successful firms was a management system designed to engage in a variety of ongoing, low-cost probes into the future. These probes included planned experiments, engagement of "futurists," the formation of strategic partnerships, and frequent brainstorming meetings to consider future scenarios. In the more successful companies, these probes created visions of multiple futures and provided a wide range of viable options to draw upon. They increased opportunities for learning within these companies and lowered the probability that they would be "surprised" by an unanticipated future. The more options these organizations envisioned the better able they were to plan and execute transitions from current to future work. Management systems in less successful companies were more likely to identify and plan for a single future, an approach that left these firms vulnerable to unanticipated changes.

Light's (1998) study of innovative nonprofit organizations found that their success was linked to rigorous internal management systems designed to "accelerate good ideas" (p. 171). All of the innovating nonprofits in this study were found to be "very well run," suggesting that effective management is a necessary but insufficient condition for ongoing innovativeness (although not all well-managed organizations were necessarily innovating). These management systems kept organizational operations running smoothly. They emphasized performance, and they loosened traditional command-and-control relationships that might stifle creativity. These systems supported the process or the "how" of innovating rather than defined the "what" to innovate. They made integrity of the process an imperative, something to be cultivated, developed, and supported. They established accountability systems that measured and tracked performance and results. They monitored all aspects of organizational operations, anticipating and planning for growth, decline, and turnover. Budgets were kept "in real time," providing flexibility in resources to support innovation. Pay was downplayed as an incentive in favor of systems that defined successful innovation as its own reward. Financial systems were also strong in these organizations. No matter how "rich" or "poor" they were, these innovating organizations created economies that optimized fiscal resources in support of innovating in a manner consistent with organizational mission and core values.

Light made similar findings regarding the internal management systems of the high performing nonprofit organizations he later studied (2002, 2004). These nonprofits were characterized by strong operations systems and strong fiscal management systems. Both were focused on programmatic support and on support of improvement processes that fed the development and maintenance of high performance over time.

Leadership

Last but not least, the tenth organizational design element for continuous improvement is leadership. Research from business and industry uniformly stresses the importance of leadership for successful continuous improvement. Leadership is a linchpin that ties together other design elements into a system of support. When this research speaks about leadership, it means more than the performance of administrative tasks. We considered these tasks part of an organization's internal management system. Most often, this research refers to leadership at the top of the organization, at the level of the executive officer or the equivalent. However, some studies consider leadership for continuous improvement less as tied to particular positions than as work that can be "distributed" and performed by persons throughout the organization.

Research identifies a number of leadership functions conducive to continuous improvement. These functions include promoting the organization's core values and identity; creating and maintaining an organizational culture that supports continuous improvement, and setting goals, priorities, and expectations for the organization's general operations and for continuous improvement. In addition, the research suggests that effective leadership for continuous improvement promotes the development of flexible organizational structures and capacities for continuous improvement processes to operate well and for fast-paced continuous organizational change. Effective leadership for continuous improvement ensures the necessary distribution of authority and influence to make continuous improvement processes work and ensures that organizational members fulfill their responsibilities effectively without micro-managing and without compromising the discretion necessary for continuous improvement processes to succeed.

These leadership functions are evident in the findings of several studies. Savolainen's (1991) research on manufacturing companies found that for continuous improvement to be effective, there needed to be champions for the process in managerial and executive leadership positions. Top executive support was essential to lend authority to and provide impetus for the process. Likewise, Lillrank and his colleagues' (2001) research emphasized the importance of executive leadership to make goals and priorities clear, to define responsibility, and to set expectations for continuous improvement. Brown and Eisenhardt's (1997) study also placed a great deal of emphasis on management systems for coordinating the sequencing of work and in conducting future probes. At the same time, they found that the more successful companies they studied also had executive leadership that operated "above" and beyond these management systems. Such leadership was not concerned with coordinating or performing the specific tasks of continuous improvement. Rather it assumed responsibility for and championed the overall process.

These findings are consistent with those of Bain's (1998) case studies. Bain found that leadership at the executive level or the equivalent was important to the success of continuous improvement. It provided active and unequivocal support for continuous improvement from the start. It lent credibility and authority to the process. While executive leadership played various direct roles in the process, it spread responsibility for continuous improvement across the organization. Finally, executive leadership performed an important accountability function to ensure that that responsibility was fulfilled wherever it was lodged.

Light's (1998) *Sustaining Innovation* project identified several "preferred states" of leadership among innovative nonprofit organizations. Among the most important was keeping innovation processes focused on the organization's core mission and values. Also important was keeping innovation in perspective. Leaders of these organizations promoted innovation relentlessly but knew when to let their organizations "catch their breaths." While they encouraged the development of new programs and practices, they also made sure that they let (even encouraged) older and less effective ones die, attending carefully to the sequencing of and the transitions between the new and the old. These leaders taught their organizations how to say "no" and when and why to say "yes" to new ideas and opportunities presented by the external environment.

Light found certain qualities of leadership to be particularly conducive to encouraging innovation. Leaders of innovating nonprofits adopted styles that were generally democratic, decentralized, and inclusive. At the same time, they helped their organizations be very clear about who had the authority and responsibility to decide what. Leaders of these organizations also had the capacity to create cultures conducive to continual innovation. They consistently called for new ideas from all parts and levels of the organization. They encouraged communication of information and new ideas throughout the organization to excess. Finally, they cultivated the values of experimentation and risk taking and in the context of risk taking the permission to fail. These qualities of leadership were also found among high performing nonprofit organizations Light (2002) subsequently studied.

Studies of continuously improving schools point to similar qualities of leadership. Rosenholtz (1989) found that the learning-enriched schools she studied had principals who made frequent use of evaluation and feedback, each directed toward continuous learning and improvement. These principals promoted the values of continuous learning and improvement and norms of collective responsibility and activity among faculty. Moreover, these principals actively sought to develop regular opportunities—tasks, time, and space—for teacher collaboration, thereby promoting continuous learning and improvement.

In a more recent study, Ulrich Reitzug and Leonard Burrello (1995) examined qualities of leadership that promote school self-renewal. Drawing on data from thirteen principals from thirteen school districts in the Southeast, Midwest, and Southwest, Reitzug and Burrello found three aspects of leadership to be particularly important. The first was the principal's ability to create a supportive environment for reflection and continuous improvement. This entails creating staffing arrangements, teams in particular, for faculty to interact, exchange ideas and share information, solve problems jointly, and develop a sense of collective responsibility. It also entails encouragement of risk-taking and nonthreatening public justification of current practice. A second aspect of leadership was the principal's ability to facilitate reflective practice among teachers. This meant continuous monitoring of instruction "by wandering around," asking teaching questions, and critiquing current practice. It also entailed challenging program regularities. The third aspect was the principal's ability to make it possible for teachers to enact the ideas and implement the programs that result from experimentation, critique, and reflection. At minimum, this involved the principal's ability to obtain sufficient money, materials, and time to make these things happen.

Allen and Calhoun (1998) found that the ongoing collaborative action research projects they studied were more successful in schools where principals were directly involved in inquiry and improvement efforts. Principals of these schools were more effective than principals of less successful schools in being able to facilitate these processes and support them with external resources. King's (2002) study found several aspects of school leadership to be related to the success of the schoolwide inquiry and improvement processes he studied. They included creating and maintaining a focus on student learning to guide inquiry and improvement, communicating high expectations for teacher performance, cultivating norms of trust and collaboration, encouraging the open exchange of ideas, and promoting broad participation and influence in schoolwide decision making for improvement resulting from inquiry. Marsh and her colleagues (2006) found that data use was more prevalent in schools with leadership that expressed strong commitment to data-driven decision making and were able to develop a strong, clear vision for data use in their schools for continuous improvement (see also Wayman et al., 2006).

Copland's (2003) study of BASRC's Cycle of Inquiry corroborated many of these findings. However, his findings went beyond affirming the importance of the executive leadership of the principal. He found that successful use of the Cycle was more likely to be found in schools where leadership functions were distributed among a number of people. In these schools, implementation was less dependent on the presence and actions of a single "visionary" leader than in less successful schools. In the more successful schools, the leadership work required for implementation of the Cycle was carried out by different people across the school community. In the more successful schools, leadership work was focused on the improvement of teaching and learning. Importantly, leadership was also focused on the integrity and the implementation of the continuous improvement process that would produce those outcomes.

COMPREHENSIVE DESIGN MODELS OF CONTINUOUSLY IMPROVING ORGANIZATIONS

At the beginning of this chapter, the point was made that elements of organizational design for continuous improvement are best thought of together in mutually reinforcing systems. One way to see how various design elements might compose such systems is to look at several comprehensive design models of continuously improving organizations. This section presents three such models.

The Self-Designing Organization

Mohrman and Cummings' (1989) model of *the self-designing organization* is derived from previous theory and research on business and industry and draws on several cases of businesses for illustration and evidence. In this model, continuous improvement of organizational structures and processes is a primary goal of an ongoing process of self-design. Self-design considers continuous improvement of structures and processes as instrumental to continuous improvement of organizational outcomes. It is self-design with the purpose of constantly improving the organization and constantly improving its performance and effectiveness. Mohrman and Cummings argue that there are a number of "organizing issues" regarding organizational structures and organizational capacities that must be addressed in order to execute self-design processes effectively and achieve continuous improvement. These issues are equivalent to design decisions. Their model consists of a series of arguments for particular design decisions.

A first design decision has to do with which organizational participants need to be involved in self-design processes and how those participants should be involved. Mohrman and Cummings (1998) argue that in small organizations with relatively "flat" structures, all participants should be involved in all stages of self-design, from initial problem identification through the implementation and assessment of new designs or strategies. In more complex organizations where self-design may operate at the level of the work unit, the process would begin at the top of the organization and "cascade downward" involving appropriate units and participants. Each unit would engage the process within the parameters set by higher levels. In the latter scenario, communication channels would tie work units engaged in self-design to higher levels of the organization to ensure efficient and effective exchange of information, feedback, and expedite negotiation across levels as lower-level participants "test boundaries, experiment . . . , and learn new things" (p. 158).

In situations where entire complex organizations pursue self-design processes for organization-wide change, Mohrman and Cummings (1989) recommend the development of "specially created design teams." These teams would be directed by upper levels and manage the process for the whole organization. Such design teams would likely be composed of selected representatives of different units with expertise appropriate to the process and to problems at hand. A higher level steering committee of representative participants might coordinate the process across design teams. Mohrman and Cummings describe a number of different ways that design teams could be structured and how different design teams might relate to each other and to the organization as a whole. These descriptions are quite insightful but it is beyond the scope of the discussion here to review them.

It is important to note that Mohrman and Cummings (1989) consider the basic structures of different organizations as "givens" and as contingencies for thinking about different ways to develop self-design processes. In relatively small organizations with simple structures, their preference is to integrate self-design processes within existing structures. What is important in these organizations is broad, cross-role participation, even if that means expanding or redefining work roles and responsibilities to include such participation. Also important is effective communication and coordination of effort within and across levels of the organization. In larger organizations and organizations with complex structures, Morhman and Cummings suggest establishing parallel structures to "house" self-design processes. Examples of such parallel structures are design teams and perhaps steering committees. The issue of integrated or parallel structures will be discussed further in Chapter 7.

Another design decision has to do with organizational culture. Mohrman and Cummings (1989) emphasize the importance of developing organizational norms to support self-design and continuous improvement. These norms include openness for sharing information, tolerance of mistakes, acknowledgement of differences in perspective and opinion, bias toward information and expertise over hierarchy, cooperation and teamwork, flexibility, and adaptation to different sit-uations. Mohrman and Cummings argue that these norms are foreign to many organizations. They see the development of these norms coming slowly through initial self-design work that builds and reinforces them, that in turn promotes further self-design work, which continues to strengthen these norms, and so on continuously. Top executive leadership would need to play a role in estab-lishing these norms.

Yet another design decision concerns resources. Mohrman and Cummings (1989) contend that organizing for self-design requires an ongoing commitment of resources that are appropriate and at sufficient levels to support the process of continuous improvement. One particularly important resource is expertise, an element of human capital. Expertise should be available and accessible and should address multiple areas, including but not limited to organizations and how they operate, change processes in general and self-design processes in particular, the nature of organizational problems to be solved, and potential solutions. Mohrman and Cummings encourage leadership and staff to look first to develop and employ internal sources of expertise at all levels of the organization. Internal expertise is likely to be developed through self-design itself. However, when internal exper-tise does not exist or cannot be developed, the necessary expertise should be sought from external sources, be it in the form of consultants, specialists, or partnerships with other organizations.

Mohrman and Cummings (1989) contend that self-design and continuous improvement depend importantly on both time and money. Self-design processes proceed more smoothly and more quickly if engaged by people who can spend considerable time in the effort. Productive involvement in these processes cannot occur, at least not for very long, unless participants' regular work schedules include it. Mohrman and Cummings go so far as to suggest that at the beginning stages, key participants might need to be dedicated to continuous improvement processes full-time. The implication is that little can be expected if involvement is "one more thing" that organizational participants assume on top of their regular responsibilities. Time needs to be created and conflicts with other duties eliminated for these processes to work well.

Mohrman and Cummings (1989) observe that a key financial cost often overlooked is the time that it takes for people to participate in the process. Beyond the cost of time are monetary costs asso-ciated with establishing and implementing the process itself (e.g., meetings, external guidance and expertise, data collection and analysis, communications, information sharing, etc.). Equally if not more important are the costs associated with implementing new designs, programs, and processes that result from improvement processes. Mohrman and Cummings acknowledge that it is difficult to specify in advance how much self-design and continuous improvement will cost. Therefore, they recommend that cost estimation and budgeting be a central part of the self-design process itself.

Finally, decisions about leadership. Mohrman and Cummings (1989) point to the importance of leadership to successful self-design and continuous improvement. They stress the importance of leadership at different levels of the organization. Leadership at the top of the organization must cre-ate the need and impetus for establishing and implementing self-design processes. Leadership must promote the norms and values that support and guide these processes and that encourage and enforce staff involvement. At whatever level, leadership must be able to muster the internal and external resources needed for self-design and continuous improvement. It must be able to monitor, guide, and keep self-design processes "on track." This may include coordinating multiple "sites" of self-design and continuous improvement within different units of the organization. Finally, leadership must attend to communication, keeping channels open and information flowing in multiple directions. Leadership itself must be open and willing to listen, learn, and change through the process. Much like the way they view expertise, Mohrman and Cummings' preference is to look internally to identify or develop key people for leadership work (note the potential costs of "freeing up" these people to perform this work). However, in the absence of internal sources of leadership, leadership may need to be secured from external sources.

Demand Requirements and Dimensions

Lillrank and his colleagues' (1998) model was developed to answer the question "How do we organize industrial activities for continuous improvement?" (p. 51). They begin with a set of propositions developed from the literature on continuous improvement and from examples of companies engaged in continuous improvement. These propositions set out seven *design requirements* or demands that must be met for continuous improvement to succeed. From design requirements, they turn to *design dimensions* that might satisfy them. The idea of design dimension is synonymous with the idea of design element.

The first design requirement for continuous improvement is the need for "a legitimate forum for exchange of ideas" (Lillrank et al., 1998, p. 52). The opportunity that people have to work on solving problems together is essential to continuous improvement, and it relates to a number of other issues, including resource needs such as time, compensation, and rewards. The second requirement is that roles and responsibilities must be structured in a way that the continuity of improvement efforts can be sustained over long periods of time. The third requirement is that the organization needs to be designed so that all parts of it are implicated by and can be involved in continuous improvement. The organization must act as a "total system" with regard to continuous improvement.

The fourth requirement is that organizational design must be supported by those persons in established centers of power and those involved in the work is affected by continuous improvement. Without this "political" support, chances of success are slim. Continuous improvement activity might be little more than symbolic and outcomes of genuine efforts would stand little chance of survival. The fifth design requirement consists of goals that define the direction of continuous improvement. This requirement is consistent with the earlier discussion of the primacy of an organization's mission and core values in guiding continuous improvement processes. The sixth requirement is that there must be structures and resources in place that support the implementation of "improvements" that flow from these processes. Finally, systems must exist to provide incentive and compensation for participation in and contributions to continuous improvement.

Following these design requirements are a number of specific design features, or in their words, dimensions that could satisfy them. Lillrank and his colleagues (1998) proposed these dimensions as alternatives that could be "tested" in field research. Roughly aligned with the design requirements, they include (a) whether continuous improvement activity, forums for exchange, and participation therein are part of ordinary work life or something beyond it; (b) whether continuous improvement activities are performed by a permanent group or by ad hoc groups; (c) whether persons engaged in continuous improvement represent one or several organizational units or functions; (d) whether persons engaged in continuous improvement represent the same or different levels of the organization; (e) whether goal setting is organization-wide or at the group level, and whether goal setting is guided centrally or occurs at the group level; (f) whether decisions about implementation of continuous improvement processes and changes that come of them are made by management or by implementing groups; and (g) whether or not incentive systems compensate for effort and reward for results.

These design dimensions were explored by Lillrank and his colleagues (1998) for more than three years in eight different companies in North America and Europe that were noted for successful continuous improvement. This research provided additional evidence of the importance of the design requirements in their model but also demonstrated that continuously improving organizations could be designed and managed in many different ways, so long as these design requirements were satisfied. All of the companies studied had established some type of long-standing, legitimate forum for exchanges and generation of ideas. How these forums were specifically designed mattered less than that they encouraged "dialogue, discussion, problem identification, and problem solutions" (p. 70). It did not matter whether continuity of improvement efforts was promoted by permanent or ad hoc groups. What mattered was that the structures provided for continuity of effort no matter who participated at any particular time. Similarly, it did not matter so much how the totality of operations was involved in continuous improvement or how established centers of power supported the enterprise. What mattered was that the totality of operations was involved and that established centers of power provided strong support.

In these cases, successful, continuous improvement was contingent on the presence of organizational goals that embodied both continuity and improvement. These goals had to be communicated to all organizational members. The process of establishing goals for continuous improvement could be structured in different ways. It could be approached from the top down or the bottom up. Goals could be set for the organization as a whole then broken down for each unit. Or goal setting could be left to individual units and be guided by an overall vision and set of organizational goals and priorities. Likewise, it did not matter what types of implementation procedures or incentive systems were in place as long as those procedures and systems were adequate.

Lillrank and colleagues' (1998) model is a contingency framework. The forms that specific design elements take can vary depending on the organization and its context. However, the form that is taken must be consistent with the function of continuous improvement. The model anticipates that organizations will need to make changes in their designs as situations and contexts change.

The "B2change" Organization

The third and most extensive model discussed in this section is Lawler and Worley's (2006) *built to change* or *b2change* organization. The b2change model rests on a logic that to be successful over time in ever-changing environments, organizations need to be designed in ways that stimulate and support change. According to Lawler and Worley,

> This means creating an organization that encourages experimentation, learns about new practices and technologies, monitors the environment, assesses performance, and is committed to continuously improving performance. The organization's strategies, structures, reward system, communication processes, and HR [human relations] management practices must be designed to change and to encourage the organization to continuously and rapidly change. (p. 21)

Creating a b2change organization is not a matter of specifying a particular organizational design. It is, Lawler and Worley (2006) argue, a commitment to "a process of organizing," to creating a series of "temporary designs that create short-term advantages," that makes organization design not only a source of support for continuous improvement but also the subject of it (p. 21). The full model of the b2change organization contains a number of processes synonymous with continuous improvement, like those discussed in Chapter 4. What is most relevant to us here are the elements of design that Lawler and Worley contend are crucial to the operation and effectiveness of a b2change organization.

Like Lillrank and his colleagues (1998), Lawler and Worley (2006) ground their discussion in a set of assumptions about the functions that b2change organizations must perform to continuously improve and remain effective over long periods of time. The first is that the b2change organization must be able to develop, sustain, and operate from a core identity, a stable set of basic beliefs and values. Identity functions as "an overarching and relatively enduring statement of how [an organization] will achieve its long-term mission" (p. 33). A second assumption is that the b2change organization must keep itself engaged with the environment. It must be able to anticipate multiple future states of the environment. A third assumption is that the b2change organization must be able to develop and maintain two relationships essential to long-term performance—critical configuration and dynamic alignment. Critical configuration refers to the relationship or the "proximity" of an organization's core identity and strategic intent to its environment. Strategic intent concerns an organization's decisions about the goods and services it will produce and the markets it will serve. Dynamic alignment refers to relationships within an organization among its core identity, strategic intent, competencies (technologies and means of production), capabilities (resources that an organization can draw upon to operate), and design (the structures and processes that enable an organization to perform effectively). A fourth assumption is that a b2change organization must possess "change capability." Change capability refers to the resources and processes needed to make adjustments in strategic intent and strategies, and even to make transformational changes to sustain configuration and alignment with identity as environments change and as the organization itself changes.

In order to perform these functions well, an organization must build structures, attract and retain human resources, develop and deploy appropriate information systems, develop effective leaders, and craft motivating reward systems, all in a manner conducive to continuous change. Like Mohrman and Cummings (1989) and Lillrank and his colleagues (1998), the issue for Lawler and Worley (2006) is not "specifying *an* organization design but committing to a process of organizing" (p. 21, emphasis in the original). For them, "designing is a dynamic process of modifying and constantly adjusting an organization's structure, systems, people, and rewards so that they provide the called-for-performance" (p. 44).

Although not specifically considered a design element in the b2change organization, it is important to say a few words about the importance of an organization's core identity. For Lawler and Worley (2006), identity is a stable, controlling force, directing change toward organizational values and purposes, even as design and activity change to respond to different demands and opportunities. The identity of a b2change organization must serve two seemingly contradictory functions. The first is to provide a stable foundation for organizational performance and the ability to change. Without such a foundation, there may be too much uncertainty for organizational members to perform or deal well with change. At the same time, its function is to create an expectation for change and a sense that ongoing change is "normal." What may constitute a stable element of identity of a b2change organization is the normalcy of continuous improvement.

From this point, Lawler and Worley (2006) turn to other elements of the b2change organization. They contend that because organizational structure is a "critical determinant of organizational effectiveness" it needs to be designed not only to meet current needs but also to change (p. 88). Lawler and Worley identify a number of structural elements that make ongoing change easier and more effective. Most of these elements concern the organization of people and their work. Consistent with the notion of "preferred organizational states of being" (Light, 1998, 2000), Lawler and Worley introduce these elements as design principles. The implication is that there may be many different ways that these principles may find expression in the structure of a b2change organization.

The first principle is that organizational structure should train the organization's attention on and maximize contact with the external environment. "The best design," Lawler and Worley (2006) contend, "puts as many employees as possible in direct contact with the external environment" (p. 90). This means shortening the distance between an organization's members and customers, other organizations and entities on which the organization depends, and the organization's competitors. This principle extends to all members of the organization and suggests a flatter organizational structure than a hierarchical one where members in particular positions may be largely separated from the environment. The idea is that proximity of organizational members to the environment is associated with their ability to know about the environment and changes in it, and with the ability of the organization to respond effectively to those changes. Such proximity also creates the opportunity for organizational members to understand how the organization functions and where problems in the relationship with the environment may occur. "Feedback" from the external environment is a point of learning for organizational members and, according to Lawler and Worley, can be a source of employee motivation to perform and organizational motivation to change.

A second principle concerns structural elements that promote responsiveness and flexibility. Lawler and Worley (2006) identify four such elements. The first concerns the design of work and work roles. Lawler and Worley suggest that fixed jobs and job descriptions should be eliminated in favor of "dynamic work assignments and relationships" (p. 93). Responsibilities need to be assigned on a temporary basis and as the needs of the organization change and as demands for people's skills change, the mix of tasks can be adjusted. A second element is the establishment of teams. Lawler and Worley argue that working in teams can promote problem identification and problem solving and it can help individuals learn and develop skills that will be needed when the organization changes. Teams can also be used to manage interactions and joint work across different parts of the organization. Temporary teams rather than permanent staffing structures may greatly enhance the ability of the organization to respond to external demands for change.

A third structural element consists of virtual or electronically based working relationships, especially among organizational members who may be separated by large geographical distances or who may be in relatively close physical proximity but unable to interact regularly in person. Such relationships can enhance the ability of an organization to change by expanding communication channels to larger numbers of people and by enhancing the flow and exchange of information through those channels. They may also make easier changes in working relationships, in reporting relationships, and in team memberships, thus reducing resistance to such changes. A fourth structural element concerns dividing large organizations into smaller units with substantial autonomy that can be close to the customer, interact in closer proximity and more effectively with the environment, and be created and eliminated relatively easily as needs arise. Moreover, such units can be changed, if necessary, with relatively less impact on other parts of the organization.

In addition to these elements, Lawler and Worley (2006) argue that certain ways of distributing decision-making authority can be more conducive than others to ongoing change. Major "organization defining" strategic decisions are often best made at the top of the organization, even in relatively flat and participative organizations. The reason for this is the need for maintaining organization-wide consistency and the integrity of organizational identity and strategic intent. But while such decisions may be best made at the top, they should be informed by broad-based input. With the exception of these major decisions, Lawler and Worley argue, continuous change is best served when organizations try to move as many decisions as possible to lower levels where there may be more contact between the organization and its environment, particularly its "customers." The point is not simply to move decision making down in the organization. It is to locate decision making in parts of the organization where information, knowledge, and skills exist to make the best decisions.

A final structural element in this model is reward systems. On the premise that reward systems should motivate people to behave in ways that support the organization's core values, strategic intent, and performance requirements, Lawler and Worley (2006) argue that reward systems in the b2change organization should be structured in ways that promote continuous improvement. This means keying rewards not only to processes of change but also to acting effectively on changes stimulated by those processes. Lawler and Worley suggest that reward systems should be designed to reflect the motivational structures of organizational participants, that is, to provide rewards that are indeed motivational to them (even though they might not be motivational to others). They also contend that structures and processes of reward systems can have ancillary benefits. At the least, the manner in which reward systems function and the ways in which they are perceived to be fair and equitable can affect the development of trust that organizational members hold of the organization and that they hold for each other. As discussed later, trust is a crucial resource for successful continuous improvement in this model.

In additional to these structural elements, Lawler and Worley (2006) identify a number of other design elements that they believe are important to the success of the b2change organization. Among the most important is human capital, that is, the knowledge, skills, and dispositions of all organizational members. According to Lawler and Worley, the b2change organization requires, at minimum, individuals with the knowledge, skills, and dispositions to meet current operational and performance needs and who are also "willing and able to change themselves to keep up with the changing organization" (p. 154).

Lawler and Worley (2006) see the "substance" of human capital, that is, the specific knowledge, skills, and dispositions required for these things, as largely idiosyncratic to individual organizations and their core values and objectives. Still, they argue that the attention that all organizations pay to the development and deployment of their human capital is crucial to their success. The management of human resources "deserves as much or more attention as the management of financial and physical assets" (p. 153). Commitment to the effective development and management of human capital must be "unflinching" at all levels of the organization. To be successful, the b2change organization must effectively develop, reward, and retain people with the knowledge, skills, and dispositions needed for organizational performance and continuous improvement. The turnover that is inevitable in an organization's workforce must be managed proactively and effectively. New learning must be rewarded.

Lawler and Worley (2006) argue that because of its orientation toward change and because change may create the need for new sets of knowledge and skills, the b2change organization should think of its human capital as "mobile." Mobility has several connotations. One is the flexible assignment of human resources to work, as work and the organization's objectives change over time. Another is the adoption of a "commitment-to-development" approach that emphasizes stability and learning in order to adapt to change. That is, the organization focuses on finding the right people then developing them over time as needs arise. A third connotation is to adopt a "travel-light" approach, which is to "acquire and discard talent as needed" (p. 156). According to this approach, there is less value placed on long-term relationships with employees and their development than on maximum flexibility to acquire and shift competencies as quickly as needed. Lawler and Worley argue that the right approach for any organization depends on the rate of environmental change, the organization's identity, and its strategic intent.

Another important design element is trust. Lawler and Worley associate trust with organizational members' commitment to the organization and its success and to their own willingness to change as the organization changes. They argue that if people perceive that change will have a positive impact on their futures they are less likely to resist it. Their trust that the organization will act with their interests in mind will likely influence whether or not they believe that change will be positive for them. That, in turn, will affect their receptivity to and engagement in change. Trust is not necessarily dependent on a particular approach to "mobility" of human capital. It is more dependent on predictability, dependability, and justification for whichever approach is used.

Yet another design element in the model of the b2change organization is leadership. For Lawler and Worley (2006), leadership is "the glue that holds structure, information systems, talent, and reward systems together" (p. 213). They believe that particular qualities of leadership are crucial for a b2change organization. Specific leadership knowledge, skills, and dispositions are idiosyncratic and contingent on the organization and its environment. So too are specific leadership practices. However, Lawler and Worley indicate that effective leadership in a b2change organization should embody some similar, basic qualities. It should personify and promote the organization's identity and core values. It must be able to communicate fully and openly with organizational members about what is going on in the organization. It must be fair and equitable in its relationship with personnel and it must be dependable and trustworthy. Finally, leadership in a b2change organization must take the environment into account and know how to engage it effectively. Lawler and Worley write that in whatever situation the organization finds itself and whatever the implications for leadership practice might be, "there needs to be a set of givens—including honesty, integrity, providing information, and helping people understand the implications of organizational strategies and decisions—that simply aren't optional" (p. 222).

A key dimension of leadership in the b2change organization is the simultaneous focus on the external environment and on internal processes and resources (including human resources). Leadership must resist settling into a "status quo." It must be continuously communicating. Lawler and Worley (2006) are clear that leaders need to adjust their practices to changing circumstances outside and inside their organizations. Those practices need to be contingent on internal and external circumstance. However, there must always be respect for and consideration of organizational identity, long-term vision and core values of the organization, and people. In the midst of an organization built for continuous change, the basic character and aim of leadership need to be a source of stability. Leadership work may change but the "brand" of leadership, the "set of givens," must be "something that people can trust" particularly during times of change (p. 222). Instability in character and aim puts both organizational performance and the ability to change effectively at risk.

Lawler and Worley (2006) also argue that an important aspect of leadership is managerial competence. The "givens" of leadership character and managerial competence are not mutually exclusive. The b2change organization requires both. Change processes have important managerial elements and their effective enactment is critical to successful change. There is no person or place in the b2change organization in which managerial competence must reside so long as it is "possessed" by the organization and is exercised effectively.

This leads to another quality of leadership in a b2change organization—the distribution or "sharedness" of leadership work. In the b2change organization, leadership is considered a "team sport" (Lawler and Worley, 2006, p. 217). Lawler and Worley argue that organizations led by single "heroic" leaders tend to be "fragile entities" (p. 217). They suffer tremendously from leader "defects" and instances of leadership failure. Organizations that become heavily dependent on a single leader often do not survive the loss of that leader. Moreover, even the most effective single leaders are rarely able to perform effectively the full work of leadership required in a b2change organization. Or they are unable to perform the full work effectively for very long.

Shared leadership is not simply important to ensure that all the work gets done or to protect the organization from leadership problems or loss. The distribution of leadership work creates proximity to leadership that may help engage members in the organization's strategy and in efforts to improve. It also develops leadership capacity in places with the most direct contact with the environment and in places closest to the sources of problems and opportunities for change. How leadership work is actually distributed depends on the organization and its context. And how that work is distributed at any one time may change as the needs of the organization change.

ORGANIZATIONAL DESIGN PRINCIPLES FOR CONTINUOUS IMPROVEMENT IN SCHOOLS

To pull it all together, lessons are presented later as a set of design principles about organizational design for continuous improvement in schools. These principles are framed according to the 10 elements of organizational design for continuous improvement discussed in the chapter. After their presentation, we conclude by revisiting considerations for thinking about organizational design that introduced the chapter.

How much confidence should we have in these design principles for schools? We have seen that overall the findings of research on the design of various types of non-education organizations are quite consistent with the findings of research on the design of schools for continuous improvement. Where there are differences, the findings from non-education organizations tend to elaborate or extend lessons from schools. There are virtually no contradictions, and the findings of research from non-education organizations make intuitive sense when applied to schools. Such consistency suggests that the basic features of organizational design for continuous improvement are largely the same for schools as for other types of organizations. This general conclusion is consistent with the findings of a recent study of expert opinion about the organizational conditions that support quality management practices in schools, including processes of continuous improvement (Detert et al., 2001). In that study, the experts consulted identified as relevant to schools many of the same organizational design elements found conducive to continuous improvement in non-education organizations.

> **Principle 1.** A school should develop norms, values, and an organizational culture conducive to continuous improvement.

The norms, values, and culture of a school provide the grounding, direction, and a source of accountability for continuous improvement. They serve the paradoxical but necessary functions of providing a source of stability necessary for organizational performance and change and at the same time provoking and promoting ongoing change. The norms and values that are particularly important for continuous improvement include openness, exchange, collaboration, flexibility, experimentation, risk-taking, adaptation, and tolerance of mistakes and failure (so long as they are encountered in the pursuit of improvement). They also include a bias toward evidence and expertise over opinion and personality, and the value of playfulness and foolishness as counterbalances to formal rational thinking and decision making. Finally, a school's norms and values should embody its organizational mission of teaching and promoting student learning and, importantly, the concept and work of continuous improvement itself.

> **Principle 2.** A school must assemble the human capital it needs for continuous improvement and for the accomplishment of its mission. A school must organize itself to engage in the ongoing development of its human capital as called for by continuous improvement.

Human capital for continuous improvement is composed of knowledge, skills, attitudes, and dispositions of a school's staff that are needed for (a) enacting the school's mission and core values, (b) engaging in processes of continuous improvement, and (c) implementing new practices and initiatives that emerge from those processes. A school can recruit and hire personnel to develop its stock of human capital. But because hiring new personnel is a limited option for many schools, a school must organize itself and establish its own capability to develop the human capital needed for continuous improvement within its own staff. This capability can include programs and processes of training and development, recruiting and retaining persons with relevant knowledge and skills, and dismissing persons whose knowledge and skills are inadequate or irrelevant. It can also include organizing staff members and their work in ways that are conducive to the ongoing development of new human capital.

> **Principle 3.** A school should organize its people and their work to promote communication, collaboration, broad interaction with the environment, feedback, and opportunities for learning, experimentation, and change.

This design principle suggests structured interdependence, "bounded" autonomy, and flexibility in task assignments and working relationships within a school. It suggests that participation in continuous improvement processes and implementation of initiatives that emerge be included among primary work responsibilities of staff members. They should not be considered "add-ons." This design principle also points to a preference for collaborative work groups, such as teams, and flat and thin organizational arrangements that reduce layers of management, lower barriers between work units and between levels of the organization, and put as many members of the school's staff as possible in direct or close contact with one another and with the environment. For schools it makes sense that there be close contact with students, parents, communities, as well as central offices, the policy environment, and so forth. Communication systems should be established that promote the free flow of information throughout the school and that promote the flow of information from outside the school in. This points to the importance of channels of communication that connect different units and levels of the school organization. It also points to the importance of structured opportunities—times, places, and reasons—for a school's staff members to regularly share information and exchange, challenge, and develop new ideas.

> **Principle 4.** Authority and influence should be spread throughout the school organization in ways that promote both upward and downward influence.

This design principle means maintaining major strategic influence at the top of the school organization but opening "executive authority" to broad-based input from staff members, constituents, and key stakeholders. It means widening participation in school-level decision making and continuous improvement processes. It also means pushing authority and influence to the faculty who have the most direct knowledge about the core operations of the school—teaching and learning—and who have direct knowledge about and receive direct feedback from the environment through their interactions with students, parents, and the community. This design principle relates to a subsequent design principle on leadership and its development and distribution throughout a school organization.

> **Principle 5.** Trust must be developed and cultivated among all members of a school organization.

Trust in organizations serves as both a glue that binds people together in common enterprise and a lubricant that enhances the ability of people to work together (Tschannen-Moran, 2004). Trust provides a sense of predictability, reliability, and stability in working relationships that is important for organizational members to deal with the uncertainty, ambiguity, and risk associated with continuous improvement. Several types of trust seem important in schools, including trust among faculty and staff members, trust in leadership, and trust in the school itself to act in the interest of individuals and to "do the right thing" in a manner consistent with its mission and core values.

> **Principle 6.** A school should develop accountability and reward systems that guide and motivate all staff members to participate in and make contributions toward continuous improvement.

These systems should also be aligned with the school's mission and core values. Specific systems are likely to be idiosyncratic to individual schools and faculties. They should be tailored and targeted to the motivational structures of those they are to guide and motivate.

> **Principle 7.** A school should develop its capacity for generating, analyzing, and using data to promote continuous improvement.

It was noted that the research on continuous improvement in schools points to the importance of a school's data capacity. Data capacity refers to the technical ability of a school to obtain or generate data that are accessible, relevant, timely, and useful for continuous improvement. It also relates to the knowledge, skills, and attitudes of school personnel to analyze and use data effectively to guide improvement efforts and to make decisions. The presence of technically sound and relevant data absent the capacity to use it effectively is as insufficient as the presence of capacity and the absence of sound and relevant data. Both are necessary. Where a school is unable to develop its own sources of good data and its own capacity to use those data well, it may turn to other sources for assistance. These sources include the central office but also external organizations and entities such as universities, consultants, school reform and improvement groups, and so forth. These inter-organizational relationships generate their own issues, but they may be beneficial. Still, it is probably better for schools to develop some threshold level of data capacity, particularly in data interpretation and use, and to supplement that capacity with external sources of assistance than to develop that data capacity exclusively from external sources.

> **Principle 8.** A school must acquire and develop adequate and sustained levels of fiscal and physical resources needed to support the processes of continuous improvement and the implementation of new initiatives that come from them.

While some of the "costs" of continuous improvement may be absorbed in general operations, continuous improvement will make new resource demands on schools, particularly as they are establishing continuous improvement processes and developing various organizational elements to support them. There are, no doubt, certain economies that come from refocusing existing resources on new ways of doing things. However, it seems clear from the literature that continuous improvement will make its own resource demands on schools. These resources include but are not limited to money, materials, facilities, and so forth. Time is also a very important resource and is easily overlooked or underestimated. Also important is the concept of slack, whereby schools are able to develop and maintain a surplus of resources that will support their responses to unexpected demands and opportunities, experimentation, learning, and implementation of new initiatives.

> **Principle 9.** Management systems in a school should be developed and directed to support the processes of continuous improvement and the implementation of initiatives generated by them.

Among other functions, the internal management systems of a school should coordinate, support, and monitor the day-to-day operations of continuous improvement processes. Those systems will need to manage data systems and information flow and obtain and allocate resources for continuous improvement. In the literature on non-education organizations, management systems are usually considered separately from leadership capacity. In the literature on schools, management is usually considered part of leadership, particularly the administrative leadership of the school principal.

> **Principle 10.** A school must develop leadership that sustains a focus on its core mission and values and that promotes and supports continuous improvement.

Consistent with the design principle concerning the distribution of authority and influence, leadership most conducive to continuous improvement tends to be democratic, participative, and inclusive. Such leadership promotes communication and the free flow of information, cultivates and sustains norms and values conducive to continuous improvement, and obtains resources necessary for it to be successful. It also monitors, rewards, and holds the school accountable for the process and outcomes of continuous improvement. Strong "executive" leadership at the top of the school organization is important for promoting and sustaining continuous improvement and ensuring its consistency with organizational mission and core values. At the same time, the distribution of leadership work throughout the school organization seems crucial for the successful enactment and outcomes continuous improvement.

A brief preface presenting several considerations for thinking about organizational design for continuous improvement begins this chapter. It is worth revisiting those considerations as ways to interpret and act upon these design principles. The first consideration was to think about organizational design for continuous improvement in terms of principles (design principles) or "preferred organizational states of being" rather than in terms a specific, absolute organizational characteristics. A second related to the concept of equifinality. This concept indicates that the details of effective organizational design for continuous improvement may vary significantly among different schools because of their environments, histories, the states of their organizational structures and capacities, among other things. What makes idiosyncratic design specifics effective is their consistency with the broader design principles or preferred organizational states of being.

Another consideration was that particular elements of organizational design for continuous improvement are best thought of as mutually interactive systems rather than discrete characteristics. The same may be said for the design principles presented earlier. The findings of research on organizational design and the comprehensive design models discussed in this chapter show important relationships among different elements of design. The general point is that while different design principles may be more salient in some school contexts than in others, or more salient for one school at some times than at other times, they all should be considered together and in interaction with each other. A related consideration is that the school organization has both formal and informal dimensions that need to be aligned.

Finally, it is important to recognize the dynamic nature of organizational design in general and continuous improvement in particular. Organizational design for continuous improvement cannot be considered static. It must be fluid and flexible and subject to change. Organizational design serves as a platform and driver for the processes of continuous improvement. At the same time, organization design is itself a focus of continuous improvement and the subject of continuous adaptation and change. Form and function are one.

QUESTIONS FOR STUDY, REFLECTION, AND ACTION

1. In what ways does organizational design matter to the practice and effectiveness of continuous improvement in schools?

2. What is the difference between adopting and implementing a process model of continuous improvement and becoming a continuously improving school organization where process and design are one? What practical problems and opportunities are associated with the former and with the latter?

3. How do each of the 10 elements of organizational design relate to continuous improvement? How might these elements relate to and influence each other? How might these elements function together as a dynamic system of organizational support for continuous improvement?

4. In what ways does the current organizational design of your school support or constrain its current improvement efforts? Be clear what kinds of improvement efforts you are thinking about. What evidence can you point to that supports your assessment?

5. Assess your school according to the 10 design principles presented at the end of the chapter. How close or how far away is your school from satisfying these principles? What design principles might your school need to focus on to make continuous improvement initially successful? What evidence can you point to that supports your analysis?

Continuous Improvement "In Action"

6

With Cristal Mendlin

You always learn by doing, but you also learn by learning, if you know what I mean.

—Yogi Berra, 2001

This chapter presents vignettes of continuous improvement in four schools. The purpose is to illustrate what continuous improvement looks like "in action." It is to bring some "real life," indeed, some of the "messiness" to the abstract nature of the discussion thus far. It is to provide opportunity to learn from the experience of others. As Yogi Berra also said, referring to his mentor Bill Dickey, "He's learning me all his experience" (2001, p. 32).

These vignettes were constructed from a small number of descriptive case studies of continuous improvement found in the education literature. In selecting cases for these vignettes, we considered several factors. We sought case studies that were developed through systematic processes of data collection and analysis and that claim to present relatively impartial perspectives of the schools and change processes under investigation. We searched for rich descriptions that also contained credible evidence of outcomes. We sought cases that illustrate different dimensions of the logic of continuous improvement described in Chapter 2. And we sought descriptions detailed enough to illustrate both continuous improvement processes and elements of school organization design that support them, as discussed in Chapters 4 and 5. Because continuous improvement is by definition something pursued over time, we looked for multiyear accounts.

In addition, we sought cases that illustrate the sorts of internal and external challenges and uncertainties discussed in Chapter 1. We looked for cases of schools that served predominantly minority or increasingly diverse student populations and schools that served large proportions of low-income students. We also looked for schools experiencing one of the more pronounced current sources of external stress and uncertainty—high-stakes student testing and accountability policies. We were not constrained in our search by the labels that cases assigned to the improvement processes they documented. While some of the cases we considered evoke language of continuous improvement, others employ different terminology (e.g., professional learning communities) to describe nearly the same things.

Using these considerations as guides, we selected case studies of four schools engaged in continuous improvement. Two are elementary schools, one is a middle school, and one is a high school. These cases tell "success stories." They illustrate what continuous improvement might look like when it is working well. Rather than simply abridge the work of others, we considered these case studies as sources of "data" to construct our own vignettes to illustrate basic elements of continuous improvement processes and elements of school organization design that support them.[21] Because the case studies are structured differently, our vignettes vary in organization and content. The reader is encouraged to go to the original studies to learn more about continuous improvement in these schools and about the research methodologies these studies employed.[22]

SHILLING ELEMENTARY SCHOOL

The first vignette of continuous improvement "in action" is of Shilling Elementary School. We developed this vignette from a Bay Area School Reform Collaborative (BASRC) research report titled *The Path Out of Underperformance: Two Cases of Title 1 Schools That Are Beating the Odds.* Issued by BASRC's Research Department in 2004, the report describes the improvement work of this school between 1999 and 2003.

This vignette illustrates several important aspects of continuous improvement: (a) the relationship of continuous improvement to changes in the school's environment and to external pressures to improve; (b) the importance of external support and initial organizational capacity, particularly for collaborative work, to the early success of continuous improvement; (c) the importance of leadership to provide systemic direction and to structure and manage continuous improvement activity; and (d) the importance of having a clear process focused on improving student learning and the role of student data to inform improvement activity. The story of Shilling Elementary School is one of small successes leading to larger accomplishments.

Shilling Elementary School is located in the Newark Unified School District in California. At the time this school was studied by BASRC, it enrolled about 590 students in kindergarten through sixth grade. The student body was 61% Latino; 23% Asian, Filipino, and Pacific Islander, 10% white, and 6% African American. Shilling was considered a Title 1 school. Half of its students came from low-income families; that is, they were eligible for the federal government's free and reduced price lunch program. English language learners (ELL) made up 45% of its students. Historically, Shilling had the largest proportions of low-income students, students of color, and ELLs of schools in its district.

(Continued)

(Continued)

In 1999, Shilling was designated by the California Department of Education as an "underperforming" school—its students were performing at the lowest levels on the state's assessments. As a result, Shilling was "invited" to join the state's Immediate Intervention/ Underperforming Schools Program (II/USP). Schools in this program were required to show growth in student performance over three years and received additional resources from the state—an external evaluator and additional funding—to carry out improvement plans. Two years later, Shilling became a member of BASRC as part of a "local collaborative," a network of schools working in concert with its district on shared improvement goals. BASRC's Cycle of Inquiry (described in detail in Chapter 4) became an important part of Shilling's movement toward continuous improvement.

Shilling's designation as an "underperforming" school and its participation in II/USP provided an initial impetus for the school to examine its own practices and assess its strengths and weaknesses. These circumstances, as well as its subsequent involvement in BASRC, launched a process of collaborative continuous improvement focused on instruction and student learning. Shilling experienced rather quick success in large part because it was able to build on capacity it already had in place—an experienced and collaborative staff that had worked together for some time and that was strongly committed to student success, strong leadership not only in the principal's office but throughout the school, and a supportive professional culture. But not until the efforts of the staff were structured, focused, and managed did they manifest themselves in productive change in instruction and student learning.

After joining BASRC, Shilling's leadership began to provide "systemic support" for teacher collaboration around curriculum and inquiry. Release days and time at staff meetings were set aside for teachers to examine student achievement data and collaboratively develop lesson plans. Monthly staff meetings were dedicated to grade-level collaboration and grade level teams were given release time three times a year so that they could develop new instructional strategies for promoting reading comprehension and literacy—the academic focus of the school. Initially, leadership directed teachers to specific topics for collaborative work. Leadership also taught teachers BASRC's Cycle of Inquiry as a process of data-based inquiry to focus and drive their collaboration (see Chapter 4). It was the adoption and implementation of this Cycle of Inquiry that Shilling's staff credited for the school's progress.

Shilling's leadership aimed to systematically employ the Cycle of Inquiry at all grade levels. Most teachers at the school had not engaged in a process like this before, and it fell to leadership— mostly the principal and the school's literacy coordinator—to make it both accessible and "implementable." The cycle was broken down into "manageable chunks." The literacy coordinator developed the structure, the time, and the timelines to work through the cycle. At the beginning, she and the principal suggested topics for teacher collaboration but later allowed the process of inquiry to "surface" topics for teachers to engage. Gradually, leadership's task shifted more to managing than directing the process. In particular, leadership helped teachers at different grade levels identify a key issue that data were telling them should be addressed, focus singularly on that issue through the cycle, then allow the cycle to identify another issue to address.

Leadership emphasized that in order to address student needs effectively, discussion, decisions, and actions had to be grounded in student data. Looking at disaggregated data was especially important in light of Shilling's diverse student population. Prior to its use of the *inquiry cycle, the school had not considered data concerning the experience and performance of different groups of students. Through the cycle, the staff looked more closely at these groups and for the first time sought to ascertain direct connections between school and classroom practices and students' experiences and performance.*

In addition to helping the school identify and define problems and point to strategies to address them, the inquiry process helped Shilling identify professional development needs of teachers and needs for various organizational supports to promote and sustain the inquiry cycle and the implementation of new programs and practices that were generated from it. The cycle also provided leaders and teachers with new insights into the change process itself. It helped them see how to engage "already hard-working" teachers in continuous improvement and not overburden them. The cycle and the data it generated helped to "manage" the change process, not simply identify and develop new programs and practices for implementation. With leadership and teachers studying the change process as they went along, the cycle helped the school look for points of leverage by which it might have an initial impact on classroom instruction and student learning and at the same time lay the foundation for greater, long-term improvement. The idea was to start with small but meaningful successes. It was also to reject the expectation of perfection, of getting it right the first time. Instead, the idea was to walk an unending path "as a learner," accumulating more and more knowledge and understanding along the way.

Shilling employed nested inquiry cycles within grade levels and across grade levels to promote collaboration and coherence in improvement efforts throughout the school. Collaborative inquiry within grade levels helped teachers continuously identify and address problems and opportunities among students with whom they worked most closely. Collaborative inquiry across grade levels helped the school as a whole identify and address problems and opportunities shared by all. Through this nested structure of inquiry cycles, teachers gained opportunities to learn from one another and to build collective knowledge. Aided by various "tools" that emanated from the process, such as instructional guides and calendars, this structure also helped to promote coherence of instructional improvement within and across grade levels.

As a member of BASRC, Shilling worked with two other elementary schools in the district with similar student populations to expand its opportunities for learning and its resources for improvement around a focus common to all three schools—improvement of literacy instruction and learning. Through structured collaboration managed carefully by the literacy coordinators of each school, teachers from all three schools meet in grade-level groups to examine lesson plans, assess student work, and discuss specific strategies for improving instruction. Each grade level had a twice-a-year opportunity to visit a demonstration classroom in another school and debrief. This cross-school collaboration allowed Shilling and the other schools to pool their resources, share professional development, and learn from each other's expertise and experience.

There were a number of ways that continuous improvement was supported at Shilling. We mentioned how the cycles were structured within and across grade levels, how leadership allocated regular blocks of time for staff to engage in the process, how it emphasized the use of data to identify and define problems and to identify strategies to address them, and how it supported the Cycle of Inquiry by focusing it and keeping it on track. School leaders also adopted and promoted a "systems perspective" that helped them and the staff think about the

(Continued)

(Continued)

school in all its interrelated elements. This perspective helped guide the process of continuous improvement toward aspects of organization that "mattered," look for places to work that might have the most impact on the whole system, and develop organizational structures and resources to support and sustain the Cycle of Inquiry. In addition, school leaders successfully leveraged human and financial resources from II/UPS and BASRC and by virtue of its Title 1 designation. It invested these resources heavily in collaborative inquiry and in the implementation of teacher professional-development activity and instructional changes generated by it.

Finally and importantly, the principal, other school leaders, and teachers were guided by a clear vision and set of core values—all students are capable learners, and all teachers, with the right guidance and assistance, can help their students succeed. Leadership kept this message and the concomitant issue of equity "on the front burner." Through the Cycle of Inquiry and through professional development, leaders worked to develop a "culture of awareness and understanding," an ever-deepening sense of who their students are, the circumstances of their lives, what they need, and the impact of race and institutional racism. From this awareness and ongoing inquiry, teachers recognized the resources and experiences that students bring with them to school and can capitalize on this in their teaching. And out of this recognition came continuous examination by teachers of their own assumptions and biases regarding students, race, and racism.

Shilling was selected by BASRC for its report because it represented a "success story." It was a Title 1 school whose participation in II/USP and BASRC set in motion a number of "promising practices" that school staff claimed resulted in significant gains in student achievement. Shilling successfully fulfilled the student performance requirements of the II/USP program, making gains that went well beyond the program's annual growth targets. During the period covered by the case study, Shilling made constant improvement on the California State Academic Performance Index (API). API is a combination of scores from norm-referenced tests and the California Standards Tests (CST). Between 2000 and 2003, schoolwide API scores rose by 44 points (scale ranging from 200 to 1,000). API scores for Hispanic and/or Latino students rose by 51 points, and scores for low-income students rose by 38 points. Shilling's third grade performed particularly well, moving to the top 10 highest performing grade levels on the 2003 CST language arts assessment of 979 California elementary schools with similar demographic characteristics.

WILL ROGERS ELEMENTARY SCHOOL

The second vignette, Will Rogers Elementary School, was drawn from the PhD dissertation research of Laura M. Stokes (1999), conducted under the auspices of the Center for Research on the Context of Learning at Stanford University. Stokes' research documented improvement work of Will Rogers during a five-year period between the 1993–1994 and 1997–1998 school years.

Like the vignette of Shilling Elementary School, this vignette illustrates the use of continuous improvement to (a) respond to external changes and pressures for improvement, (b) address the unmet needs of a school's student body, (c) illustrate the importance of having a specific process to guide its work and to develop organizational structures and capacities to support this process, and (d) show that developing the capacity for continuous improvement may take time. Like the first vignette, this vignette shows the importance of leadership to cultivate and manage the process of continuous improvement, the importance of data in that process, and the role of external supports to get the process of continuous improvement going.

Will Rogers Elementary School is a neighborhood school located in the Santa Monica-Malibu Unified School District in California. The school is located in a racially and economically diverse residential community. At the time of this study, Rogers enrolled about 700 students and larger percentages of students of color than average in the district. Of its students, 43% were Latino, 39% white, 15% African American, and 3% Asian-Pacific Islander and American Indian. Thirty-one percent were limited English proficient and half were eligible for free or reduced-price lunch. The annual student mobility rate was 10%.

In order to address persistently low levels of academic achievement among low-income and racial and ethnic minority students, Rogers sought and received a grant through California's SB 1274 Demonstration Project in School Restructuring. This statewide initiative promoted a practitioner inquiry-based approach to continuous school improvement. It provided $25 million each year between 1993 and 1997 to 144 elementary and secondary schools throughout the state. It also established the California Center for School Restructuring (CCSR) to oversee the initiative and provide guidance and oversight to participating schools. Rogers joined this project in 1992 with a planning grant and received annual implementation grants of $100,000 from 1993 through 1997. The school district provided additional funding through the Los Angeles Annenberg Metropolitan Project (LAAMP) to promote a parallel continuous improvement process at the school. Part of this Annenberg initiative was to build "systematic" inquiry into teachers' work through the development of voluntary inquiry groups.

An important part of continuous improvement at Rogers was a protocol of processes designed at the CCSR for schools receiving SB 1274 restructuring grants. The CCSR described the protocol as a "school-centered, organizational learning system built on authentic inquiry," rather than mere "show and tell." In performing the protocol, schools were to identify critical questions associated with student learning and present analyses of evidence, especially samples of student work, that demonstrate the extent to which all students in the school were achieving. The protocol also called for assessment of the inquiry process itself, asking schools to assess involvement of the school community in inquiry and in planning as a result of that inquiry. This protocol was the first of a number of "tools" that Rogers employed in establishing and implementing processes of continuous improvement.

Rogers' approach to continuous improvement evolved substantially from year to year. At the beginning, Rogers' principal envisioned a "whole-school process" of becoming an inquiry school. She believed, as did many of Rogers' teachers, that creating processes of inquiry at the school level was crucial to improving teaching and student learning at the classroom level. Between 1992 and 1994, with resources from the SB 1274 grant, the principal created organizational conditions to support inquiry and improvement processes. She established a new participatory governance council, which included teachers and parents, and revamped school decision-making processes to make them more teacher centered and consensus based. She created a "web of interdependent working groups" to drive programmatic changes in such areas as bilingual education and special education. Students and faculty were grouped into four

(Continued)

(Continued)

"houses" to create more intimate learning communities for students and professional communities for teachers. The school schedule was reorganized to provide 90 minutes each week for grade-level teacher teams to work on curriculum and for house groups to plan student activities. The principal established two three-day institutes, one "preservice" or before-the-school-year institute and one at mid-year, for inquiry-based planning and assessment. While much of these inquiry and continuous improvement processes were led by teachers, the principal played a quiet but crucial role in cultivating and managing them.

The first year of continuous improvement at Rogers was devoted more to identifying problems and priorities than to developing specific efforts to address them. That 1993–1994 school year, the institutes focused primarily on developing "essential questions" at the school level and assessing the status of the school with regard to those questions. The staff selected mathematics as its focus. The staff crafted five questions concerning student learning, instructional practice, and student assessment, which were then tied to specific goals for improvement. Between institutes, these questions were explored in grade-level teams, mostly during the 90-minute planning periods established by the principal.

Grade-level teams were charged with working from the essential questions to develop sub-questions of particular relevance to working with their own students. Pursuant to the CCSR protocol, they were charged with collecting and assessing student achievement data related to their sub-questions. Each team was allowed flexibility in this data collection and assessment process. However, each was required to collect and assess samples of student work. Some teachers were paid through the SB 1274 grant to serve as leaders of team-level inquiry. This first year, the mid-year institute was used largely for teams to work separately, to discuss their own findings rather than to share and discuss them with other teams or with the entire school. This first year, team findings were much of the "show-and-tell" variety, highlighting successes, with little critical self-analysis and little attention to problems and areas in need of improvement.

While not what the protocol envisioned, the principal saw this as an important first step. She understood that there was a learning curve and that this "floundering" first year would lay a foundation for development of the process in years to come. The principal and teachers agreed that they were learning a great deal about the process of inquiry, about being open and self-critical, and about the time it takes to achieve change. In the process, the staff learned something about their students' learning in mathematics and identified as a problem the lack of curricular coherence in the subject across grade levels. The staff also learned that it was literacy not mathematics that was the most important issue to address for the next few years.

At the preservice institute before the next school year, the staff identified three essential questions concerning literacy. Teachers also began to create additional assessment tools and rubrics that would generate better evidence for inquiry, including "running records" of student learning as well as their own self-designed tests of student reading comprehension and writing. Their intention was to create tools that would provide measures of student learning and direction for improving teaching practice and the school's instructional program.

That year's mid-year institute showed progress from the previous year's inquiry processes. Most team findings had advanced from show-and-tell to more critical and analytic assessments of student learning and instructional practices. At the same time, reports highlighted several issues about the protocol that required attention. Among them were differences in teachers' willingness and ability to assemble running records of student learning and the school's capacity to manage all the data that were generated at the team level. After the mid-year institute, one teacher developed a schoolwide computerized system to manage running records data. By late spring, with peer and principal encouragement and with opportunities for professional development, most teachers had completed running records for all their students. By the end of the year, the school printed for the faculty all students' running record scores for the year with students' and teachers' names removed. This made the data "real, concrete, urgent, and scary." These data demonstrated that not all students were reading as well as many teachers had assumed, and they had a much greater impact on the faculty than grade-level data. It was an occasion that spurred evolution of the inquiry process. It led to schoolwide development of student learning standards, achievement benchmarks for each grade level, and a more systematic set of assessments to create a more coherent picture of achievement across the school.

Also, during this second year, the school district joined LAAMP and launched its own inquiry-based reform project. This initiative was to begin with small groups of volunteers at each school throughout the district. These groups were expected to meet several times a month to study subjects that they thought were important to their own school's improvement. They were to be supported by a "critical friend," an external facilitator paid for by the district. There were no specific expectations for data collection or reporting. A small group of teachers at Rogers volunteered for this work and used the resources that accompanied it to support what they were already doing related to the SB 1274 process. The district provided LAAMP funding for a second inquiry group the next year. These groups' activities revolved primarily around reflective conversation about problematic topics. They functioned more as a forum for exchanging ideas than as platforms for systematic inquiry and planning. Still, because some teachers participated both in the LAAMP groups and the school-level inquiry and improvement process, the two likely informed each other.

By the third year of the initiative, Rogers had made substantial progress developing its capacity for collective inquiry into student learning. The school had developed the technical ability to collect and analyze a variety of student achievement data. At that year's preservice institute, discussion of the school's essential questions was grounded in data from the previous year. The school decided to narrow its focus for the year on student reading comprehension and worked to ensure that all grade levels had a shared focus for their inquiry in that area. Data from the previous year revealed racial differences in student achievement, especially gaps between African American students and other students at each grade level. The school decided to disaggregate the data further to better understand the problem. A handful of teachers formed their own inquiry group to study underlying patterns of literacy development among Latino students.

The mid-year institute that third year marked another step in the development of whole-school inquiry and continuous improvement. It was the first time that Rogers elevated grade-level team inquiry to a full school-level analysis. Each team presented its findings to the entire staff for discussion rather than only discuss them within the team. The team interested in investigating achievement among Latinos decided to augment its data collection with student

(Continued)

(Continued)

interviews. Coupled with data showing racial disparities in academic achievement, the student voice "galvanized" the faculty's attention on a school-level problem that could not be dismissed. As a result, issues of race and equity began "moving to center stage." This led to new inquiry and discussion after the mid-year institute on inequities in learning opportunities and achievement.

By the fourth year of this effort, three strands of inquiry were operating concurrently. Most teachers were participating in at least one strand. One strand was the whole-school inquiry and improvement process and another consisted of the district's LAAMP inquiry groups. As the school-level process became more efficient and institutionalized as the "normal way of doing business," a third strand emerged—small ad hoc groups of teachers assembled around self-initiated studies to explore issues in-depth. At the same time that school-level inquiry and improvement processes became routinized, these ad hoc groups added a new layer of inquiry. At the school-level teachers began to believe that the house system established before the introduction of these inquiry processes had become a way to segregate students and perpetuate performance differences among them. At the mid-year institute that year, the faculty voted to "deconstruct" the house system. The principal and teachers also began to refocus the year's essential questions around school and classroom change consistent with the notion of anti-racist pedagogy. The idiosyncratic nature of the ad hoc inquiry groups produced a spate of initiatives, including student engagement surveys and processes for more systematic teacher self-assessment.

The SB 1274 grant expired at the end of the fourth year, but Rogers' staff remained committed to continuing the school-level inquiry and improvement process. A number of activities paid for with SB1274 funds, including teacher inquiry leaders, were covered by new funds acquired by the principal. The LAAMP inquiry groups continued as did the small ad hoc teacher inquiry groups. In the fifth year of the effort and the last year of the case study, the school decided at its preservice institute that with its efforts well underway to improve literacy teaching and learning, it should return to its earlier focus on mathematics. After that preservice institute, the school continued to collect and analyze data on literacy instruction and student learning and began systematic assessment of the math program. Grade-level teams continued to develop their capacity for inquiry, although one or two wrestled with internal problems, mostly concerning working relationships among team members. On the basis of this assessment of the math program, teachers began to develop benchmarks and new student assessments for math learning, a process that extended well into the school year. A small group of teachers developed a supplemental math program to assist struggling students and two-thirds of the faculty volunteered to participate in a new teacher-initiated mentor-buddy system to help low-performing students. Another teacher voluntarily taught an evening computer skills class to parents.

These three strands created a variety of opportunities for school, group, and individual learning and continuous improvement. School-level inquiry processes provided the opportunity for learning about and defining broad problems and established a forum for developing schoolwide initiatives to address them. Grade-level teams and small inquiry groups supported individual learning and improvement in a way that the school-level processes could not. They also provided informal contexts for the "incubation" of innovative ideas and practices.

At the same time, implementing these processes created a number of organizational challenges. In this last year of the case study, the amount of time and energy that teachers spent engaged in school-level improvement processes, notably the work on literacy and mathematics, limited their ability to engage in smaller ad hoc projects. The level of inquiry work at school and small group levels presented other tradeoffs too. For some teachers the time required to participate in inquiry activity took time away from teaching and from working with other teachers on matters that did not pertain directly to inquiry and improvement processes. Ironically, the processes of inquiry themselves began to eat away at the time needed to develop and implement responses to the findings of inquiry.

The case study of Will Rogers Elementary School did not set out to analyze systematically the outcomes of continuous improvement at the school but rather its implementation. Still, the study reported that internal school assessments revealed gains in student achievement across grade levels, especially during the fourth and fifth years. In the fifth year, disaggregations of achievement data by race revealed that achievement gaps were beginning to narrow. According to the case study, by engaging in these processes of inquiry and continuous improvement, teachers had become more improvement oriented and had developed greater capacity for change. The staff had developed an ability to identify problems to address and new technical skills of inquiry. It had learned to better manage conflict and to extend inquiry beyond "finding answers" to identifying new problems and opportunities. It had begun to embed inquiry processes into school routines. In addition, the case study found that in the minds of staff members, the knowledge gained from their own systematic inquiry seemed more valid and valuable than knowledge available to them from other sources.

GUSTAV FRITSCHE MIDDLE SCHOOL

The third vignette, developed from one of several case studies of National School Change Award winners, is of Gustav Fritsche Middle School. This collection was developed by Lew Smith and is contained in his recent book *Schools That Change* (2008). Smith's case of Fritsche Middle School covers a 12-year period from 1988 to 2000.

This vignette tells the story of how a school used continuous improvement as a transformational response to external demands for improvement. It illustrates (a) the crucial role of the principal to create a context for, to initiate, and to guide the early stages of continuous improvement; (b) the need for faculty commitment to continuous improvement and the importance of developing collaborative working relationships among members of the school community; and (c) with emphasis, the importance of establishing a focus on improving student learning and the importance of data and inquiry to guide action. This vignette also points to the role of external support for continuous improvement, particularly the support from the central office.

Gustav Fritsche Middle School is located in Milwaukee, Wisconsin. In 2001, the end of the period of the case study, Fritsche enrolled about 1,040 students in the sixth through eighth grades. Student enrollment was about 37% African American, 16% Latino, 40% white, 4% Asian American, and 3% other races and ethnicities. Although not reported in the case, the school's

(Continued)

(Continued)

Web site indicates that about two-thirds of students were eligible for participation in the federal government's free and reduced-price lunch program. In addition, about 6% of students were classified as ELL, and 17% were classified as special education.

In the 1970s, Fritsche Middle School had been one of the better schools in Milwaukee, but in the 1980s, it had become one of the worst. It was not a place where teachers wanted to work. The building was dirty and unkempt. Students roamed the halls doing what they pleased. Fights were common, and the school was considered unsafe. There were neither rules nor anyone willing to enforce any that might be suggested. The principal was barely visible. His office door was usually closed, and he was virtually unknown to students. It was "every staff member for herself or himself." Teachers did not work together, and many did not even like each other. Cliques reigned, staff meetings were few and far between, and when they did occur, there was little in the way of meaningful discussion or exchange of ideas. With safety and survival such great concerns, student achievement was not given much attention.

The coming of continuous improvement to Fritsche was gradual and incremental. It began with the appointment of a new principal in 1988, who was described by the faculty as "a go-getter; very driven; a constant learner; and a good listener, open to suggestions." He was seen as both creative in his thinking and crafty in getting people to try new things. At the same time, he knew what he wanted to accomplish for the school, and as one teacher stated, "Won't be pushed aside."

The new principal embodied the organizational improvement principles and processes he would end up promoting in the school. He was forward thinking and would continually question the status quo with simple questions such as, "Why does it have to be this way?" He continually sought out opportunities to learn something new and generate information to help the school move forward. He crafted and promoted a clear set of values and goals for renewing the school to become one of the best middle schools in Milwaukee, to make Fritsche as good as the three "highly lauded," open enrollment middle schools in the district that were known for their superior image and high academic achievement. He announced that in five years, Fritsche was going to be recognized as a National Blue Ribbon school. "Blue ribbon" became the school's rallying cry. From his first day, the principal challenged and encouraged teachers and students to improve continuously. "Blue ribbon" and a "we can do it" message became his mantras. From his first day, the principal began to develop the organizational capacity of the school for introducing ongoing processes of improvement.

The principal sought to engender ownership and confidence in his staff and in the student body to improve. He placed responsibility for the school and its performance directly on their shoulders. The school was not something that existed apart from them. What the school was and how it performed reflected directly on them. At the same time that he increased the pressure, the principal increased the support. He reversed course of earlier principals and made himself accessible to all. He adopted a nickname that was easier to remember and pronounce than his lengthy Greek name. He worked to reshape the school's climate by never staying in his office, by developing a system of student discipline, and by increasing administrative support of teachers to implement that system. He began to shift the school's stance from being reactive to problems to being proactive to take advantage of new ideas and opportunities. Finally, he worked hard to develop trust among administration, teachers, and students. Even small efforts, such as buying students alarm clocks to help them get to school on time, were meant to communicate the message that "we care" that you work at and attend this school, and we want you to succeed.

As "promised," after the principal's first five years, the school applied for blue ribbon recognition. While praised at the state level, Fritsche failed to secure the national award. On the foundation laid, the staff was able to join the principal to ask "why" and to pursue an answer collectively. Through joint effort, the principal and staff identified three areas that needed to be addressed. While the school had done much to reestablish order and safety and to create a welcoming and supportive environment, the quality of classroom instruction had not changed substantially, and student academic achievement remained "flat," lagging behind many other Milwaukee middle schools. While the principal had served as a dynamic change leader, little had been done to develop leadership more broadly across the school organization. Through additional inquiry led by the principal, the school moved further toward becoming what he had learned from the corporate literature to be a "learning organization," to develop and institutionalize processes of continuous improvement.

An important next step in this direction came as Fritsche began to adopt a number of "exemplary" middle school practices, including student advisories, integrated curricula, block scheduling, peer mediation, and looping—a practice of keeping students and teachers together for several years. The move toward block scheduling demonstrated further emergence of continuous improvement. In spring of 1995, the principal initiated the idea of block scheduling by putting an article on the subject in mailboxes of the entire faculty, and then he waited to see who might "take the bait." A team of teachers came forward to try it. This launched an action research project that selected a group of students to have a different schedule with longer teaching blocks in the core academic subjects—mathematics, science, social studies, and English. Data were collected to assess classroom teaching practices and to compare this pilot group with a "control" group of students that remained on the regular school schedule. These teachers found that block scheduling provided them time to develop new instructional strategies and classroom activities that were more engaging and exciting for students. Students in the pilot group out-performed other students on all internal and external assessments and they testified positively about their new learning experiences. The principal had teachers in the pilot project present their findings to the rest of the staff, and upon hearing them, more teachers stepped forward to try block scheduling. In spring 1996, the faculty voted to implement schoolwide block scheduling the following fall. Fritsche's process for continuous improvement had fully emerged: "Learn something new, gather research about its effectiveness, pilot it, assess the results . . . , and make adjustments as needed."

In the following years, this cycle of improvement played out in several ways. During the 1996–1997 school year, teachers experimented with different physical configurations of classrooms, the inclusion of special education students began, and teachers created a professional development agenda focused on curriculum integration and cooperative learning. After studying the first year of schoolwide implementation, teachers decided to continue block scheduling for another three years. The next year, data collection, study, and deliberation refocused teachers' professional development agenda on issues of problem based-learning and Socratic teaching methods (the focus on cooperative learning continued). Also that year, the special education inclusion initiative was evaluated. In addition, several teachers brought the idea of looping to the principal's attention, and the principal told them to find out more. The process began again. Looping was investigated in 1997, piloted in 1998, and adopted for the

(Continued)

(Continued)

entire sixth and seventh grades in 1999. Gradually through these various initiatives, the entire staff was brought into this participative, collaborative change process.

By 2000, the principal and staff at Fritsche had developed the organizational structures, capacities, and methods of continuous improvement and had employed them to turn the school into one that mirrored many middle school reforms. The school's three grade levels were reorganized into house structures. Each house was organized into teams that created small learning communities for teachers and students. Each house was organized heterogeneously to include gifted, academically at-risk, and special education students. The school day ran according to a block schedule of extended class periods, integrated curricula, thematic units, and problem-based learning.

This progress was not enough. The principal became increasingly frustrated in his relationship with the school district's central office over resources he thought were needed for the school. After winning "many battles, but weary of the continuous struggle," the principal introduced the idea to his assistant principals of becoming one of Wisconsin's first public charter schools. Given the circumstances with the central office, going charter seemed to be the "next logical step" of continuous improvement. In 1999, after volunteering his time to help the state develop a version of charter legislation that could gain passage politically, the principal was at the point of being able to submit Fritsch's application to become a charter school. The state required that half of a school's staff sign a petition declaring an intention to become a public charter school. Three-quarters of Fritsch's staff signed. The last step required by law was to obtain approval from the Milwaukee school board. After overcoming several hurdles and after a timely election that placed more persons sympathetic to charter schools on the board, Fritsch's charter application was approved by the board and then the state.

Becoming a charter school was an important chapter in this school's story for several reasons. First, charter status gave the school more latitude in its improvement processes, program development, staff, and budget. Second, the school was able to lever additional funding directly from the state rather than be dependent solely on district revenues. Third, the process served to unite further the school's administration, staff, parents, and community members in a common cause. It also set the stage for another step in the school's improvement process.

One particularly relevant part of Fritsche's charter application was a commitment to total quality management. This meant more systematic emphasis on processes of continuous data collection, analysis, and use of data in decision making at both classroom and school levels. Spurred on by the principal, who with a number of teachers had visited schools outside of Wisconsin that were successfully implementing these processes, the faculty was encouraged to engage in constant assessment of student progress and use these assessments to drive instructional improvement.

This part of the story is told in the case study through the example of "the best mathematics teacher in the school and perhaps the district." Despite being recognized for teaching excellence, the principal directly challenged this teacher to do even better. He described the data-driven processes he wished to promote, and she accepted the challenge. In the two years that followed, this teacher concentrated on constant assessment of her students' progress. Through the information and insights that these assessments provided, she added to her teaching repertoire methods that were more responsive to her students and more effective in promoting student learning. As an expression of his commitment to improvement, the principal visited this teacher's classroom frequently and discussed with her what he observed. They discussed what student assessments could reveal about this teacher's teaching and her students' learning. The result of the challenge to do better, the introduction of more systematic ways of generating information about teaching and learning, and guided support for improvement was a change from what the principal characterized as a good classroom to a high-performing one.

During this period, student achievement rose substantially at Fritsche. In 1996, only 39% of eighth graders read at or above grade level. In math, the figure was 38%, in science 34%, and in social studies 36%. Four years later, these percentages had risen by at least 10 points in each subject. The proportion of students performing at or above grade level in reading had risen to 51%, in math to 63%, in science to 48%, and in social studies to 49%. The proportion of eighth graders performing at or above grade level in math had risen to three times the district average. Fritsche's sixth graders outperformed other sixth graders in the Milwaukee school district on average by two times in writing and four times in mathematics.

Teachers' perceptions of the school also changed substantially. By 2000, most felt that they had "a new school." They saw Fritsche as a learning community, a place where change was encouraged and supported. They felt respected and perceived a new sense of unity, a common purpose. As one teacher put it, "You felt good to be a member of the Fritsche team." Parents and students echoed this positive perspective about the school and exuded a sense of excitement about its future.

BLUE MOUNTAIN HIGH SCHOOL

The fourth vignette is of Blue Mountain High School. This vignette was developed from the more extensive case study of the school by Andy Hargreaves and Corrie Giles that was published first in Hargreaves' book *Teaching in the Knowledge Society* (2003) and in a subsequent article by Giles and Hargreaves (2006). Their case of Blue Mountain covers roughly an eight-year period from 1994 through early 2000s.

This vignette tells the story of a newly created school focused on student and adult learning and designed for organizational learning and continuous improvement. This vignette (a) illustrates how continuous improvement can be used by a school to respond to its community and to manage the challenges of externally mandated accountability reforms, (b) highlights organizational processes and structures that support organizational learning and continuous improvement, (c) reflects the role of data and assessments in promoting student learning and the importance of focusing continuous improvement on developing school-level organizational conditions conducive to improving instruction and student learning, and (d) shows the importance of whole-school involvement in continuous improvement and the importance of focusing continuous improvement on itself in order to make it a more effective process.

Blue Mountain High School is located in a middle- to upper-middle income community in Ontario, Canada. It is a relatively new school, opening its doors in 1994 to about 620 students in Grades 9 through 13. With space for twice that enrollment, Blue Mountain projected growth

(Continued)

(Continued)

by an average of 100 students a year until it reached capacity. Of the students who attended Blue Mountain, 30% were nonwhite, minority students, predominantly of East Indian descent.

Blue Mountain was planned from the start to be a learning organization, with systems thinking and continuous improvement permeating almost everything. The force that drove the school's development and operation was a vision of the school as a community that put the student and high-quality life-long learning at the center. According to a teacher interviewed for the case study, "[A]11 that matters [at this school] is the student." Students and student learning were put at the center of a professional community that emphasized adult learning, involvement of all staff members in defining and working toward the school's goals for student learning, and continuous improvement to build the school's capacity for achieving these goals.

This vision was supported by a system of norms and expectations. Central to this system was an ethic of care that emphasized reciprocal nurturing and mutual responsibility. This ethic applied to relationships of teachers, administrators, and other staff members with students. It also applied to relationships among adults in the school. This ethic was the "emotional glue" to hold the school together. Related to it were expectations for continuous and self-renewing adult learning, collaboration, inquiry, and joint problem solving. Teachers were expected to work hard; to be creative, take risks, and experiment with new ideas; and to be innovative in their teaching to engage students more effectively in learning. Blue Mountain also expected teachers to understand the "big picture" of the school, its problems and opportunities, and what it was trying to accomplish. Teachers were expected to contribute at the school level and were given the freedom and encouragement to look for problems wherever in the school they might be and to suggest and follow-through on possible solutions.

The vision for the school was enacted through a multilevel system of teams, structurally interconnected and focused on the school's goals for student learning. This system was the "enabling structure" for organizational learning and continuous improvement. It was created to support and institutionalize inquiry, goal-setting, problem-solving, and improvement processes and to help the school "survive" inevitable turnover in the principalship. The district had a policy of rotating principals among schools every six years or so. The system of teams was designed to provide teachers with schoolwide perspectives on issues and to prevent "compartmentalization" of teacher learning and improvement within departments or other substructures. The system was designed to enhance communication and the flow of information across the school so that all staff members could see the "big picture" and be more aware of the likely consequences of individual preferences and actions for the whole-school community. Moreover, these teams were designed to involve the whole school in learning and continuous improvement processes.

This system was composed of six types of teams. Some were "standing" teams and others were "ad hoc" teams. The "driving force" behind continuous improvement at Blue Mountain were Key Process Teams. These teams were the primary forums for inquiry, planning, and decision making; teacher professional development; and adult learning at the school. Each team focused on a particular issue of concern to the school as a whole, such as curriculum, student assessment and evaluation, school climate and morale, and so forth. They met at least once a month and were led by teacher members. They received guidance from and were to report to a Leadership Team (described later). The number of Key Process Teams varied over the years of the case study, fluctuating between 10 and four, depending on the issues at hand. Regardless of the number of teams operating at any one time, all teachers at Blue Mountain were required to be members of at least one Key Process Team.

A Leadership Team played a central role in cultivating and reinforcing the school's vision and in setting and maintaining the strategic direction of the school. This committee was composed of the principal, the vice principal, the teacher heads of the Key Process Teams, and two student representatives. The Leadership Team identified problems and opportunities presented to the school. It monitored learning and continuous improvement processes across the system of teams. It was a communications hub for other teams and for the school as a whole. The Leadership Team identified issues and priorities for Key Process Teams and Management Teams (described later) to engage. It also weighed policy and programmatic alternatives generated by these teams.

A third type of team was Management Teams. These teams were temporary and "event-driven." Their membership was composed of volunteers from the school's staff, and perhaps parents and students, who might have particular interest or experience in the task at hand. These teams were to implement specific tasks that emerged from the Key Process Teams or the Leadership Team. They were also responsible for planning and organizing the "predictable rituals and ceremonies" that took place during the school year, such as commencement.

In addition to these three types of teams was a School Advisory Council. This council was established prior to the school's opening and was instrumental in designing the school building and creating the vision for the school. Its members consisted of the principal, teachers, parents, and community members. The Council served as a formal link between the school and the community and an extended source of accountable for the school. It could advocate in the community and at the school district on behalf of the school. And it could monitor the work of the school and its achievement of student learning goals.

Another type of team at Blue Mountain was Subject Discipline Groups. While other teams focused at the school level and fostered cross-department and cross-curricular linkages, Subject Discipline Groups provided opportunities for teachers to engage in discipline-specific inquiry, planning, and development. They also provided opportunities for discipline-specific teacher learning and professional development. The work of these groups could inform school-level improvement efforts through Key Process Teams and the Leadership Team.

Blue Mountain also constituted other teams to address particular needs as they arose. For example, the school created a Professional Learning Committee to examine the implications of the implementation of legislated standards and accountability reforms on teachers' opportunities for professional learning and development.

Finally, there was a Student Parliament at Blue Mountain. This student governance group consisted of eight members elected at large from the student body and 50 additional student members from each teacher-student advisory group in the school. A teacher served as the Parliament's staff advisor. The Parliament, linked to the system of teams through the Leadership Team, met once a week and was charged with considering schoolwide issues before addressing other concerns. This focus kept students aware of the "big picture" and aware of the implications for the whole school of their recommendations and actions.

These teams supported a general system of organizational learning and continuous improvement. This system eschewed finding "quick-fix" answers to problems that might bring

(Continued)

(Continued)

superficial or short-term accomplishments. Instead, it focused on deeper, "sustainable" improvement in the school and in student learning. It was also intended to provide enactive learning experiences for teachers and other staff members to develop capabilities for continuous improvement.

Each year the staff engaged in a series of school-level assessments. These assessments focused on student learning and progress toward meeting student learning goals. They also focused on the school as an organization, processes of learning and inquiry, and how these processes and the organizational conditions of the school related to improvement and to the achievement of student learning goals. Data from these assessments were used for setting goals for student learning and for organizational improvement. They were also used for improving the effectiveness of teams and improvement processes themselves. These data were fed back to the entire school community. Student assessment data were computerized so that they could be shared regularly with faculty and parents. Both student and organizational assessment data became grist for Blue Mountain's Leadership Team in goal setting and providing direction to the planning and development work of Key Process Teams and Management Teams.

In addition to this process of schoolwide assessment, teachers made extensive use of alternative student assessments for their particular subject areas and at their particular grade levels. These alternative assessments were likely to be developed by the teachers themselves. Variations of portfolio assessments and exhibitions were commonplace. These assessments provided information from the classroom and department levels that complemented and contextualized information from school-level assessments.

These processes were largely successful. The school established a series of seven collaboratively determined goals for student learning that it called "exit outcomes." These goals anchored the school's organizational learning and improvement activities. Soon after the school opened, it developed an initial curriculum model, pursuant of student learning goals. This model used themes of technology and globalism to integrate discipline-based subject matter. This initial effort led to others to integrate English and history curricula, math and science curricula, and construction (vocational studies) and community studies curricula in cross-disciplinary team teaching. Teachers experimented with sharing classes of 50 to 60 students, creating experiments with new ways to organize subject matter and new ways to teach. Teachers in business studies, in student guidance, and of special needs students developed an integrated approach to supporting students struggling to find a sense of direction at school and in their lives. Technology teachers collaborated with other teachers across curricular areas to design and build with students a house in the school's community. With a local university and a consultant from the school district office, the school experimented with a "global camp" that 10th-grade students could attend for week-long sessions. The camp was designed to expand student learning opportunities and help them see "the interconnectedness of everything we do."[23]

Part of the logic of continuous improvement is the ability to help organizations adapt productively to internal and external changes. Blue Mountain High School was able to engage productively with its community and to allay community concerns about its vision and improvement activity through the system of teams, especially the School Advisory Team. The system of teams and learning and improvement processes helped the school to socialize new staff members and prepare for leadership succession. By distributing the work of organizational *learning and school improvement through the system of teams, Blue Mountain was able to reduce its dependency on a few key leaders and change agents and increase the likelihood that its efforts would be sustained after these individuals were gone.*

The system of teams and processes also helped Blue Mountain manage the challenges of externally mandated, standardized accountability reforms, at least initially. One year after Blue Mountain opened, a newly elected provincial government centralized authority, stripped school districts of their ability to raise tax revenues locally, reduced district budgets, and introduced a centralized, subject-based curriculum and student testing program. The provincial government also passed legislation to increase teachers' time in the classroom to seven out of eight periods per day. On top of this, new austerity measures at the district level increased student enrollment at Blue Mountain beyond projections and reduced the size of the school's middle-level administrative staff. The number of counselors and teacher-librarians was also cut. These changes increased classroom and administrative responsibilities for teachers and reduced the amount of time they had to work together on teams and engage in learning and improvement activities.

The case study from which this vignette was drawn indicates that Blue Mountain was able to adapt to and buffer some of the demands of these external pressures. However, the case study raises the question of whether the degree of external pressures on the school would eventually overwhelm the school and, ironically, compromise its ability to function as a learning-and-continuously-improving organization. The authors of the case study point to substantial increases in teachers' workload and stress; loss of time that had previously been used for team work, learning, and continuous improvement; substantial pressure to revert to more conventional discipline-specific curricula; erosion of working relationships; and a "corrosion of caring" from increases in stress and threats to what the school had accomplished since its inception. The case study ends leaving open the question of sustainability.

SUMMARY

These four vignettes provide valuable insight into the practice of continuous improvement in schools and illustrate different ways in which the steps and the key qualities of continuous improvement processes discussed in Chapter 4 can manifest themselves in practice. They highlight a number of the organizational design elements discussed in Chapter 5 that support those processes.

Several themes can be seen across these vignettes. One theme is the primacy of student learning as a focal point and a driver for continuous improvement. These schools pursued a range of improvement objectives; however, most all of these objectives were directed in one way or another at improving student learning. Another theme is the systemic nature of continuous improvement. The stories of continuous improvement in these schools illustrate how over time process and organization can work together in mutually reinforcing manner. Instrumental to the success of continuous improvement in these schools was the adoption or development of explicit processes of continuous improvement and the important roles that inquiry, data, and learning played in those processes.

Yet another theme that can be seen is the function of continuous improvement as a whole-school property that is inclusive of persons across the school organization and that directs attention to any aspect of the school where improvement may be warranted. Principal leadership is a crucial element of each school's story. It is leadership that is strategic and that evolves even as leadership may be cultivated among teachers and diffused throughout the school as continuous improvement takes hold. What also comes across in these vignettes is the long, steady, and persistent work of principals, teachers, and other members of school communities that may be required in order for continuous improvement to take hold and be successful.

QUESTIONS FOR STUDY, REFLECTION, AND ACTION

1. In what ways does each vignette illustrate the following themes? Compare and contrast the vignettes on each theme. How does each theme relate to the success of continuous improvement in each school?

   - Student learning as a focal point and driver of continuous improvement
   - Integration of continuous improvement processes and organizational design
   - Continuous improvement as a whole-school endeavor
   - Principal leadership and leadership development across the school

2. How do each of these themes relate to each other in the vignettes? For example, how does the theme of *focus on student learning* relate to the theme of *leadership*? How does the theme of *integration of process and organizational design* relate to the theme of *continuous improvement as a whole-school endeavor*?

3. Imagine the next chapter of Blue Mountain High School in which the school not only sustains its progress but also pushes it even further. What might the storyline of this next chapter be? What specific actions might the school have taken to respond to the challenges it was facing and to sustain the work of continuous improvement?

4. Imagine a fifth vignette, one of your school embarking on continuous improvement. Compose this vignette as a success story that begins in the present and extends three to five years into the future. How would the story begin? How would it unfold? What would we see the principal, teachers, and others doing? What accomplishments would be evident?

5. If this fifth vignette is thought of as a vision of successful continuous improvement at your school, how close or how far away is your school from making this vision a reality? How would you explain the gap between the current reality and the reality expressed by the vision? What concrete steps might be taken to move from the current reality to the envisioned reality?

Becoming a Continuously Improving School

7

If you start me up. If you start me up, I'll never stop. Never stop, never, stop, never stop.

—Mick Jagger and Keith Richards, 1981

As we approach the end of this book, we come to two overarching questions. Should schools pursue continuous improvement? And if they pursue it, how might they do so successfully?

TO PURSUE CONTINUOUS IMPROVEMENT

Should schools pursue continuous improvement?

The short answer to the question is yes, they should. Schools now operate and will continue to operate in rapidly changing environments. The future they will face will be more uncertain and more demanding. The demographic, economic, and political terrains of schooling are shifting substantially at the same time that new demands for student learning and new accountability pressures are being placed on schools (see Chapter 1). These changes and challenges create new uncertainties for schools, not only about what the future will hold but also about what schools will need to do to address them. As they are currently organized and operated, most schools are unlikely to succeed in this future. Or at least it is unlikely that they will be much more effective than they are now. Thus, a compelling rationale exists for schools to develop the processes and organizational design elements for continuous improvement (see Chapter 2). Indeed, continuous improvement may be the most effective option now known for schools to be successful in this future.

Supporting this argument is accumulating evidence that continuous improvement or similar processes are instrumental to the long-term success of organizations, to long-term organizational improvement, and to the innovativeness of organizations in changing and uncertain environments (see Chapter 3). This evidence comes largely from studies of non-education organizations, including businesses and industries and also nonprofit organizations and public agencies. The evidence from studies of schools and school districts, while relatively sparse, is consistent with the broader evidence from non-education organizations. The similarity of empirical findings across organizational types (including schools) lends substantial support to the argument that continuous improvement can be effective for schools.

Of course, there are several arguments to the contrary. One argument is that continuous improvement is not for every organization. For some organizations, the changes that would be required to become continuously improving are not worth the financial and personnel costs (Lawler & Worley, 2006). Nor would the added value to performance be significant enough to justify the investment. Moreover, the argument goes, continuous improvement may best be reserved for organizations that operate in the most highly competitive, turbulent, and chaotic environments (Brown & Eisenhardt, 1998). The implication is that there may not be a compelling reason to pursue continuous improvement in organizations, like schools, that operate in changing and challenging environments but not in environments that are overly competitive and volatile nor where organizational survival is continually at stake. Applied to schools, this argument is shaky at best. While perhaps not as chaotic and fraught with the sorts of survival threats that other organizations experience, the changing demands, uncertainties, and pressures on schools seem only a matter of degree. Certainly, the stakes associated with the effective education of children and youth are high.

Another counter argument is that the very organizational tendencies that continuous improvement is supposed to overcome are simply too strong in schools for continuous improvement to take root and grow (see Chapter 3). These include inertial and isomorphic tendencies and tendencies toward stability and rigidity in the presence of risk, uncertainty, and external "threat." Yet another argument is that most schools lack leadership and the human, technical, and financial resources necessary to engage in continuous improvement successfully. Moreover, the argument goes, most schools lack the external support from district central offices, or they confront competing and conflicting policy pressures that act as countervailing and compromising forces. These arguments are supported by a number of studies that have examined why school engagement in self-initiated and self-directed improvement and innovation often fails (e.g., Giles & Hargreaves, 2006; Gordon, 1984; Smylie & Wenzel, 2003). These arguments are also shaky. The logic of continuous improvement and the preponderance of evidence indicate that continuous improvement may be the very approach needed to address such shortcomings in school organization and support. Returning to the general conclusion, continuous improvement is perhaps the best option we have now for developing schools organization to be effective in the future.

HOW CAN SCHOOLS BECOME CONTINUOUSLY IMPROVING ORGANIZATIONS?

If schools pursue continuous improvement, how might they go about it successfully? This is not an easy question to answer. Becoming a continuously improving organization is itself a complex and continuous organizational change process. First steps and good starts matter; for if initiated successfully, continuous improvement should build upon itself as a virtuous circle.

Unfortunately, the education literature gives little guidance on good beginnings. Nor does the literature on non-education organizations provide much help. These literatures focus primarily on what continuous improvement looks like or should look like when it is "up and running." They are largely descriptive of models and processes, their implementation and outcomes, and their organizational supports. Little documentation and analysis exist of how continuous improvement is introduced into schools or other organizations or what schools and other organizations do over time to remain continuously improving.

To complicate matters further, schools can take many routes to becoming continuously improving organizations (Burke, 2008). As Paul Light (1998) found in his study of nonprofit organizations, there is "no one true path" to continuous improvement and innovation (p. 238). David Hopkins (2001) also made this observation in his study of school reform. Because of differences in the contexts and in the capacities of schools when they begin improvement processes, there are likely to be many efficacious courses to follow. One particular way might be extremely successful in one school and may only partially successful or wholly unsuccessful in another—equifinality again.

Still, several sources provide insight into how schools might get started to become continuously improving organizations. One source is the collection of vignettes of continuously improving schools presented in Chapter 6. We can also turn back to several works on non-education organizations discussed in earlier chapters that speak specifically to the development of continuous improvement.

Insights From the Vignettes

Each of the four vignettes presented in Chapter 6 describes a school in the process of becoming and operating as a continuously improving organization. Looking across these vignettes, several themes emerge. First, in each vignette, the move toward continuous improvement was triggered by some force, some "dissonance," some impetus from inside or outside the school. For Shilling Elementary School and Will Rogers Elementary School, the impetus came from external accountability systems and placement of these schools in state "remediation" programs. These two schools also found themselves participants in school reform networks that provided additional impetus and accountability for pursuing continuous improvement. For Gustav Fritsche Middle School, the impetus came from the district central office and a new principal who was directed to "turn the school around." For Blue Mountain High School, a newly developed school, the impetus came from the philosophy of strong founding leadership and the development of an organizational culture with continuous learning and improvement at its core.

Second, each school adopted and organized around an explicit and systematic process or "technology" for continuous improvement. While these schools may have phased in these processes over time, a theme discussed later, their attention to process was deliberate and strategic. While schools adapted them along the way, these processes were not ad hoc or "process produced" (i.e., made up as they went along). Moreover, the process adopted by each school reflected many of the essential elements and key qualities outlined in Chapter 4. Shilling Elementary organized around the Cycle of Inquiry that was developed and promoted by the Bay Area School Reform Collaborative (BASRC), the reform network of which it was a member. Rogers Elementary used the process protocol developed by the California Center for School Restructuring (CCSR) and supported by the Los Angeles Annenberg Metropolitan Project (LAAMP), the school reform network of which Rogers was a member. The processes used by both Fritsche and Blue Mountain were "home grown," developed by each school's leadership. However, each was explicit, systematic, and grounded in leadership's understandings of processes of goal setting, problem solving, organizational inquiry, and organizational improvement.

A third theme that is evident in these vignettes is that these schools embarked on the road to continuous improvement gradually, in incremental steps that could be supported by their organizational capabilities at the time but that also pressed them forward. Each of these schools "ramped up" to continuous improvement through the learning, motivation, and momentum derived from "small wins." These schools "grew" continuous improvement from small-group activity to an organization-wide enterprise. They trained their efforts first on "easier" problems and graduated to "tougher" ones. These were incremental build-ups, snowball processes, whereby engagement in continuous improvement could be developed and sustained through strategic expansion of involvement by teachers and other members of the school community. At Shilling and Rogers, continuous improvement began within grade levels and then was extended across grade levels and to the whole school. Rogers proceeded in like manner. It moved from less to more systematic data collection and inquiry and from "show and tell" to critical self-analysis. At Fritsche, the foci of continuous improvement developed from less threatening noninstructional issues to more difficult issues of classroom instruction and student learning. Because Blue Mountain was a new school founded on principles of continuous learning and improvement, there was less need for gradual development than in the other schools.

A fourth theme is the importance of school administrative leadership, particularly the school principal. Although the processes of continuous improvement and the organizational elements to support them rely ideally on the "leadership work" of many in the school, the role of principals in developing and sustaining continuous improvement is crucial (see Chapter 5). These vignettes illustrate the importance of the principal in establishing, communicating, and sustaining a vision for the school grounded in the concept of continuous improvement and guided by a mission and core values concerning student learning. In large part by these principals' hands, continuous improvement processes were initiated, and the imperatives for them were communicated. As more and more teachers and others became involved in the work and leadership of continuous improvement, these principals adapted their roles accordingly to manage the process strategically over time. Indeed, whether directive initially or facilitative as the process became established, these principals acted as stewards of continuous improvement.

In addition, the principals in these vignettes worked to develop their schools' capacities for continuous improvement, from developing structures (e.g., teams); to allocating time, obtaining resources, and creating opportunities for the work of continuous improvement; to developing the knowledge and skills of teachers and others to perform this work; to developing data capacity for the inquiry that drives continuous improvement (see Chapter 5). These principals continuously monitored the processes of continuous improvement and the internal capacities of their schools to engage those processes successfully. Finally, these principals worked the boundaries and the external environments of their schools, cultivating external support for continuous improvement from the central office and buffering fledgling processes of continuous improvement from external threats.

A fifth theme that emerges from the vignettes is that for most of these schools, continuous improvement focused on more than improving educational practices and student outcomes. A focus on student learning was central to the mission and core value in each. But these processes were also focused on improving school organizational capacity for future improvement. Directly or indirectly, these schools built organizational capacity for continuous improvement through continuous improvement. At Shilling, initial continuous improvement activity was used to identify needs for teacher professional development and the need to develop different aspects of school organization to sustain the inquiry cycle and support the implementation of new programs and practices that would be generated by it. At Rogers and Blue Mountain, continuous improvement was used to develop systems of student assessment and sources of student data that would become part of the organizational infrastructure to support future inquiry and improvement. In all the vignettes, engaging successfully in processes of continuous improvement built organizational capacity for ongoing improvement by promoting cultures of collaboration, inquiry, and problem solving. In various ways, the process of continuous improvement in each school was turned on itself to further develop and enhance its effectiveness in the future.

Lessons From the Literature

In addition to these vignettes of schools, there are several pieces of literature on non-education organizations discussed in earlier chapters that provide lessons on becoming a continuously improving school. One of these is Light's (1998) study of nonprofits and government agencies. These were organizations for which continuous improvement and innovation had become "ordinary practice." According to Light, these organizations became and sustained themselves as continuously innovating by mixing, matching, and developing preferred states of organizational being as needed. They did not follow one script but instead drew on "a broad inventory" of preferences as they designed themselves and operated over time. Recall from Chapter 5 that these preferences included a "stay thin" organizational design that minimized layers of management, use of self-managed teams, decentralized decision making, and organization-wide communication. They also included development of structural opportunities for experimentation and evaluation of new ideas and establishment of a reward system to encourage risk taking. These organizations committed themselves to developing diverse workforces that would provide a range of perspectives that in turn would increase the odds of generating new ideas for improvement and innovation. Light also identified a number of leadership practices that were instrumental in developing these organizations as continuously improving and innovating. These practices included continuous cultivation of organizational mission and core values and the institution of rigorous management systems and organizational cultures to support continuous improvement and innovation over time.

While largely idiosyncratic in how they established themselves as continuously improving and innovating, there were some common elements. These organizations were in "absolute agreement" that the starting point for continuous improvement and innovation is to "ask hard questions and [give] honest answers about why the organization exists, whom it serves, and how it will know if it is succeeding" (Light, 1998, p. 60). In addition, from the very beginning, organizations need to establish effective management systems to monitor and control the financial and operational elements of the organization and to monitor the environment. Continuous improvement and innovation depend on solid management systems, and organizations cannot succeed at either if they are wrestling with getting basic operations right.

A second common element is that no substitute exists for the organizing power of the core mission of the organization. From the beginning, these organizations used their core missions to drive improvement and innovation. They could measure outcomes and progress because they knew the outcomes they were pursuing and they knew the organizational values that would guide the pursuit. They could celebrate success because they knew when it occurred and they could make corrections when it did not.

A third common element was that these organizations strategically and proactively engaged their environments. If markets for these organizations did not exist, they were created. If markets existed, they were "harnessed as a lever" for improvement and innovation (Light, 1998, p. 255). To become and sustain themselves as continuously improving and innovating, these organizations had to actively monitor, manage, and cultivate their environments. They could not sustain improvement and innovation if they were passive or merely reactive to them.

A fourth element was that at the same time that they built strong management systems and engaged their environments, these organizations took "a few simple steps to increase the odds that acts of innovation [would] occur and endure" (Light, 1998, p. 255). Among these steps were removing barriers to internal collaboration among staff members and external collaboration with other organizations, providing time and space for experimentation, and creating an expectation for continually developing new ideas. These organizations worked from the beginning to establish faith as a core value for sustaining innovativeness. Light observed, "There is simply no way to persevere in the face of the stress and uncertainty associated with true innovation without faith in something larger than oneself" (p. 256). The same might be said for establishing and sustaining continuous improvement.

John Bessant and David Francis (1999) made a number of similar observations from studies of British and Japanese industries conducted through the Centre for Research in Innovation Management at the University of Brighton in the United Kingdom. Like the nonprofits and government agencies in Light's (1998) study, these industries began their movement toward continuous improvement by establishing a strategic focus. They made a concerted effort to "learn" how to become continuously improving, using systematic training programs to develop and "embed" key organizational behaviors conducive to continuous improvement. They provided training in problem-finding and problem-solving processes and in specific continuous improvement processes and techniques.

These companies also established structures and processes to support continuous improvement, such as quality circles and teams. They set up management systems to receive and respond to ideas developed throughout the organization. And they developed reward systems to recognize and reinforce improvement. In addition, these companies developed "innovation routines" that communicated expectations and provided opportunities for experimentation, trial-and-error learning, and risk taking. Finally, they established formal monitoring systems to assess and improve their continuous improvement processes. These consisted of various measurement and feedback systems that created opportunities for "generative learning" that contributed to the long-term development of continuous improvement capability (Light, 1998, p. 1109).

Finally, we can look to Edward Lawler III and Christopher Worley's (2006) analysis of the b2change organization. A crucial part of their work focuses on answering the question, "How can you change a traditional organization into a b2change organization?" (p. 285). Drawing on examples from various companies successfully engaged in continuous improvement, Lawler and Worley argue that becoming a b2change organization involves five key initiatives. These initiatives are discussed later in the order in which Lawler and Worley believe they should be implemented.

The first initiative is to "create a change-friendly identity" for the organization (Lawler & Worley, 2006, p. 290). This means reframing the organization's identity from one based on stability to one focused on changes in the environment and on the belief that change is a natural, necessary, desirable, and even "friendly" property of the organization. The second initiative is to "pursue proximity" with the environment (p. 293). Because long-term performance depends on how effectively an organization addresses current and future demands from the environment, it must be positioned and have the capacity to continuously anticipate and identify those demands. So early on, organizations must develop inquiry and strategic planning capabilities. They need to develop processes, such as structured conversations, to think about and to "play" with alternative futures (note the plural), and to picture and create "a wide range of possible environmental success paths" (p. 295).

A third initiative is to "build an orchestration capability" (Lawler & Worley, 2006, p. 298). This refers to an organization's ability to execute change. In order to build this capability, an organization needs to develop the change-management skills of its people. It needs to hire personnel with skills in organization development and it needs to train and develop current managers and employees accordingly. The organization needs to develop the physical and fiscal resources to support continuous improvement. However, it is not enough to merely obtain requisite resources. Those resources need to "work together" in a coordinated manner. Organizations need to ensure that resources are developed and employed systemically and systematically, thus the need to develop organizational capability to orchestrate resources in a strategically coordinated manner. For example, they argue that organizations might need to merge strategic planning and human resource functions into "an organization effectiveness function" (p. 301). Organizations will also need to develop the capability to "embrace change then reflect on its experience" (p. 303). In other words, organizations must develop the meta-routines of assessing and continuously improving their own continuous improvement processes.

A fourth initiative is to "adopt strategic adjustment as a normal condition" (Lawler & Worley, 2006, p. 304). By this, Lawler and Worley mean that to become b2change, organizations need to shift their members' perceptions about the "importance, frequency, ease, and desirability of change" (p. 304). They need to make change a normal condition. This means creating structures, instituting systems of "talent" development and management to increase and employ necessary knowledge and skills, and developing rewards to motivate and support change. It also means putting as many people as possible into contact with the external environment to increase the sensitivity of the organization to the need for change, increase the amount of "intelligence" available to the organization, and create new potential for flexibility and responsiveness. It means pushing decision making down in the organization, infusing leadership work throughout the organization, and diffusing information widely.

The fifth initiative is to "seek virtuous spirals" (Lawler & Worley, 2006, p. 308). This means bringing all the previous initiatives together into a system of mutually reinforcing, positive influences that promote continuous improvement.

SUMMARY AND CONCLUDING CONSIDERATIONS

Bringing together the arguments from this literature with insights from the vignettes, several things stand out as particularly important for schools to consider as they begin their pursuit of continuous improvement. They are not offered here as sequential steps. With the possible exception of the first consideration and perhaps the fifth, the particular contexts and current capabilities of individual schools will dictate the order, combinations, and emphases placed on each and how attention to them might evolve as continuous improvement takes root.

1. Identify, clarify, and promote the mission, vision, and core values of the school, as these establish the foundation, the direction, the strategic focus, and the touchstone of accountability for continuous improvement. They are as much prerequisites of continuous improvement as anything else.

2. Establish an imperative for change and for continuous improvement. Schools must begin to think that "business as usual" is inadequate—if not now, it soon will be. Members of the school community must come to believe that stability is "out" and continuous improvement is "in" as a preferred state of "organizational being" if the school is to achieve its mission in the future.

3. Adopt or develop a systematic process or "technology" for continuous improvement. This process should reflect the key elements and qualities described in Chapter 4. It would organize and coordinate the initial and ongoing "work" of continuous improvement; promote the active monitoring and engagement of school environments, a key function noted in the vignettes and the literature; and introduce and institutionalize systems of inquiry, learning, and evidence-based strategic decision making, as well as promote the working relationships and norms and expectations of continuous learning associated with them. Whether used to introduce improvement activity incrementally as described in the vignettes or more dramatically and completely, such a process would create the prospects for bringing different initiatives together into an ongoing spiraling system of improvement. The continuous improvement process should establish early on the "meta-routines" of continuously monitoring, assessing, and improving the process itself.

4. Develop the school's organizational capacity to support the process and outcomes of continuous improvement. This book has strongly emphasized the importance of the relationship between the process of continuous improvement and the organizational contexts in which that process functions. Schools embarking on continuous improvement may need to develop the organizational elements necessary to initiate continuous improvement and to implement the first initiatives that come from it. Schools may need to pay particular attention to developing the knowledge and skills of teachers and other staff members to initially engage in this work. As indicated earlier, continuous improvement will likely make the development of organizational capacity a "permanent" organizational state, meaning that a continuously improving school will likely always be attending to its capability for further improvement.

5. Establish effective leadership for continuous improvement. It is clear that changing from a conventional school to a continuously improving school does not happen by itself. It requires systematic and strategic leadership. Whether performed primarily by the principal or by a wider group across the school, effective leadership for each of the four areas discussed earlier is imperative. It is as imperative for leadership to effectively direct and manage continuous improvement once initiated, however it may evolve.

Several issues and dilemmas will need to be considered as schools embark on continuous improvement. Among them are the following.

What Mission? What Core Values?

A crucial element in continuous improvement is the focus on the organization's mission and core values and on the accomplishment of goals that follow from them. To a large extent, the literature on the concept and practice of continuous improvement treats these things neutrally. As argued earlier, the concept of continuous improvement connotes change in a valued direction. But there are many possible directions that could be embodied in a school's mission, vision, and core values. Which ones should guide and govern organizational activity? As Willis Hawley and Gary Sykes (2007), among others, clearly argue, student learning should be the overarching driver of continuous improvement in schools and school districts. Improvement of school organization and organizational processes, including instruction, should be instrumental to improving student learning.

But what does it mean to improve student learning? What academic and nonacademic learning outcomes should a school pursue? As argued in Chapter 1, such questions take us into ambiguous and contested territory. The point here is twofold. The first is that it seems absolutely necessary that as schools embark on continuous improvement, they must be clear about the student learning outcomes that they value and that they commit themselves to pursue (Knapp et al., 2006). The second is that while many student learning outcomes have value and might be pursued, some are likely to be more worthy than others at this time and in anticipation of the future.

This takes us back again to Chapter 1 and to the arguments presented there that schools will be required to shift from pursuing student learning outcomes that might have been appropriate in the past to learning outcomes that will be required in an uncertain future. We are reminded of the National Research Council's (2000) call for schools to move beyond promoting the acquisition of "simple literacy" skills to promoting the development of "high literacy." We are reminded of calls for schools to prepare students to engage in nonroutine, creative, "right-brain work"; to be able to engage in "expert thinking" and "complex communication"; to be able to forge productive relationships with others; and to become curious, self-sustaining, lifelong learners. And we are reminded of Howard Gardner's (2006) argument for the cultivation of "five minds for the future": the disciplined mind, the synthesizing mind, the creating mind, the respectful mind, and the ethical mind. It will be imperative for schools to come to terms with these arguments.

The Paradox of Stability for Change

Another issue in embarking on continuous improvement concerns the paradox of the need for stability to create change. Carrie Leanna and Bruce Barry (2000) contend that certain sources of stability in organizational life enable rather than impede change. More specifically, they argue that "flexibility becomes impossible to sustain in the face of constant uncertainty" (p. 755). The ambiguity can be overwhelming psychologically and constant uncertainty provides no foundation or "traction" for change to take hold (see Burke, 2008). Kenneth Kerber and Anthony Buono (2005) observe that continuous improvement can itself be problematic:

> If used inappropriately, [it] can contribute to organizational chaos, as continuous changes and transitions confuse and frustrate rather than enlighten and support organizational members and key stakeholders. The feeling of being in "permanent white water" and the need to constantly adapt and adjust can be a daunting experience. (p. 27)

This suggests several things. The first is that continuous improvement need not always be continuous. Organizations may reach plateaus where they are performing well enough to take a break from improving, at least until circumstances warrant. Light (1998) reassures organizations striving for continuous improvement and innovation in this regard when he writes, "[T]here is nothing wrong with slowing down. To be successful innovating organizations need not continue innovating for all time" (p. 243). However, he continues that ultimately "the greatest challenge facing an innovating organization is to know when to start innovating and when to stop" (p. 244).

A related matter concerns which aspects of school organization need to be stable and which need to remain flexible and provisional for continuous improvement to be successful. As Chapter 1 suggests, schools have an inclination to seek stability in programs and practices. Their tendency is to find, put in place, and perpetuate for long periods of time presumably effective practices. Translated, the problem of school improvement is the introduction and sustainability, even the "scaling up" of "best practices." Continuous improvement turns this notion on its head. In continuously improving organizations, it is not programs, practices, or even roles and responsibilities that should remain stable. Instead, for continuously improving organizations, what is most important is stability in organizational mission, core values, and processes. The fundamental organizational logic, as James March (1981) reasoned some time ago, is not stability in behavior. Specific actions resulting from organizational processes are not and should not be stable if an organization is to respond effectively to changing demands and opportunities.

"Threshold" Capacity

A third consideration is whether schools must first have developed some "threshold" of organizational capacity to embark successfully on continuous improvement. Must schools have developed some minimal levels of readiness; of physical and fiscal resources; of knowledge, skills, and attitudes; of working relationships among personnel? What leadership must be present in the principal and in other administrative staff, not to mention within the teaching faculty? The notion of threshold capacity is implicit in Lawler and Worley's (2006) discussion of moving from traditional to continuously changing organizations. It is an element of David Hopkins' (2001) contingency view of school improvement strategies. It is also a key finding of research on improvement among schools in the Chicago Annenberg Challenge (Smylie & Wenzel, 2003). Schools engaged this self-initiated, collaborative reform more effectively if they entered the Challenge with strong participative leadership and with strong working relationships among faculty members, among other organizational resources and capacities. Schools that lacked such initial capacities struggled with or failed in this reform.

The broader argument is that different approaches to organizational improvement make different demands on schools. These demands require certain organizational resources and capabilities for schools to be successful at those approaches. If those resources are absent, underdeveloped, or not employed effectively, schools are not likely to engage those demands well. The issue is whether continuous improvement makes certain demands on schools that require some threshold capacity to even get started or whether the demands are such that virtually no threshold capacity is required, that continuous improvement once initiated can generate whatever capacity will be needed as it moves forward. We will return to this matter shortly.

External Support

At the same time that continuous improvement is meant to help schools engage and adapt to their environments more effectively, certain aspects of their environments may be more or less conducive to becoming continuously improving organizations. Of particular importance to the initial development of continuous improvement is the support that schools receive from their central offices and from the broader policy environment. Central offices can do much to promote continuous improvement at the school level by providing time, material and financial resources, and opportunities for the hiring and development of personnel to perform the work of continuous improvement. Central offices can adapt standard operating procedures and regulations to create an environment more conducive to inquiry, experimentation, and innovation. Central offices can create norms and expectations, even incentives and accountability systems that might motivate schools toward continuous improvement. More important, central offices can create an "uncluttered" playing field by creating coherence among various programs and policies to which schools are subject. Coherence of demands on schools from the broader policy environment may also be important for supporting the development of continuous improvement at the school level.

However likely or unlikely it is that central offices and broader policy environments can support the development of school-level continuous improvement in these ways, it is not difficult to imagine the consequences of lack of support or of countervailing demands and influences. For example, Corrie Giles and Andy Hargreaves (2006) documented how the resilience and sustainability of innovation and improvement processes in the continuously learning and improving schools they studied was seriously undermined by the introduction of large-scale, standardized, high-stakes government reform initiatives (see Chapter 6). Likewise, research on Chicago Annenberg schools documented how difficult it can be to initiate and sustain organizational changes or new programs and practices that compete with large-scale and strongly enforced initiatives from the central office and the state legislature (Smylie & Wenzel, 2003). The question turns to how central offices can, at minimum, reduce barriers to continuous improvement at the school level if not support it directly and with conviction or, perhaps, how central offices and schools can develop together into broader systems of continuous improvement.

The Need for Revolutionary Change

Finally, we return to the arguments in Chapter 1 about the current state of schools. If most schools are that stable and persistent, if they are so reticent to change, if surrounding institutional forces press them to remain fairly stable and homogeneous, how can schools come to develop the organizational properties and processes of continuous improvement? How can they change from relatively stable organizations to organizations disposed to and capable of sustainable flexibility, adaptability, innovation, and higher levels of performance? Why would schools respond to the new demands that are placed upon them by turning toward continuous improvement as opposed to a different form or level of stability?

For many schools the movement to continuous improvement would be a radical undertaking. It would mean change in identity, orientation, and culture; change in organizational processes, structures and capabilities; and change in relationships with their environments. It would not only mean abandoning tendencies toward inertia and isomorphism but also adopting opposite tendencies of adaptation and differentiation. These are fundamental changes. What are the chances that schools can make such changes? Make them on their own? Make them without strong external impetus and support?

Punctuated equilibrium theory suggests they cannot (see Chapter 2). This theory would lead us to believe that to become continuously improving organizations, schools would need a major perturbation to the equilibrium they have long enjoyed, a significant "jolt to the system" that could not be ignored. They would require some force to knock them out of their present orbits into the orbit of continuous improvement. They would need to be "transformed" or, in other school reform parlance, "turned around" to continuous improvement (Murphy & Meyers, 2007) through new leadership and staff, external mandates and accountability, radical restructuring, and new school development. These sorts of forces are evident in the vignettes of schools in Chapter 6.

It is well a matter of situation and contingency. Certainly, there are schools with organizational orientations, capabilities, and leadership that may make the turn to continuous improvement on their own, with a lot of hard work but without the kind of major external shock and upheaval anticipated by punctuated equilibrium theory. On the other hand, there certainly are schools that would require a strong shock and fundamental transformation to begin on the course of continuous improvement. This goes back to the issue of threshold capacity. But it also goes back to an observation made at several points in this book that all organizations, even those that are successfully engaged in continuous improvement, will at times need to contemplate and engage in more radical and revolutionary change. It is not a question of whether schools will confront this prospect. It is a question of when, how, and under what conditions they will confront it. For some schools, one of those points of revolutionary change may be to "start them up" on the path of continuous improvement (see Murphy & Meyers, 2007).

It is good to recall Karl Weick and Robert Quinn's (1999) observation that continuous improvement and revolutionary change are not mutually exclusive. Continuous improvement can reduce the need for revolutionary change and make it more effective and less costly when it must occur. The challenge is how to effectively engage continuous improvement and revolutionary change and to manage effectively the transitions between them. The challenge is to create a continuously improving school organization that is ambidextrous and effective in different types and degrees of change over time. Many schools will find this challenge daunting. They may have little choice but to engage it. By all counts it will be what the future demands.

QUESTIONS FOR STUDY, REFLECTION, AND ACTION

1. How might your school establish an imperative for pursuing continuous improvement? How might the evidence and the arguments presented in this book and how might the assessments of your school performed in response to questions at the ends of earlier chapters be used in this regard?

2. What leadership "work" needs to be performed to begin continuous improvement at your school? Given assessments of your school in response to earlier questions, what aspects of this leadership work might best be performed by the principal? By teachers and others in the school? What needs to be done to develop leadership for moving continuous improvement forward?

3. Using the essential elements of the process of continuous improvement outlined in Chapter 4 as a guide, what are the first steps that your school might take to launch itself from its present orbit into a virtuous circle of continuous improvement? What initial goals might it set? What evidence might it use to set these goals? How would your school gather information about, assess, and decide among different strategies for achieving these goals? What evidence might your school use to assess implementation and the attainment of these goals and to identify the next goals for improvement?

4. What sources of external support would be helpful to your school as it embarks on continuous improvement? From the central office? From parents and the community? From unions and other external groups? How might your school cultivate and engage these sources of support and at the same time buffer itself from external sources of threat and disruption?

5. If your school is a candidate for "turn around," radical restructuring, or other form of revolutionary change, how might that process proceed so that your school emerges ready for continuous improvement?

Endnotes

CHAPTER 1

1. See Armstrong's (2001) analysis of religious fundamentalism, Putnam's (2000) analysis of the collapse of American community, and Bishop's (2008) analysis of social and political self-segregation.

2. The statistics reported in this section were the most current available when this book was put into production. It is beyond the scope of this work to explore possible explanations of these changes and challenges.

3. A few examples of differences among neighboring states are instructive. In 2005, average per pupil funding in New Jersey was $2,712 greater in high-poverty districts than in low-poverty districts. That year average per pupil funding in New York was $3,068 less in high-poverty than in low-poverty districts. Average per pupil funding in Illinois was $2,235 less in high-poverty districts than in low-poverty districts. But in Indiana, average per pupil funding was $322 greater in high-poverty districts than in low-poverty districts. In Minnesota, per pupil funding was on average $1,629 greater in high-poverty than in low-poverty districts. Some variations among states are due to court orders.

4. For long-term trends in student scores on the National Assessment of Educational Progress (NAEP) see Perie, Moran, and Lutkus (2005). For international comparisons of student achievement in mathematics and science see Gonzales et al. (2004, 2008) and in reading literacy see Baer, Baldi, Ayotte, and Green (2007).

5. The U.S. Department of Labor's (1999) report *futurework* concluded that today's job applicants are not well prepared for either today's or tomorrow's jobs even with regard to the most basic of skills. The American Management Association (2001) found that 34 percent of applicants tested by potential employers lacked basic reading and math skills required of the jobs for which they were applying.

6. Several studies have found that students who exercise choice options may do better academically in their new schools (e.g., Hess, 2003). It should not be surprising that students who attend higher-performing schools may achieve at higher levels than if they attended lower-performing schools.

CHAPTER 2

7. For an introduction to the concept of organizational self-design see Hedberg, Nystrom, & Starbuck (1976), Mohrman and Cummings (1989), Weick (1977), Weick and Berlinger (1989), and Wildavsky (1972). For an introduction to the concept of organizational improvisation see Bastien and Hostager (1988), Miner, Bassoff, and Moorman (2001), Moorman and Miner (1998), and Weick (1993, 1998). For an introduction to the concept of high reliability organizations see Bigley and Roberts (2001), Guy (1990), LaPorte and Consolini (1991), Stringfield (1995), Stringfield, Reynolds, and Schaffer (2008), Weick and Sutcliffe (2007), and Weick,

Sutcliffe, and Obstfeld (1999). For an introduction to the concept of organizational learning see Argyris and Schön (1996), Duncan and Weiss (1979), Easterby-Smith and Araujo (1999), Easterby-Smith, Crossan, and Nicolini (2000), Fiol and Lyles (1985), Knoke (2001), Landau (1973), Leithwood and his colleagues (1995, 1998), Mulford (1998), and Senge (1990).

8. Defining continuous improvement as an organizational process is synonymous with Marshak's (2004) concept of continuous organizational "morphing." See also Quinn's (1980) description of "logical incrementalism."

9. Kerber and Buono (2005) also observe "As the pace of change in our . . . environment continues to accelerate, organizational success will be increasingly dependent on our capacity for continuous adaptation" (p. 32). And Burgelman (1991) argues that organizational survival now depends "to a significant extent" on the ability of organizations to adjust continually to changes in their environments (p. 255).

10. An illustration of this possibility comes from Greve's (1995) study of U.S. radio stations and the "contagion of strategy abandonment," a phenomenon that occurs when leading organizations begin to abandon particular strategies and other organizations follow suit. Greve found that while this behavior weakened organizational inertia it also led to uncritical and potentially harmful abandonment of strategies that actually worked well for many stations at the time (see also Greve & Taylor, 2000).

CHAPTER 3

11. The education and non-education literatures were searched for evidence of outcomes of continuous improvement. Among the criteria used to select studies for this chapter was that studies focus on improvement processes that were implemented over substantial periods of time and that were integrated into organizational designs or routines. Studies that focused on short-term or one-time projects or ancillary improvement processes were not included. In addition, studies had to report the findings of original data collection and analysis. Preference was given to studies with credible descriptions of research design and methodology. This chapter draws mostly from systematic analytical studies of continuous improvement or "like" processes that often include comparison organizations and from studies focusing on organizations that have been successful over long periods of time or that have made substantial and sustained gains in performance and examining organizational features and processes that explain that success. Although the studies selected for this chapter are among the strongest methodologically, they are not without limitations. Thus, evidence from individual studies should be approached with some caution.

12. Quinn (1980) also reports that he has observed the same types of incremental practices function effectively in large government and semipublic organizations.

13. In contrast, histories of the comparison companies, particularly those with "unsustained" performance, reveal that unfocused, undisciplined, nonstrategic, noncontinuous, impulsive change, even change aimed at achieving the "big win," is much less effective and can set companies into a downward performance spiral from which it is hard to recover.

14. Collins (2005) acknowledges that these interviews are no substitute for a rigorous multi-year comparative study that would examine both social sector and business organizations in-depth and historically. Still, these leaders' perspectives provide some evidence of how good-to-great principles apply to a broader range of organizations.

15. The Chicago Challenge was a six-year reform initiative that provided monetary and professional support to more than 200 city public schools organized in networks with external partners. This Challenge was one of a number of Challenges established by the Annenberg Foundation in the mid-1990s, mostly in large city school systems.

16.   BASRC was established in the San Francisco Bay area and was another big city Challenge funded by the Annenberg Foundation to promote large-scale school improvement.

17.   Organizational learning was defined not only in terms of school capacity for organizational learning but also by teacher engagement in particular activities, such as taking initiatives and risks and participating in ongoing and collaborative professional development, all consistent with continuous improvement.

CHAPTER 4

18.   Other models available to schools today include those developed by Fidler (2002), Knapp and his colleagues (2006), Leithwood and his colleagues (2001), Loucks-Horsley and her colleagues (2003), and Marsh and her colleagues (2006). Another prominent model is part of the Baldrige National Quality Program (2006). Also, the Center for Continuous Instructional Improvement, recently established as part of the Consortium for Policy Research in Education (CPRE) at the University of Pennsylvania, promises to be a useful source of models and strategies.

19.   One notable exception to this is the research that has been conducted on BASRC's Cycle of Inquiry (see Chapter 3).

CHAPTER 5

20.   Ten years after Bentzen's study, Gordon (1984) challenged the notion that schools could truly and effectively engage in self-renewal (or continuous improvement). He argued that most schools lack the organizational arrangements and the inherent capacity for changing themselves. Specifically, he pointed to structures that isolated individual teachers and made work individualistic and to belief systems that reinforced conventional ways of thinking and teaching and that perpetrated norms of independence, autonomy, and privacy. Because of these factors, most schools need help from outside entities to change and the need for external assistance makes *self*-renewal, by definition, impossible. This argument can be taken to mean that external support may be important for self-renewal, or continuous improvement, and that successful self-renewal may hinge on the structure of people and work and on organizational norms, values, and culture.

CHAPTER 6

21.   Our vignettes use school names and other descriptive information presented in the case studies, and they honor any agreements of anonymity between the researchers and the schools that we could discern. We use material from the case studies with full acknowledgment that we are representing the work of others, and we take full responsibility for any errors made in telling the stories of these schools.

22.   There are many case studies in the education literature and in the literature on business and management that provide other useful illustrations of continuous improvement "in action." They vary considerably in detail. Few present comprehensive views of the theory in practice. Few describe particularly well the dynamics of enacting processes of continuous improvement over time. A primary part of the logic of continuous improvement is how it helps an organization deal with unexpected problems and opportunities. However, most cases focus on the circumstances by which an organization comes to adopt a process of continuous improvement (usually a strong external stress), initial implementation of this process, and initial

indicators of success. The dynamic long view is largely absent. Most cases claim relationships between continuous improvement and organizational performance and effectiveness. However, these claims often rest on tenuous evidence of outcomes.

Even with such limitations, the case literature contains many entries that can illuminate different aspects of continuous improvement practice. There are several descriptions of schools chosen as winners in the Baldrige National Quality Award Program (e.g., Daniels, 2006; Siri & Miller, 2001) and of other schools widely publicized and recognized as models of organizing for continuous improvement, notably Adlai E. Stephenson High School in Lincolnshire, Illinois (e.g., DuFour, 1995; Honawar, 2008; Kanold, 2006; see also Sergiovanni, 2004). There are a number of descriptions of efforts to introduce continuous improvement as part of larger reform initiatives (e.g., Copland, 2003; Roesner, 1995; Weller & Weller, 1998). There are also several accounts of continuous improvement processes that are part of district-level reform activity in Community School District #2 in New York City (e.g., Elmore & Burney, 1998; Stein & D'Amico, 2002) and in San Diego, California (e.g., Hubbard, Stein, & Mehan, 2006; Stein, Hubbard, & Mehan, 2004).

Useful descriptions of continuous improvement practice in non-education organizations can be found in Choi's (1995) study of a U.S. auto parts supplier; Lillrank and his colleagues' (2001) research at Saab, ABB, and General Electric; Mitki and his colleague's (1997) account of an American-Israeli paper mill; Rindova and Kotha's (2001) study of Yahoo and Excite! Internet companies; Lemmer and Brent's (2001) case of Kraft Foods; and Carman's (1993) account of the Southern Pacific Railroad. Descriptions of continuous improvement processes in non-education organizations can also be found in the work of Collins (2001); Collins & Porras, (1994) and Lawler and Worley (2006).

23. The case study from which this vignette was drawn provides no data on student achievement.

References

AdvancED. (n.d.a). *Accreditation standards for quality schools.* Schaumburg, IL: National Study of School Evaluation.

AdvancED. (n.d.b). *Breakthrough school improvement: An action guide.* Schaumburg, IL: National Study of School Evaluation and AdvancED Research and Development Division.

Allen, L., & Calhoun, E. F. (1998). Schoolwide action research. *Phi Delta Kappan, 79,* 706–710.

Allensworth, E., Correa, M., & Ponisciak, S. (2008, May). *From high school to the future: ACT preparation—too much, too late.* Chicago: Consortium on Chicago School Research.

Amburgey, T. L., Keppy, D., & Barnett, W. P. (1993). Resetting the clock: The dynamics of organizational change and failure. *Administrative Science Quarterly, 38,* 51–73.

American Heritage Dictionary of the English Language, 4th edition. (2006). Boston: Houghton Mifflin.

American Management Association. (2001). *One-third of job applicants flunked basic literacy and math tests last year, American Management Association survey finds.* Retrieved January 4, 2008, from http://www.amanet.org/press/amanews/bjp2001.html

Anderson, J. C., Rungtusanatham, M., & Schroeder, R. G. (1994). A theory of quality management underlying the Deming management method. *Academy of Management Review, 19,* 472–509.

Argyris, C., & Schön, D. A. (1974). *Theory in practice: Increasing professional effectiveness.* San Francisco: Jossey-Bass.

Argyris, C., & Schön, D. A. (1996). *Organizational learning II: Theory, method, and practice.* Reading, MA: Addison-Wesley.

Armstrong, K. (2001). *The battle for God.* New York: Ballantine.

Arroyo, C. G. (2008, January). *The funding gap.* Washington, DC: The Education Trust.

Baer, J., Baldi, S., Ayotte, K., & Green, P. (2007). *The reading literacy of U.S. fourth-grade students in an international context: Results from the 2001 and 2006 Progress in International Reading Literacy Study (PIRLS).*(NCES 2008-017). Washington, DC: National Center for Education Statistics, Institute of Education Sciences, U.S. Department of Education.

Bain, A. (1998). Social defenses against organizational learning. *Human Relations, 51*(3), 413–429.

Baldrige National Quality Program. (2006). *Education criteria for performance excellence.* Gaithersburg, MD: National Institute of Standards and Technology.

Bascia, N., & Hargreaves, A. (Eds.). (2000). *The sharp edge of educational change.* New York: RoutledgeFalmer.

Bastien, D. T., & Hostager, T. J. (1988). Jazz as a process of organizational innovation. *Communication Research, 15,* 582–602.

Bay Area School Reform Collaborative. (2004, April). *The path out of underperformance: Two cases of Title 1 schools that are beating the odds.* Retrieved September 18, 2006, from http://www.springboardschools.org/research/other_research.html

Bentzen, M. M. (1974). *Changing schools: The magic feather principle.* New York: McGraw-Hill.

Berliner, D. C., & Biddle, B. J. (1996). *The manufactured crisis: Myths, fraud, and the attack on American's public schools.* New York: Basic Books.

Berra, Y. (2001). *When you come to a fork in the road, take it!* New York: Hyperion.

Bessant, J., & Francis, D. (1999). Developing strategic continuous improvement capability. *Internal Journal of Operations & Production Management, 19,* 1106–1119.

Bhuiyan, N., & Baghel, A. (2005). An overview of continuous improvement: From the past to the present. *Management Decision, 43*(5), 761–771.

Bigley, G. A., & Roberts, K. H. (2001). The incident command system: High-reliability organizing for complex and volatile task environments. *The Academic of Management Journal, 44*(6), 1281–1299.

Bishop, B. (2008). *The big sort: Why the clustering of like-minded America is tearing us apart.* New York: Houghton Mifflin.

Blau, P. M., & Scott, W. R. (1962). *Formal organizations.* San Francisco: Chandler.

Bostingl, J. J. (1996). *Schools of quality: An introduction to total quality management in education* (2nd ed.). Alexandria, VA: Association for Supervision and Curriculum Development.

Box, G. E. P., & Draper, N. R. (1969). *Evolutionary operation: A statistical method of process improvement.* New York: Wiley.

Boyd, W. L. (2003). Public education's crisis of performance and legitimacy. In W. L. Boyd & D. Miretzky (Eds.), *American educational governance on trial: Change and challenges. 102nd yearbook of the National Society for the Study of Education, Part I* (pp. 1–19). Chicago: National Society for the Study of Education.

Brown, S. L., & Eisenhardt, K. M. (1997). The art of continuous improvement: Linking complexity theory and time-based evolution in relentlessly shifting organizations. *Administrative Science Quarterly, 42,* 1–34.

Brown, S. L., & Eisenhardt, K. M. (1998). *Competing on the edge: Strategy as structured chaos.* Boston, MA: Harvard Business School Press.

Bryson, J. M. (1995). *Strategic planning for public and nonprofit organizations* (rev. ed.). San Francisco: Jossey-Bass.

Burgelman, R. A. (1991). Intraorganizational ecology of strategy making and organizational adaptation: Theory and field research. *Organization Science, 2*(3), 239–262.

Burke, W. W. (2008). *Organization change: Theory and practice* (2nd ed.). Los Angeles: Sage.

Burns, T., & Stalker, G. M. (1994). *The management of innovation* (rev. ed.). Oxford: Oxford University Press.

Caffyn, S. (1999). Development of a continuous improvement self-assessment tool. *International Journal of Operations & Production Management, 19*(11), 1138–1153.

Callahan, R. E. (1962). *Education and the cult of efficiency.* Chicago: University of Chicago Press.

Carman, J. M. (1993). Continuous quality improvement as a survival strategy: The Southern Pacific experience. *California Management Review, 35,* 118–132.

Case-Winters, A. (2004, May). Our misused motto. *Presbyterians Today.* Available at http://www.pcusa.org/today/believe/past/may04/reformed.htm

Choi, T. (1995). Conceptualizing continuous improvement: Implications for organizational change. *Omega, International Journal of Management Science, 23*(6), 607–624.

Collins, J. (2001). *Good to great: Why some companies make the leap . . . and others don't.* New York: Harper Business.

Collins, J. (2005). *Good to great and the social sectors: Why business thinking is not the answer.* Boulder, CO: Author.

Collins, J., & Porras, J. I. (1994). *Built to last: Successful habits of visionary companies.* New York: HarperCollins.

Collins, J., & Porras, J. I. (2002). *Built to last: Successful habits of visionary companies* (paperback ed.). New York: Collins Business Essentials.

Copland, M. A. (2003). Leadership for inquiry: Building and sustaining capacity for school improvement. *Educational Evaluation and Policy Analysis, 25,* 375–395.

Crowson, R. L., & Morris, V. C. (1991). The superintendency and school leadership. In P. W. Thurston & P. P. Zodhiates (Eds.), *Advances in educational administration: Vol. 2* (pp. 191–215). Greenwich, CT: JAI.

Cuban, L. (1990). Reforming again, again, and again. *Educational Researcher, 19*(1), 3–13.

Cuban, L. (2004). *The blackboard and the bottom line: Why schools can't be businesses.* Cambridge, MA: Harvard University Press.

Cummings, T. G., & Worley, C. G. (2005). *Organization development and change* (8th ed.). Mason, OH: South-Western College Publications.

Cyert, R. M., & March, J. G. (1959). A behavioral theory of organizational objectives. In M. Haire (Ed.), *Modern organization theory* (pp. 76-90). New York: Wiley.

Daniels, S. E. (2006). Oklahoma school district goes over the top. *Quality Progress, 39*(5), 51–59.

Darling-Hammond, L., & Rustique-Forrester, E. (2005). The consequences of student testing for teaching and teacher quality. In J. L. Herman & E. H. Haertel (Eds.), *Uses and misuses of data for educational accountability and improvement. The 104th yearbook of the National Society for the Study of Education, Part 2* (pp. 289–319). Malden, MA: Blackwell.

Datnow, A., Hubbard, 1., & Mehan, H. (2002). *Extending educational reform: From one school to many.* New York: RoutledgeFalmer.

Dean, A., Carlisle, Y., & Baden-Fuller, C. (1999). Punctuated and continuous change: The UK water industry. *British Journal of Management, 10,* S3–S18.

Dean, J. W., Jr., & Bowen, D. E. (1994). Management theory and total quality: Improving research and practice through theory development. *Academy of Management Review, 19,* 392–418.

Delbridge, R., & Barton, H. (2002). Organizing for continuous improvement: Structures and roles in automotive components plants. *International Journal of Operations & Production Management, 22,* 680–692.

Deming, W. E. (2000). *Out of crisis.* Cambridge, MA: MIT Press.

Detert, J. R., Louis, K. S., & Schroeder, R. G. (2001). A cultural framework for education: Defining quality values and their impact in U.S. high schools. *School Effectiveness and School Improvement, 12,* 183–212.

DiMaggio, P. J., & Powell, W. W. (1983). The iron cage revisited: Institutional isomorphism and collective rationality in organizational fields. *American Sociological Review, 48,* 147–160.

Downs, A. (1972). Up and down with ecology: The "issue-attention" cycle. *The Public Interest, 28,* 38–50.

Dufour, R. (1995). Restructuring is not enough. *Educational Leadership, 52*(7), 33–36.

Duncan, R., & Weiss, A. (1979). Organizational learning: Implications for organizational design. In B. M. Staw (Ed.), *Research in Organizational Behavior: Vol. 1* (pp. 75–123). Greenwich, CT: JAI Press.

Easterby-Smith, M., & Araujo, L. (1999). Organizational learning: Current debates and opportunities. In M. Easterby-Smith, L. Araujo, & J. Burgoyne (Eds.), *Organizational learning and the learning organization* (pp. 1–21). Thousand Oaks, CA: Sage.

Easterby-Smith, M., Crossan, M., & Nicolini, D. (2000). Organizational learning: Debates past, present, and future. *Journal of Management Studies, 37*(6), 783–796.

Education Finance Statistics Center. (2005a). *Percentage distribution of total revenue for public elementary and secondary education in the United States, by region and revenue source: 1989–90 to 2002–05.* Retrieved July 7, 2008, from http://nces.ed.gov/EDFIN/tables/tab_change_rev_src.asp

Education Finance Statistics Center. (2005b). *Total revenues for elementary and secondary schools, fall enrollment, and total revenues per pupil: Fiscal years 1970 to 2005.* Retrieved July 7, 2008, from http://nces.ed.gov/EDFIN/tables/tab_public_effort_show.asp

Elmore, R. F., & Burney, D. (1998). *Continuous improvement in Community District 2, New York City* (OERI research contract #RC-96-7002). Pittsburgh, PA: University of Pittsburgh, Learning Research and Development Center.

Evans, R. (2001). *The human side of school change.* San Francisco: Jossey-Bass.

Farkas, S., & Duffett, A. (2008, June). *High-achieving students in the era of NCLB, Part 2: Results from a national teacher survey.* New York: Thomas B. Fordham Institute.

Federal Interagency Forum on Child and Family Statistics. (2009). *America's children: Key national indicators of well-being, 2009.* Washington, DC: U.S. Government Printing Office.

Feldman, M. S., & Pentland, B. T. (2003). Reconceptualizing organizational routines as a source of flexibility and change. *Administrative Science Quarterly, 48,* 94–118.

Fidler, B. (2002). *Strategic management for school development.* London: Paul Chapman.

Fink, D. (2000). *Good schools/real schools: Why school reform doesn't last.* New York: Teachers College Press.

Fiol, C. M., & Lyles, M. A. (1985). Organizational learning. *Academy of Management Review, 10,* 803–813.

Fiske, E. B., & Ladd, H. F. (2000). *When schools compete: A cautionary tale.* Washington, DC: Brookings Institution.

Fox-Wolfgramm, S. J., Boal, K. B., & Hunt, J. G. (1998). Organizational adaptation to institutional change: A comparative study of first-order change in prospector and defender banks. *Administrative Science Quarterly, 43,* 87–126.

Friedman, T. (2006). *The world is flat: A brief history of the twenty-first century.* New York: Farrar, Straus, and Giroux.

Fullan, M. (1992). *Successful school improvement: The implementation perspective and beyond.* New York: Open University Press.

Fullan, M. (1993). *Change forces: Probing the depth of educational reform.* New York: Routledge.

Fullan, M. (2005). *Leadership and sustainability: System thinkers in action.* Thousand Oaks, CA: Corwin.

Fullan, M., Miles, M. B., & Taylor, G. (1980). Organization development in schools: The state of the art. *Review of Educational Research, 50,* 121–183.

Gardner, H. (2006). *Five minds for the future.* Boston, MA: Harvard Business School Press.

General Accounting Office. (1994). *U.S. companies improve performance through quality efforts* (GAO/NSIAD-91-190). Washington, DC: Author.

Gersick, C. J. G. (1991). Revolutionary change theories: A multilevel exploration of the punctuated equilibrium paradigm. *Academy of Management Review, 16,* 10–36.

Gilbreth, F., & Gilbreth, E. (1948). *Cheaper by the dozen.* New York: Gorsset & Dunlap.

Giles, C., & Hargreaves, A. (2006). The sustainability of innovative schools as learning organizations and professional learning communities during standardized reform. *Educational Administration Quarterly, 42,* 124–156.

Goh, S. C., Cousins, J. B., & Elliott, C. (2006). Organizational learning capacity, evaluative inquiry and readiness for change in schools: Views and perceptions of educators. *Journal of Educational Change, 7,* 289–318.

Gold, B. A. (1999). Punctuated legitimacy: A theory of educational change. *Teachers College Record, 101,* 192–219.

Gonzales, P., Guzmán, J. C., Pantelow, L., Pahlke, E., Jocelyn, L., Kastberg, D., & Williams, T. (2004). *Highlights from the Trends in International Mathematics and Science Study (TIMSS) 2003.* (NCES 2005-005). Washington, DC: National Center for Education Statistics, U.S. Department of Education.

Gonzales, P., Williams, T., Jocelyn, L., Roey, S., Kastberg, D., & Brenwald, S. (2008). *Highlights from TIMSS 2007: Mathematics and science achievement of U.S. fourth- and eighth-grade students in international context* (NCES 2009-001). Washington, DC: National Center for Education Statistics, U.S. Department of Education.

Goodlad, J. I. (1975). *The dynamics of educational change.* New York: McGraw-Hill.

Gordon, D. (1984). *The myths of school self-renewal.* New York: Teachers College Press.

Greve, H. R. (1995). Jumping ship: the diffusion of strategy abandonment. *Administrative Science Quarterly, 40,* 444–473.

Greve, H. R., & Taylor, A. (2000). Innovations as catalysts for organizational change: Shifts in organizational cognition and search. *Administrative Science Quarterly, 45,* 54–80.

Guy, M. E. (1990). High-reliability management. *Public Productivity & Management Review, 13,* 301–313.

Hackman, J. R., & Wageman, R. (1995). Total quality management: E mpirical, conceptual, and practical issues. *Administrative Science Quarterly, 40,* 309–342.

Hambrick, D. C., & D'Aveni, R. A. (1988). Large corporate failures as downward spirals. *Administrative Science Quarterly, 33,* 1–23.

Hannan, M. T., & Freeman, J. (1984). Structural inertia and organizational change. *American Sociological Review, 49,* 149–164.

Hannaway, J., & Woodroffe, N. (2003). Policy instruments in education. *Review of Research in Education, 27,* 1–24.

Hargreaves, A. (2003). *Teaching in the knowledge society: Education in the age of insecurity.* New York: Teachers College Press.

Hargreaves, A., & Fink, D. (2006). *Sustainable leadership.* San Francisco: Jossey-Bass.

Hargreaves, D. H., & Hopkins, D. (1994). *Development planning for school improvement.* London: Cassell.

Harry, J., & Schroeder, R. (2006). *Six Sigma: The breakthrough management strategy revolutionizing the world's top corporations.* Westminster, MD: Random House/Currency.

Hatch, M. J. (2006). *Organizations: Modern, symbolic, and postmodern perspectives* (2nd ed). New York: Oxford University Press.

Haveman, H. A. (1992). Between a rock and a hard place: Organizational change and performance under conditions of fundamental environmental transformation. *Administrative Science Quarterly, 37,* 48–75.

Hawley, W. D. with Rollie, D. L. (Eds.). (2007). *The keys to effective schools: Education reform as continuous improvement* (2nd ed.). Thousand Oaks, CA: Corwin.

Hawley, W. D., & Sykes, G. (2007). Continuous school improvement. In W. D. Hawley with D. L. Rollie (Eds.), *The keys to effective schools: Education reform as continuous improvement* (2nd ed., pp. 153–172). Thousand Oaks, CA: Corwin.

Hedberg, B. (1981). How organizations learn and unlearn. In P. C Nystrom & W. H. Starbuck (Eds.), *Handbook of organizational design: Vol. 1. Adapting organizations to their environments* (pp. 3–27). New York: Oxford University Press.

Hedberg, B. L. T., Nystrom, P. C., & Starbuck, W. H. (1976). Camping on seesaws: Prescriptions for a self-designing organization. *Administrative Science Quarterly, 21,* 41–65.

Hedges, L. V., & Nowell, A. (1999). Changes in the black-white gap in achievement test scores. *Sociology of Education, 72,* 111–135.

Hess, F. M. (2003). Breaking the mold: Charter schools, contract schools, and voucher plans. In W. L. Boyd & D. Miretzky (Eds.), *American educational governance on trial: Change and challenges. 102nd yearbook of the National Society for the Study of Education, Part I* (pp. 114–135). Chicago: National Society for the Study of Education.

Hill, J. G., & Johnson, F. (2005). *Revenues and expenditures for public elementary and secondary districts: School year 2002–03 (fiscal year 2003).* (NCES 2006-312). Washington, DC: National Center for Education Statistics, Institute of Education Sciences, U.S. Department of Education.

Honawar, V. (2008). Working smarter by working together. *Education Week, 27*(31), 25–27.

Honig, M. I. (Ed.).(2006). *New directions in education policy implementation.* Albany: State University of New York Press.

Hopkins, D. (2001). *School improvement for real.* New York: RoutledgeFalmer.

Hubbard, L., Stein, M. K., & Mehan, H. (2006). *Reform as learning: When school reform collides with school cultural and community politics.* New York: Routledge.

Huff, J. O., Huff, A. S., & Thomas, H. (1992). Strategic renewal and the interaction of cumulative stress and inertia. *Strategic Management Journal, 13,* 55–75.

Hussar, W. J., & Bailey, T. M. (2007, December). *Projections of education statistics to 2016* (35th ed.). Washington, DC: Institute of Education Sciences, National Center for Education Statistics, U.S. Department of Education.

Imai, M. (1986). *Kaizen: The key to Japan's competitive success.* New York: McGraw-Hill.

Juran, J. M. (1992). *Juran on quality by design.* New York: Free Press.

Kanold, T. D. (2006). The flywheel effect: Educators gain momentum from a model for continuous improvement. *Journal of Staff Development, 27*(2), 16–21.

Kaplan, R. S., & Norton, D. P. (1996, January/February). Using the balanced scorecard as a strategic management system. *Harvard Business Review OnPoint,* 2–12.

Karathanos, D., & Karathanos, P. (1996). The Baldrige Education Pilot Criteria 1995: An integrated approach to continuous improvement in education. *Journal of Education for Business, 71,* 272–276.

Kelly, D., & Amburgey, T. L. (1991). Organizational inertia and momentum: A dynamic model of strategic change. *Academy of Management Journal, 34*(3), 591–612.

Kerber, K., & Buono, A. F. (2005). Rethinking organizational change: Reframing the challenge of change management. *Organizational Development, 23*(3), 23–38.

Kewal Ramani, A., Gilbertson, L., Fox, M. A., & Provasnik, S. (2007, September). *Status and trends in the education of racial and ethnic minorities* (NCES 2007-039). Washington, DC: Institute of Education Sciences, National Center for Education Statistics, U.S. Department of Education.

King, M. B. (2002). Professional development to promote schoolwide inquiry. *Teaching and Teacher Education, 18,* 243–257.

Kingdon, J. W. (1995). *Agendas, alternatives, and public policies* (2nd ed.). New York: Longman.

Knapp, M. S., Swinnerton, J. A., Copland, M. A., & Monpas-Huber, J. (2006, October). *Data-informed leadership in education.* Seattle: University of Washington, Center for the Study of Teaching and Policy.

Knoke, D. (2001). *Changing organizations.* Boulder, CO: Westview.

Koberg, C. S. (1986). Adaptive organizational behavior of school organizations: An exploratory study. *Educational Evaluation and Policy Analysis, 8,* 139–146.

Krishnan, R., Shani, A. B., Grant, R. M., & Baer, R. (1993). In search of quality improvement: Problems of design and implementation. *Academy of Management Executive, 7*(4), 7–20.

Kruse, S. D. (2001). Creating communities of reform: Continuous improvement planning teams. *Journal of Educational Administration, 39,* 359–383.

Landau, M. (1973). On the concept of a self-correcting organization. *Public Administration Review, 33,* 533–542.

LaPorte, T. R., & Consolini, P. M. (1991). Working in practice but not in theory: Theoretical challenges of "high-reliability organizations." *Journal of Public Administration Research and Theory, 1*(1), 19–48.

Laughlin, R. C. (1991). Environmental disturbances and organizational transitions and transformations: Some alternative models. *Organization Studies, 12*(2), 209–232.

Lawler, E. E. III, & Worley, C. G. (2006). *Built to change: How to achieve sustained organizational effectiveness.* San Francisco: Jossey-Bass.

Leanna, C. R., & Barry, B. (2000). Stability and change as simultaneous experiences in organizational life. *Academy of Management Review, 25*(4), 753–759.

Lee, H.-J. (2004). The role of competence-based trust and organizational identification in continuous improvement. *Journal of Managerial Psychology, 19,* 623–639.

Leithwood, K., & Aitken, R. (1995). *Making schools smarter.* Thousand Oaks, CA: Corwin.

Leithwood, K., Aitken, R., & Jantzi, D. (2001). *Making schools smarter: A system for monitoring school and district progress* (2nd ed.). Thousand Oaks, CA: Corwin.

Leithwood, K., & Louis, K. S. (1998). Organizational learning in schools: An introduction. In K. Leithwood & K. S. Louis (Eds.), *Organizational learning in schools* (pp. 1–14). Exton, PA: Swets & Zeitlinger.

Lemmer, I., & Brent, J. (2001). Kraft foods. In L. Carter, D. Giber, & M. Goldsmith (Eds.), *Best practices in organization development and change* (pp. 11–38). San Francisco: Jossey-Bass.

Lerman, R. I., & Schmidt, S. R. (1999, August). *An overview of economic, social, and demographic trends affecting the U.S. labor market.* Washington, DC: The Urban Institute.

Levitt, B., & March, J. G. (1988). Organizational learning. *Annual Review of Sociology, 14,* 319–340.

Levy, F., & Murnane, R. J. (2004). *The new division of labor: How computers are creating the next job market.* New York: Russell Sage Foundation.

Lewin, K. (1935). *A dynamic theory of personality.* New York: McGraw-Hill.

Lezotte, L. W., & McKee, K. M. (2002). *Assembly required: A continuous school improvement system.* Okemos, MI: Effective Schools Products.

Lezotte, L. W., & McKee, K. M. (2006). *Stepping up: Leading the charge to improve our schools.* Okemos, MI: Effective Schools Products.

Light, P. C. (1998). *Sustaining innovation: Creating nonprofit and government organizations that innovate naturally.* San Francisco: Jossey-Bass.

Light, P. C. (2000). *Making nonprofits work.* Washington, DC: Brookings Institution.

Light, P. C. (2002). *Pathways to nonprofit excellence.* Washington, DC: Brookings Institution.

Light, P. C. (2004). *Sustaining nonprofit performance: The case for capacity building and the evidence to support it.* Washington, DC: Brookings Institution.

Light, P. C. (2005). *Four pillars of high performance: How robust organizations achieve extraordinary results.* New York: Mc-Graw-Hill.

Lillrank, P., Shani, A. B., Kolodny, H., Stymne, B., Figuera, J. R., & Lui, M. (1998). Learning from the success of continuous improvement change programs: An international comparative study. In R. W. Woodman & W. A. Pasmore (Eds.), *Research in organizational change and development: Vol. 11* (pp. 47–71). Stamford, CT: JAI Press.

Lillrank, P., Shani, A. B., & Lindberg, P. (2001). Continuous improvement: Exploring alternative organizational designs. *Total Quality Management, 12*(1), 41–55.

Lindberg, P., & Berger, A. (1997). Continuous improvement—design, organization, and management. *International Journal of Technology Management, 14*(1), 86–101.

Lipman, P. (2002). Making the global city, making inequality: The political economy and cultural politics of Chicago school policy. *American Educational Research Journal, 39,* 379–419.

Lipsky, M. (1980). *Street-level bureaucracy.* New York: Russell Sage Foundation.

Locke, E., A., & Jain, V. K. (1995). Organizational learning and continuous improvement. *International Journal of Organizational Analysis, 3*(1), 45–68.

Loucks-Horsley, S., Love, N., Stiles, K. E., Mundry, S., & Hewson, P. W. (2003). *Designing professional development for teachers of science and mathematics* (2nd ed.). Thousand Oaks, CA: Corwin.

Louis, K. S., & Miles, M. (1990). *Improving the urban high school: What works and why.* New York: Teachers College Press.

Lugg, C. A., Bulkley, K., Firestone, W. A., & Garner, C. W. (2002). The contextual terrain facing educational leaders. In J. Murphy (Ed.), *The educational leadership challenge: Redefining leadership for the 21st century. 101st yearbook of the National Society for the Study of Education Part I* (pp. 20–41). Chicago: National Society for the Study of Education.

March, J. G. (1981). Footnotes to organizational change. *Administrative Science Quarterly, 26,* 563–577.

March, J. G. (1991). Exploration and exploitation in organizational learning. *Organization Science, 2*(1), 71–87.

March, J. G. (1994). *A primer on decision making: How decisions happen.* New York: Free Press.

Marsh, J. A., Pane, J. F., & Hamilton, L. S. (2006). *Making sense of data-driven decision making in education.* Santa Monica, CA: RAND.

Marshak, R. J. (2004). Morphing: The leading edge of organizational change in the twenty-first century. *Organization Development, 22*(3), 8–21.

Masuch, M. (1985). Vicious circles in organizations. *Administrative Science Quarterly, 30,* 14–33.

Maudus, G., & Clarke, M. (2001). The adverse impact of high-stakes testing on minority students: Evidence from one hundred years of test data. In G. Orfield & M. L. Kornhaber (Eds.), *Raising standards or raising barriers? Inequality and high-stakes testing in public education* (pp. 85–106). New York: Century Foundation.

McDonnell, L. M. (2008, May). *The changing nature of federalism in education: A paradox and some unanswered questions.* Paper prepared for The States' Impact on Federal Education Policy invitational conference, Washington, DC.

McLaughlin, M. W., & Mitra, D. (2003). *The cycle of inquiry as the engine of school reform: Lessons from the Bay Area School Reform Collaborative.* Stanford, CA: Center for Research on the Context of Teaching, Stanford University.

McLaughlin, M. W., & Talbert, J. E. (2000, May). *Assessing results: Bay Area School Reform Collaborative, Year 4.* Stanford, CA: Center for Research on the Context of Teaching, Stanford University.

McLaughlin, M. W., & Talbert, J. E. (2002, October). *Bay Area School Reform Collaborative Phase One, 1996–2001, Summary Report.* Stanford, CA: Center for Research on the Context of Teaching, Stanford University.

McNeil, L. (2000). *Contradictions of school reform: Educational costs of standardized testing.* New York: RoutledgeFalmer.

McNichol, E. C., & Lav, I. J. (2008). *29 states face total budget shortfall of at least $48 billion in 2009.* Washington, DC: Center on Budget and Policy Priorities.

Meyer, J., & Rowan, B. (1977). Institutionalized organizations: Formal structure as myth and ceremony. *American Journal of Sociology, 83,* 340–363.

Meyer, J., & Rowan, B. (1978). The structure of educational organizations. In M. W. Meyer & Associates, *Environments and organizations* (pp. 78–109). San Francisco: Jossey-Bass.

Miner, A. S., Bassoff, P., & Moorman, C. (2001). Organizational improvisation and learning: A field study. *Administrative Science Quarterly, 46,* 304–337.

Mintrop, H., & Trujillo, T. (2007). The practical relevance of accountability systems for school improvement: A descriptive analysis of California schools. *Educational Evaluation and Policy Analysis, 29,* 319–352.

Mintzberg, H. (1979). *The structuring of organizations.* Upper Saddle River, NJ: Prentice Hall.

Mitki, Y., Shani, A. B., & Meiri, Z. (1997). Organizational learning mechanisms and continuous improvement: A longitudinal study. *Journal of Organizational Change Management, 10*(5), 426–446.

Mohrman, S. A., & Cummings, T. G. (1989). *Self-designing organizations: Learning how to create high performance.* Reading, MA: Addition-Wesley.

Moorman, C., & Miner, M. (1998). Organizational improvisation and organizational memory. *Academy of Management Review, 23,* 698–723.

Mulford, B. (1998). Organizational learning and educational change. In A. Hargreaves, A. Lieberman, M. Fullan, & D. Hopkins (Eds.), *International handbook of educational change* (pp. 616–641). Dortretch, The Netherlands: Kluwer.

Murnane, R. J. (2009). Educating urban children. In R. P. Inman (Ed.), *Making cities work: Prospects and policies for urban American* (pp. 269–295). Princeton, NJ: Princeton University Press.

Murphy, J., & Meyers, C. V. (2007). *Turning around failing schools: Leadership lessons from the organizational sciences.* Thousand Oaks, CA: Corwin.

Nadler, D. A., Gerstein, M. S., & Shaw, R. B. (1992). *Organizational architecture: Designs for changing organizations.* San Francisco: Jossey-Bass.

Nagaoka, J., & Roderick, M. (2004). *Ending social promotion: The effects of retention.* Chicago: Consortium on Chicago School Research.

National Center for Education Statistics. (2006). *The condition of education 2006.* Washington, DC: Institute for Education Sciences, U.S. Department of Education.

National Center for Education Statistics. (2007). *The condition of education 2007.* Washington, DC: Institute for Education Sciences, U.S. Department of Education.

National Education Association. (2008). *The KEYS-CSI Model.* Retrieved July 25, 2008, from http://www.keysonline.org

National Research Council. (2000). *How people learn.* Washington, DC: National Academy Press.

Nisbett, R., & Ross, L. (1980). *Human inference: Strategies and shortcomings of social judgment.* Englewood Cliffs, NJ: Prentice-Hall.

Nohria, N. (1996). *From the m-form to the n-form: Taking stock of changes in the large industrial corporation* (Working Paper 96-054). Cambridge, MA: Harvard University Business School.

North Central Association. (2004). *School improvement checklist.* Washington, DC: Author.

O'Day, J. A. (2002). Complexity, accountability, and school improvement. *Harvard Educational Review, 72*(3), 293–329.

Odden, A. (1991). *Education policy implementation.* Albany: State University of New York Press.

Ogawa, R. T., Crowson, R. L., & Goldring, E. B. (1999). Enduring dilemmas of school organization. In J. Murphy & K. S. Louis (Eds.), *Handbook of research on educational administration* (pp. 277–296). San Francisco: Jossey-Bass.

Orfield, G., & Lee, C. (2007, August). *Historic reversals, accelerating resegregation, and the need for new integration strategies.* Los Angeles: The Civil Rights Project, University of California-Los Angeles.

Orlikowski, W. J. (1996). Improvising organizational transformation over time: A situated change perspective. *Information Systems Research, 7*(1), 63–92.

Pallas, A., Natriello, G., & McDill, E. L. (1995). Changing students/changing needs. In E. Flaxman & A. H. Passow (Eds.), *Changing populations changing schools. 94th yearbook of the National Society for the Study of Education, Part II* (pp. 30–58). Chicago: National Society for the Study of Education.

Perie, M., Moran, R., & Lutkus, A. D. (2005). *NAEP 2004 trends in academic progress: Three decades of student performance in reading and mathematics* (NCES 2005-464). Washington, DC: National Center for Education Statistics, Institute of Education Sciences, U.S. Department of Education.

Perrow, C. (1984). *Normal accidents.* New York: Basic Books.

Peters, T. J., & Waterman, R. H. (1982). *In search of excellence: Lessons from America's best-run businesses.* New York: HarperCollins.

Planty, M., Hussar, W., Snyder, T., Provasnik, S., Kena, G., Kinkes, R., Kewal Ramani, A., & Kemp, J. (2008). *The condition of education 2008* (NCES 2008-031). Washington, DC: National Center for Education Statistics, Institute of Education Sciences, U.S. Department of Education.

Putnam, R. D. (2000). *Bowling alone: The collapse and revival of American community.* New York: Simon & Schuster.

Quinn, J. B. (1980). *Strategies for change: Logical incrementalism.* Homewood, IL: Richard D. Irwin.

Reed, R., Lemak, D. J., & Montgomery, J. C. (1996). Beyond process: TQM content and firm performance. *Academic of Management Review, 21,* 173–202.

Reitzug, U., & Burrello, L. C. (1995). How principals can build self-renewing schools. *Educational Leadership, 52*(7), 48–50.

Reynolds, D. (Ed.). (1999). *International handbook of school effectiveness research: An international survey of research on school effectiveness.* New York: Routledge.

Rhoten, D., Carnoy, M., Chabran, M., & Elmore, R. (2003). The conditions and characteristics of assessment and accountability: The case of four states. In M. Carnoy, R. Elmore, & L. Siskin (Eds.), *The new accountability: High schools and high-stakes testing* (pp. 13–53). New York: RoutledgeFalmer.

Rindova, V. P., & Kotha, S. (2001). Continuous "morphing": Competing through dynamic capabilities, form, and function. *Academy of Management Journal, 44,* 1263–1280.

Roesner, L. (1995). Changing the culture at Beacon Hill. *Educational Leadership, 52*(7), 28–32.

Romanelli, E., & Tushman, M. L. (1994). Organizational transformation as punctuated equilibrium: An empirical test. *Academy of Management Review, 37*(5), 1141–1166.

Rosenholtz, S. J. (1989). *Teachers' workplace: The social organization of schools.* New York: Longman.

Rowan, B. (1990). Commitment and control: Alternative strategies for the organizational design of schools. *Review of Research in Education, 16,* 353–389.

Rowan, B. (2002). The ecology of school improvement: Notes on the school improvement industry in the United States. *Journal of Educational Change, 3,* 283–314.

Rudolph, J. W., & Repenning, N. P. (2002). Disaster dynamics: Understanding the role of quantity in organizational collapse. *Administrative Science Quarterly, 47,* 1–30.

Rumsfeld, D. (2002). U.S. Department of Defense news briefing, February 12. Retrieved January 14, 2008, from http://www.defenselink.mil/transcripts/transcript.aspx?transcriptid=2636

Rumsfeld, D. (2003). U.S. Department of Defense news briefing, April 11, 2003. Retrieved December 15, 2008, from http://www.defenselink.mil/transcripts/transcript.aspx?transcriptid=2367

Sallis, E. (2002). *Total quality management in education* (3rd ed.). New York: RoutledgeFalmer.

Sarason, S. B. (1973). *The culture of the school and the problem of change.* Boston: Allyn and Bacon.

Sarason, S. B. (1996). *Revisiting "The culture of the school and the problem of change."* New York: Teachers College Press.

Sastry, M. A. (1997). Problems and paradoxes in a model of punctuated organizational change. *Administrative Science Quarterly, 42,* 237–275.

Savolainen, T. I. (1991). Cycles of continuous improvement: Realizing competitive advantage through quality. *International Journal of Operations & Production Management, 19,* 1203–1222.

Scott, W. R. (2002). *Organizations: Rational, natural, and open systems* (5th ed.). Upper Saddle River, NJ: Prentice-Hall.

Scott, W. R. (2007). *Institutions and organizations* (3rd ed.). Thousand Oaks, CA: Sage.

Schwartz, G. (2005). Obstacles, challenges, and potential: Envisioning the future. In G. Schwartz & P. U. Brown (Eds.), *Media literacy: Transforming curriculum and teaching. 104th yearbook of the National Society for the Study of Education, Part I* (pp. 229–250). Malden, MA: Blackwell.

Sebring, P. B., Allensworth, E., Bryk, A. S., Easton, J. Q., & Luppescu, S. (2006, September). *The essential supports for school improvement.* Chicago: Consortium on Chicago School Research, University of Chicago.

Senge, P. M. (1990, Fall). The leader's new work: Building learning organizations. *Sloan Management Review,* 7–23.

Seo, M.-G. (2003). Overcoming emotional barriers, political obstacles, and control imperatives in the action-science approach to individual and organizational learning. *Academy of Management Learning & Education, 2,* 7–21.

Sergiovanni, T. J. (2004). *Strengthening the heartbeat: Leading and learning together in schools.* San Francisco: Jossey-Bass.

Shewhart, W. A. (1931). *Economic control of quality of manufactured product.* New York: D. Van Nostrand.

Shewhart, W. A. (1939). *Statistical method from the viewpoint of quality control.* Washington, DC: The Graduate School, Department of Agriculture.

Shipps, D., Kahne, J., & Smylie, M. A. (1999). The politics of urban school reform: Legitimacy, city growth, and school improvement in Chicago. *Educational Policy, 13*(4), 518–545.

Shuchman, M. L., & White, J. S. (1995). *The art of the turnaround: How to rescue your troubled business from creditors, predators, and competitors.* New York: American Management Association.

Silins, H. C., Mulford, W. R., & Zarins, S. (2002). Organizational learning and school change. *Educational Administration Quarterly, 38,* 613–642.

Simon, H. A. (1986). Theories of bounded rationality. In C. B. McGuire & R. Radner (Eds.), *Decision and organization: Vol. 2* (pp. 161–176). Minneapolis: University of Minnesota Press.

Simon, H. A. (1991). Bounded rationality and organizational learning. *Organization Science, 2,* 125–134.

Siri, D. K., & Miller, R. (2001). Continuous improvement through Baldrige in education. *Leadership, 31*(1), 12–14.

Slatter, S. (1984). *Corporate recovery: A guide to turnaround management.* Harmondsworth, Middlesex, England: Penguin.

Smith, L. (2008). *Schools that change: Evidence-based improvement and effective change leadership.* Thousand Oaks, CA: Corwin.

Smylie, M. A., & Corcoran, T. B. (2009). Nonprofit organizations and the promotion of evidence-based practice in education. In J. D. Bransford, D. J. Stipek, N. J. Vye, L. M. Gomez, & D. Lam (Eds.), *The role of research in educational improvement* (pp. 111–135). Cambridge, MA: Harvard Education Press.

Smylie, M. A., & Crowson, R. L. (1993). Principal assessment under restructured governance. *Peabody Journal of Education, 68*(2), 64–84.

Smylie, M. A., & Wenzel, S. A. (2003, October). *The Chicago Annenberg Challenge: Successes, failures, and lessons for the future. Final technical report of the Chicago Annenberg Research Project.* Chicago: Consortium on Chicago School Research, University of Chicago.

Sørensen, J. B., & Stuart, T. E. (2000). Aging, obsolescence, and organizational innovation. *Administrative Science Quarterly, 45,* 81–112.

Sporte, S. E., Smylie, M. A., Allensworth, E. M., & Miller, S. R. (2003, June). *Chicago school reform and changes in the social organization of schools: A tale of unintended consequences.* Presentation at the Focus on Illinois Education Research Symposium, Illinois Education Research Council, Champaign, IL.

Staw, B. M., Sanderlands, L. E., & Dutton, J. E. (1981). Threat-rigidity effects in organizational behavior: A multilevel analysis. *Administrative Science Quarterly, 26,* 501–524.

Stein, M. K., & D'Amico, L. (2002). The district as a professional learning laboratory. In A. M. Hightower, M. S. Knapp, J. A. Marsh, & M. W. McLaughlin (Eds.), *School districts and instructional renewal* (pp. 61–75). New York: Teachers College Press.

Stein, M. K., Hubbard, L., & Mehan, H. (2004). Reform ideas that travel far afield: The two cultures of reform in New York City's District #2 and San Diego. *Journal of Educational Change, 5,* 161–197.

Stein, S. J. (2004). *The culture of education policy.* New York: Teachers College Press.

Stokes, L. M. (1999). *Becoming an inquiring school.* Unpublished Ph.D. dissertation, Stanford University.

Stringfield, S. (1995). Attempts to enhance students' learning: A search for valid programs and highly reliable implementation techniques. *School Effectiveness and Improvement, 6*(1), 67–96.

Stringfield, S., Reynolds, D., & Schaffer, E. C. (2008). Improving secondary students' academic achievement through a focus on reform reliability: The first five years of The High Reliability Schools Project. *School Effectiveness and School Improvement, 19*(4), 409–428.

Taylor, F. W. (1911). *The principles of scientific management.* New York: Harper.

Teddlie, C., & Reynolds, D. (2000). *The international handbook of school effectiveness research.* London: Falmer.

Thompson, J. G. (1967). *Organizations in action.* New York: McGraw-Hill.

Timar, T. B., & Kirp, D. L. (1987). Educational reform and institutional competence. *Harvard Educational Review, 57*(3), 308–330.

Torbert, W. R. (1992). The true challenge of generating continual quality improvement. *Journal of Management Inquiry, 1*(4), 331–336.

Tschannen-Moran, M. (2004). *Trust matters: Leadership for successful schools.* San Francisco: Jossey-Bass.

Tsoukas, H., & Chia, R. (2002). On organizational becoming: Rethinking organizational change. *Organization Science, 13*(5), 567–582.

Tushman, M. L., Newman, W. H., & Romanelli, E. (1986). Convergence and upheaval: Managing the unsteady pace of organizational evolution. *California Management Review, 29*(1), 29–44.

Tushman, M. L., & O'Reilly, C. A. III. (1996). Ambidextrous organizations: Managing evolutionary and revolutionary change. *California Management Review, 38*(4), 8–30.

Tushman, M. L. & Romanelli, E. (1985). Organizational evolution: A metamorphosis model of convergence and reorientation. *Research in Organizational Behavior, 7,* 171–122.

Tyack, D. B. (1974). *The one best system: A history of American urban education.* Cambridge, MA: Harvard University Press.

Tyack, D. B. (1991). Public school reform: Policy talk and institutional practice. *American Journal of Education, 100,* 1–19.

Tyack, D. B., & Cuban, L. (1995). *Tinkering toward Utopia: A century of public school reform.* Cambridge, MA: Harvard University Press.

Tye, B. B. (2000). *Hard truths: Uncovering the deep structure of schooling.* New York: Teachers College Press.

U.S. Bureau of the Census. (2004). *U.S. interim projections by age, sex, race, and Hispanic origin.* Retrieved January 4, 2008, from http://www.census.gov/ipc/www/usinterimproj/

U.S. Bureau of the Census. (2007a). More than 300 counties now "majority-minority." Retrieved January 4, 2008, from http://www.census.gov/PressRelease/www/releases/archives/population/010482.html

U.S. Bureau of the Census. (2007b). *Statistical abstract of the United States: 2007.* Washington, DC: Author.

U.S. Bureau of the Census. (2009). *Statistical abstract of the United States: 2009.* Washington, DC: Author.

U.S. Bureau of Labor Statistics. (2007, December). *Occupational outlook handbook, 2008–09 edition.* Washington, DC: U.S. Bureau of Labor Statistics, U. S. Department of Labor.

U.S. Citizenship and Immigration Services. (1998). *The triennial comprehensive report on immigration.* Washington, DC: U.S. Citizenship and Immigration Services, U.S. Department of Homeland Security.

U.S. Department of Labor. (1999, September). *Futurework: Trends and challenges for work in the 21st century.* Washington, DC: Author.

Valli, L., & Buese, D. (2007). The changing roles of teachers in an era of high-stakes accountability. *American Educational Research Journal, 44,* 519–558.

Vince, R. (2002). The impact of emotion on organizational learning. *Human Resource Development International, 5,* 73–85.

Von Bertalanffy, L. (1950). An outline of general systems theory. *British Journal of the Philosophy of Science, 1,* 134–165.

Walsh, K. (2003). *After the test: How schools are using data to close the achievement gap.* San Francisco: Bay Area School Reform Collaborative.

Watson, G. (1967). *Toward a conceptual architecture of a self-renewing school system.* Washington, DC: National Training Laboratories, Institute for Applied Behavioral Science. [ERIC Document Collection Service ED012515]

Wayman, J. C., Midgeley, S., & Stringfield, S. (2006, April). *Leadership for data-based decision making: Collaborative educator teams.* Paper presented at the annual meeting of the American Educational Research Association, San Francisco.

Weick, K. E. (1976). Educational organizations as loosely-coupled systems. *Administrative Science Quarterly, 21,* 1–19.

Weick, K. E. (1977). Organization design: Organizations as self-designing systems. *Organizational Dynamics, 6*(2), 31–46.

Weick, K. E. (1979). *The social psychology of organizing* (2nd ed.). New York: McGraw Hill.

Weick, K. E. (1993). The collapse of sensemaking in organizations: The Mann Gulch disaster. *Administrative Science Quarterly, 38,* 628–652.

Weick, K. E. (1998). Improvisation as a mindset for organizational analysis. *Organization Science, 9*(5), 543–555.

Weick, K. E., & Berlinger, L. R. (1989). Career improvisation in self-designing organizations. In M. B. Arthur, D. T. Hall, & B. S. Lawrence (Eds.), *Handbook of career theory* (pp. 313–328). New York: Cambridge University Press.

Weick, K. E., & McDaniel, R. R., Jr. (1989). How professional organizational work: Implications for school organization and improvement. In T. J. Sergiovanni & J. H. Moore (Eds.), *Schools for tomorrow: Directing reforms to issues that count* (pp. 330–355). Boston: Allyn & Bacon.

Weick, K. E., & Quinn, R. E. (1999). Organizational change and development. *Annual Review of Psychology, 50,* 361–386.

Weick, K. E., & Sutcliffe, K. M. (2007). *Managing the unexpected: Resilient performance in an age of uncertainty* (2nd ed.). San Francisco: Jossey-Bass.

Weick, K. E., Sutcliffe, K. M., & Obstfeld, D. (1999). Organizing for high reliability: Processes of collective mindfulness. In B. M. Staw & R. Sutton (Eds.), *Research in organizational behavior: Vol. 23* (pp. 81–123). Greenwich, CT: JAI Press.

Weiler, H. (1993). Control versus legitimation. In J. Hannaway & M. Carnoy (Eds.), *Decentralization and school improvement* (pp. 55–83). San Francisco: Jossey-Bass.

Weller, L. D., & Weller, S. J. (1998). Raising test scores through the continuous improvement model. *The Clearing House, 71*(3), 159–164.

Wildavsky, A. (1972). The self-evaluating organization. *Public Administration Review, 32,* 509–520.

Wilson, K. G., & Daviss, B. (1994). *Redesigning education: A Nobel Prize winner reveals what must be done to reform American education.* New York: Teachers College Press.

Wirt, F., & Kirst, M. (2005). *Political dynamics of American education* (3rd ed.). Berkeley, CA: McCutchan.

Yong, J., & Wilkinson, A. (1999). The state of total quality management: A review. *The International Journal of Human Resource Management, 10,* 137–161.

Zangwill, W. I., & Kantor, P. B. (1998). Toward a theory of continuous improvement and the learning curve. *Management Science, 44*(7), 910–920.

Zhou, L. (2008). *Revenues and expenditures for public elementary and secondary education: School year 2005–06 (fiscal year 2006).*(NCES 2008-328). Washington, DC: National Center for Education Statistics, Institute of Education Sciences, U.S. Department of Education.

Zhou, L., & Gaviola, N. (2007). *Revenues and expenditures for public elementary and secondary districts: School year 2004–05 (fiscal year 2005).*(NCES 2007-355). Washington, DC: National Center for Education Statistics, Institute of Education Sciences, U.S. Department of Education.

Zumda, A., Kuklis, R., & Kline, E. (2004). *Transforming schools: Creating a culture of continuous improvement.* Alexandria, VA: Association for Supervision and Curriculum Development.

Index